EMQs for
Medical Students
Volume 3

Adam Feather
Paola Domizio
Kevin Hayes
Charles H Knowles
John S P Lumley

PASTEST
Dedicated to your success

© 2004 PasTest Ltd

Egerton Court
Parkgate Estate
Knutsford
Cheshire, WA16 8DX

Telephone: 01565 752000

First edition 2004
Reprinted 2005

ISBN: 1 904627 07 2

A catalogue record for this book is available from the British Library.

The information contained within this book was obtained by the authors from reliable sources. However, while every effort has been made to ensure its accuracy, no responsibility for loss, damage or injury occasioned to any person acting or refraining from action as a result of information contained herein can be accepted by the publisher or the authors.

PasTest Revision Books and Intensive Courses

PasTest has been established in the field of postgraduate medical education since 1972, providing revision books and intensive study courses for doctors preparing for their professional examinations. Books and courses are available for the following specialties:

MRCP Part 1 and Part 2, MRCPCH Part 1 and Part 2, MRCOG, DRCOG, MRCGP, MRCPsych, DCH, FRCA, MRCS and PLAB.

For further details contact:

PasTest Ltd, Freepost, Knutsford, Cheshire, WA16 7BR
Tel: 01565 752000   Fax: 01565 650264
Email: enquiries@pastest.co.uk   Web site: www.pastest.co.uk

Typeset by Saxon Graphics Ltd, Derby
Printed and bound by the Cromwell Press Ltd, Wiltshire

Contents

Contributors List

Adam Feather
Senior Lecturer in Medical Education
St. Bartholomew's and The Royal London Hospital Medical School
Consultant Physician
Newham Healthcare Trust
London

Paola Domizio BSc MB BS FRCPath ILTM
Professor of Pathology Education
Department of Histopathology
Barts and the London Queen Mary's School of Medicine
West Smithfield
London

Mr Kevin Hayes MRCOG
Lecturer in Medical Education and Obstetrics and Gynaecology
St George's Hospital Medical School
Cranmer Terrace
SW17 0RE

Charles H Knowles MBBChir PhD FRCS
Specialist Registrar in Surgery,
Centre for Academic Surgery
Royal London Hospital
London
and
Honorary Clinical Lecturer in Surgery
University of London

John S P Lumley MS FRCS
Professor of Vascular Surgery
University of London
Honorary Consultant Surgeon
Great Ormond Street Children's Hospital
Medical College and Hospital of St Bartholomew, London
Member of Council, Royal College of Surgeons of England
Past World President, International College of Surgeons

Preface to EMQs for Medical Students – Volume 3

The new volume is in response to the demand for further questions of this type that are becoming widely used throughout medical schools in the UK. Whereas in the previous two volumes a systems approach was used, this volume mixes questions, testing the reader across all disciplines. No excuses are made for the use of some previous option lists with minor modifications or occasionally repeating a question; this should reassure the readers that there is a limit to the number of medical lists that can be thrown at them. It also serves to reinforce important topics.

We are also pleased to note that the format of the question is similar to that in the previous volumes and the introduction has been retained. This, we hope, will also provide reassurance that not everything is changing all the time in medical education.

Each examination is 2 hours in duration. Each correct answer scores one mark and there is no negative marking for incorrect answers. Where there is more than one answer for a given vignette each answer scores one mark if they are independent of one another. If they are dependent of one another to complete a given syndrome or clinical picture they score the given part of one mark, i.e. if there are three answers, each score one third of a mark.

Abbreviations

AIHA	Autoimmune haemolytic anaemia
Alb	Albumin
ALL	Acute lymphoblastic leukaemia
AMA	Anti-mito chrondrial antibody
AML	Acute myelogenous Leukamia
APCKD	Adult polycystic kidney disease
AR	Autosomal recessive
ASmaA	Anti-smooth muscle antibody
AV	Atrioventricular
BAR	Bronchoalveolar lavage
BER	Best eye response
BMI	Body mass index
BMR	Best motor response
BVR	Best vocal response
BV	Bacterial vaginosis
CESDI	Confidential enquiry into stillbirths & deaths
CIN	Cervical intraepithelial neoplasia
CLL	Chronic lymphatic leukaemia
CML	Chronic myeloid leukaemia
COCP	Combined oral contraceptive pill
COPD	Chronic obstructive pulmonary disease
CPN	Community psychiatric nurse
CTPA	CT scan with pulmonary angiography
CSF	Cerebrospinal fluid
CT	Computerised tomogram
CURE	Clopidogrel in Unstable angina to prevent Recurrent Events
DIC	Dissiminated intravascular coagulation
EBV	Ebstein-Barr virus
EO	Eyes open
FBC	Full blood count
GBS	Group B Streptococcus
GCSF	Granulocyte colony-stimulating factor
GI	Gastrointestinal
GSI	Genuine stress incontinence
HAV	Hepatitis A virus
Hb	Haemoglobin
HCV	Hepatitis C virus
HNPCC	Hereditary nonpolyposis colorectal cancer
HPV	Human papillomavirus
IBD	Irritable bowel disease

IHD	Ischaemic heart disease
IMB	Intermenstrual bleeding
IVU	Intravenous urogram
LGV	Lymphogranuloma venerum
LLETZ	Large loop excision of the transformation zone
MALT	Lymphoma of mucosa associated lymphoid tissue
MCV	Mean corpuscular volume
MS	Mitral stenosis
MSU	Mid stream urine
NHL	Non-Hogkins lymphoma
NSAIDs	Non-steroidal anti-inflammatory drug
OA	Osteoarthritis
OGD	Oesophagastroduodenoscopy
PBC	Primary bilary cirrhosis
PCB	
PCOS	Polycystic ovary syndrome
PET	Pre-eclamptic toxaemia
PID	Pelvic inflammatory disease
Pl+	Platelets
PSA	Serum prostatic specific antigen
PV	Per vagina
QTc	Corrected QT interval
rT3	Reverse T3
RTA	Road traffic accident
RPOC	Retained products of conception
SA	Sinoatrial
SACD	Subacute combined degeneration of the cord
SARS	Severe acute respiratory syndrome
SCC	Squamous cell carcinoma
SDH	Subdural haemorrhage
SIADH	Syndrome of inappropriate antidiuretic hormone secretion
SLE	Systemic lupus erythematosus
TED	Thromboembolic disease
TR	Tricuspid regurgitation
UKEs	Urea & electrolytes
UTI	Urinary tract infection
VMA	Vanyillyl mandelic acid

NORMAL VALUES

Haematology
Haemoglobin
Males	13.5–17.5 g/dl
Females	11.5–15.5 g/dl

MCV   76–98 fl
PCV   35–55%
WCC $4–11 \times 10^9$/l
Neut. $2.5–7.58 \times 10^9$/l
Lymph. $1.5–3.5 \times 10^9$/l
Plt $150–400 \times 10^9$/l

ESR   0–10 mm in the 1st hour

PT   10.6–14.9 s
PTT   23.0–35.0 s
TT   10.5–15.5 s
Fib   125–300 mg/dl

$Vitamin_{B12}$ 160–900 pmol/l
Folate   1.5–10.0 µg/l
Ferritin
Males	20–250 µg/l
Females	10–120 µg/l

Immunoglobulins
IgM   0.5–2.0 g/l
IgG   5–16 g/l
IgA   1.0–4.0 g/l

Biochemistry
Na^+ 135–145 mmol/l
K^+ 3.5–5.0 mmol/l
Urea   2.5–6.5 mmol/l
Cr   50–120 µmol/l

ALT   5–30 iu/l
AST   10–40 iu/l
Bili.   2–17 µmol/l
Alk P   30–130 iu/l
Alb.   35–55 g/l
γGT   5–30 iu/l
αFP   <10 ku/l

CCa^{2+} 2.20–2.60 mmol/l
PO_4^{2-} 0.70–1.40 mmol/l

CK	23–175 iu/l
LDH	100–190 iu/l
Amylase	<200 u/l
Lactate	0.5–2.2 mmol/l
Mg^{2+}	0.75–1.00 mmol/l
Urate	0.1–0.4 mol/l
CRP	0–10 mg/l

Diabetes

Glucose	
Random	3.5–5.5 mmol/l*
Fasting	<7 mmol/l
HbA_{1c}	<7.0%

Endocrinology

TSH	0.17–3.2 mu/l
fT_4	11–22 pmol/l
fT_3	3.5–5 pmol/l
Cortisol	
0900	140–500 nmol/l
2400	50–300 nmol/l
Growth hormone	<10 ng/ml
Cholesterol	<5.2 mmol/l
Triglycerides	0–1.5 mmol/l
LDL	< 3.5 mmol/l
HDL	> 1.0 mmol/l
Total/HDL	< 5.0
FSH	1–25 u/l
LH	1–70 u/l
Prolactin	< 400 mu/l

Blood Gases

pH	7.35–7.45
$PaCO_2$	4.6–6.0 kPa
PaO_2	10.5–13.5 kPa
HCO_3^-	24–30 mmol/l
BE	–2–2.0 mmol/l

CSF

Protein	<0.45 g/l
Glucose	2.5–3.9 mmol/l (two-thirds plasma)
Cells	< 5 (WCC)
Opening pressure	6–20 cmH_2O

---

* If > 5.5 then OGTT 2 hrs: 7–11.1 = IGT
                                                    > 11.1 = DM

PAPER 1

Paper 1 questions ✓✓✓✗

1. THEME: ANAEMIA

A   Anaemia of chronic disease
B   Aplastic anaemia
C   Autoimmune haemolytic anaemia
D   B12 deficiency
E   Iron deficiency
F   Myelodysplasia
G   Pancytopenia secondary to multiple myeloma
H   Sickle cell disease
I   Sideroblastic anaemia
J   Thalassaemia trait

The following patients have all presented with anaemia. Please choose the most appropriate cause from the above list. The items may be used once, more than once or not at all.

1. A 73-year-old woman presents to her GP with lethargy and malaise. Of note she has recently been placed on clopidogrel for unstable angina. Her routine blood tests show FBC: Hb 6.8 g/dl, MCV 68 fl, WCC 9.2 × 10⁹/l, Plt 491 × 10⁹/l; U&Es: Na⁺ 136 mmol/l, K⁺ 3.9 mmol/l, urea 4.7 mmol/l, Cr 88 μmol/l.

2. A 79-year-old man, who has recently been started on phenytoin post neurosurgery, is readmitted under the physicians with a severe pneumonia and is noted to have bleeding gums and 'heavy' bruising over his limbs. Investigations reveal FBC: Hb 4.9 g/dl, MCV 88 fl, WCC 2.2 × 10⁹/l, Plt 11 × 10⁹/l; blood film 'pancytopenia with few reticulocytes seen', bone marrow trephine shows 'hypocellularity with increased fat spaces'.

3. A 67-year-old woman is admitted to hospital with severe lumbar back pain associated with recurrent chest infections and general malaise. Investigations show FBC: Hb 3.9 g/dl, MCV 98 fl, WCC 1.9 × 10⁹/l, Plt 27 × 10⁹/l; U&Es: Na⁺ 130 mmol/l, K⁺ 5.9 mmol/l, urea 24.4 mmol/l, Cr 412 μmol/l, ESR 122 mm/h; CCa²⁺ 3.37 mmol/l.

4. A 51-year-old Asian woman is seen in the pre-operative assessment clinic prior to her planned breast lumpectomy. Routine investigations reveal FBC: Hb10.3 g/dl, MCV 58 fl, WCC 5.5 × 10⁹/l, Plt 369 × 10⁹/l, ferritin 92 µg/l.

5. An 83-year-old woman is admitted to hospital with a severe community-acquired pneumonia. Investigations reveal FBC: Hb 7.9 g/dl, MCV 102 fl, WCC 3.2 × 10⁹/l, Plt 254 × 10⁹/l; blood film 'significant reticulocytosis'. 'Cold' IgM antibodies are later shown to be responsible.

2. THEME: RESPIRATORY FAILURE

√√ ✗ √√

A Asbestosis
B Asthma
C COPD
D Guillain–Barré syndrome
E Idiopathic pulmonary fibrosis
F Legionella pneumonia
G Mycoplasma pneumonia
H Pickwickian syndrome
I Pulmonary embolism
J Pulmonary oedema

The following patients have all presented with respiratory failure. Please choose the most appropriate cause from the above list. The items may be used once, more than once, in combination or not at all. (The ABGs have all been taken on room air.)

1. A 71-year-old retired boiler lagger is referred to medical outpatients with a 6-month history of worsening exertional dyspnoea. On examination he is dyspnoeic at rest but does not have finger clubbing or cyanosis. Auscultation reveals bibasal, fine inspiratory crepitations. His chest radiograph shows pleural and diaphragmatic plaques with diffuse lower zone changes. ABGs show pH 7.39, $PaCO_2$ 4.1 kPa, PaO_2 7.9 kPa, Sats 91%, HCO_3^- 25 mmol/l, base excess 1.9 mmol/l.

2. A 61-year-old obese man presents to his GP with exertional dyspnoea, early morning headaches and daytime somnolence. Subsequent spirometery reveals an obstructive problem and ABGs show pH 7.37, $PaCO_2$ 7.9 kPa, PaO_2 7.3 kPa, Sats 87%, HCO_3^- 34 mmol/l, base excess 6.9 mmol/l. He improves with overnight nasal ventilation.

3. A 49-year-old woman presents in the A&E department with acute shortness of breath. On examination she is peripherally 'shutdown', clammy, tachycardic and hypotensive. ABGs show pH 7.13, $PaCO_2$ 3.5 kPa, PaO_2 7.9 kPa, Sats 89%, HCO_3^- 15 mmol/l, base excess 7.3 mmol/l, and her chest radiograph shows alveolar shadowing in a 'bat wing' configuration.

4. A 35-year-old woman becomes acutely unwell with shortness of breath and a dry non-productive cough. Investigations reveal U&Es: Na^+ 127 mmol/l, K^+ 4.9 mmol/l, urea 7.4 mmol/l, Cr 122 μmol/l. Her chest radiograph is relatively unremarkable but ABGs show pH 7.33, $PaCO_2$ 3.7 kPa, PaO_2 6.3 kPa, Sats 82%, HCO_3^- 20 mmol/l, base excess 2.9 mmol/l. The diagnosis is later confirmed by urine antigen testing.

5. A 56-year-old man presents to his GP with a 4-month history of increasing exertional dyspnoea. On examination he has marked clubbing of the fingernails and is short of breath on relatively mild exertion. Auscultation of his chest reveals fine inspiratory crepitations. Subsequent investigations confirm a restrictive pattern on spirometry.

3. THEME: ASCITES

A   Alcoholic cirrhosis
B   Chronic hepatitis B infection
C   Colonic carcinoma
D   Constrictive pericarditis
E   Ischaemic cardiomyopathy
F   Ovarian carcinoma
G   Pericarditis
H   Peritoneal mesothelioma
I   Renal cell carcinoma
J   Tuberculosis

The following patients have all presented with ascites. Please choose the most appropriate cause from the above list. The items may be used once, more than once, in combination or not at all.

1. A 51-year-old woman presents to her GP with increasing abdominal swelling. Subsequent investigations reveal a grossly elevated Ca-125, her chest radiograph is unremarkable but there are adenocarcinoma cells within the ascitic fluid.

2. A 49-year-old woman presents in A&E with increasing exertional dyspnoea, and swelling of her abdomen and ankles. On examination she has tar stained fingers on her right hand, her pulse is 120 bpm regular and BP = 105/70. Her JVP is elevated to the angle of her jaw but Kussmaul's sign is negative. Her apex beat is grossly displaced into the posterior axillary line and she has a marked pansystolic murmur which is clearly heard throughout the precordium. Her ECG shows SR 120 bpm , left axis deviation and deep Q waves in leads V_1–V_4.

3. A 71-year-old retired docker presents to his GP with increasing abdominal swelling, lethargy and malaise. On examination he is clinically anaemic and has gross ascites but no organomegaly, masses or lymphadenopathy. Subsequent CT scan of the abdomen shows infiltration of the peritoneum and ascites. The diagnosis is later confirmed by laparoscopy and biopsy.

4. A 57-year-old man presents to his GP with night sweats, increasing exertional dyspnoea, lethargy and abdominal swelling. Subsequent investigations reveal FBC: Hb 6.4 g/dl, MCV 79 fl, WCC 12.2 × 10^9/l, Plt 494 × 10^9/l and his chest radiograph confirms multiple large round lesions throughout both lung fields.

5. A 29-year-old Asian woman presents to her GP with acute abdominal pains and diarrhoea. She is admitted to hospital where subsequent colonoscopy is unremarkable, as are her chest radiograph and ECG. Subsequent CT scan of the abdomen with contrast confirms terminal ileitis with associated para-aortic and coeliac lymphadenopathy.

4. THEME: HEADACHE

✓ ✓ ✓ ✓ ✗

A   Benign intracranial hypertension
B   Cervical spondylosis
C   Giant cell arteritis
D   Meningitis (bacterial)
E   Meningitis (viral)
F   Sagittal sinus thrombosis
G   Staphylococcal abscess
H   Subarachnoid haemorrhage
I   Subdural haemorrhage
J   Tension headache

The following patients have all presented with a headache. Please choose the most appropriate cause from the above list. The items may be used once, more than once or not at all.

1. A 23-year-old woman who has recently been started on the oral contraceptive pill presents in A&E with a sudden severe headache radiating across the top of her head. Fundoscopy reveals papilloedema but CT head scan and lumbar puncture are relatively normal. A repeat CT with contrast confirms the diagnosis showing a 'positive delta sign'.

2. A 19-year-old woman with a BMI of 34 presents to her GP with a 6-month history of intermittent headaches associated with visual blurring. She is referred to a neurologist but routine investigations including ESR, CT head scan and lumbar puncture are normal. Her symptoms improve with weight loss and diuretics.

3. A 21-year-old man presents in A&E with a 12-hour history of severe headache. On examination he is unwell, distressed and photophobic. He has marked meningism and cannot tolerate fundoscopy. There is no rash or other clinical signs. CSF examination reveals raised lymphocyte count, normal protein and glucose concentrations.

4. A 64-year-old man presents to his GP with a 24-hour history of right-sided weakness associated with a 3–4-day history of a worsening headache. On examination he has a grade 3/5 right hemiparesis but nothing else of note. A CT head scan shows an isodense, concave rim over the left frontal and parietal lobes with significant mass effect to the right.

5. A 71-year-old woman presents to her GP with severe headaches over the forehead and associated with pain in her shoulders. Her cervical spine radiographs show mild osteoarthritic changes but her ESR = 110 mm/h.

5. THEME: EPONYMOUS SIGNS

A   Cullen's sign
B   De Musset's sign
C   Duroziez's sign
D   Gower's sign
E   Grey Turner's sign
F   Nikolsky's sign
G   Quinke's sign
H   Romberg's sign
I   Troisier's sign
J   Trousseau's sign

Each of the following presentations are associated with an eponymous sign or signs. Please choose the most appropriate from the above list. The items may be used once, more than once, in combination or not at all.

1. A 48-year-old Bengali woman presents in A&E with lethargy and several tonic–clonic seizures. Routine investigations show CCa^{2+} 1.83 mmol/l, PO_4^{2-} 2.10 mmol/l, Alkaline phosphatase 498 iu/l.

2. A 38-year-old Somalian woman presents in A&E with severe shortness of breath on exercise. On examination she has 'titubation of her head' and a loud early diastolic murmur heard best with patient leaning forward in expiration. There are no features of infective endocarditis.

3. A 61-year-old man presents to his GP with a 3-month history of weight loss, lethargy and abdominal fullness on eating. On examination he has a large epigastric mass and is clinically anaemic.

4. A 37-year-old alcohol abuser is admitted to hospital with severe upper abdominal pains. He has marked abdominal tenderness and investigations show amylase 1080 iu/l and a marked metabolic acidosis.

5. A 63-year-old woman is seen by her GP with a severe blistering rash involving the upper and lower limbs, truncal areas and the mucous membranes of her mouth. Whilst examining apparent normal areas of skin, firm pressure leads to shearing off of the skin.

6. THEME: ILIAC FOSSAE MASSES

A Appendix mass
B Caecal carcinoma
C Crohn's disease
D Iliac artery aneurysm
E Iliac lymphadenopathy
F Ovarian cancer
G Ovarian cyst
H Pelvic kidney
I Psoas abscess
J TB ileitis
K Undescended testis

The following are descriptions of patients who have presented with masses in their iliac fossae. Please select the most appropriate diagnosis from the above list. The items may be used once, more than once or not at all.

1. A 19-year-old man presents with a 3-day history of right iliac fossa pain with nausea, anorexia and fever. On examination he is pyrexial, temperature 38.2°C and a tender indistinct mass in the right iliac fossa associated with guarding.

2. A 25-year-old woman is seen in A&E with a 3-day history of severe colicky right iliac fossa pain, and diarrhoea. On questioning she admits to several previous less severe episodes over a 2-year period and weight loss of over 7 kg during this time. On examination there is a tender indistinct mass in the right iliac fossa.

3. A 32-year-old man complains of several months weight loss, night sweats and dull abdominal pain. More recently he has noticed a swelling in his left groin. On examination of this swelling you also find a moderate sized indistinct mass in the left iliac fossa. There is no history of foreign travel.

4. A 66-year-old woman presents to her GP because she has noticed a large mass in her abdomen. Other than a dull lower abdominal ache and a slight decrease in appetite she has had no other symptoms. On observation of the abdomen there is a large left iliac fossa mass, which on palpation has an easily defined upper border but which you cannot get below.

5. A 72-year-old man is referred to clinic with anaemia (Hb 9.4 g/dl, MCV 69.6 fl). He is otherwise asymptomatic. On examination you feel a distinct hard mobile mass in the right iliac fossa.

7. THEME: NIPPLE DISCHARGE

A   Carcinoma of the breast
B   Fibrocystic disease of the breast
C   Intraduct papilloma
D   Lactating breast
E   Mammary duct ectasia
F   Mammary duct fistula
G   Paget's disease of the nipple
H   Prolactinoma

The following patients have all presented with nipple discharge. Please select the most appropriate diagnosis from the above list. The items may be used once, more than once or not at all.

1. A 35-year-old woman presents with a 2-month history of unilateral painless serosanginous nipple discharge. Examination is unremarkable with no lumps palpable in either breast.

2. A 65-year-old woman presents with a 2-month history of cheese-like nipple discharge from her right breast and nipple retraction. Breast examination reveals a slit like retraction of her right nipple with no lumps palpable in her breast.

3. A 27-year-old woman is referred from the fertility clinic with a several month history of watery whitish discharge from her breasts. She also complains about recent problems with her vision for which she is waiting to see her GP. Examination of her breasts is unremarkable but on neurological examination she has bitemporal hemianopia.

4. A 66-year-old woman has been referred by her GP with unilateral heavily bloodstained nipple discharge.

5. A 40-year-old woman presents with a green–brown watery discharge from both nipples. She has a long history of mastalgia.

8. THEME: HAEMATURIA

A   Anticoagulant therapy
B   Catheter trauma
C   Cystitis
D   Glomerulonephritis
E   Polycystic kidney disease
F   Prostate carcinoma
G   Pyelonephritis
H   Renal cell carcinoma
I   Squamous cell carcinoma of bladder
J   Transitional cell carcinoma of bladder
K   Urethritis
L   Urolithiasis

The following patients have all presented with haematuria. Please select the most appropriate diagnosis from the above list. The items may be used once, more than once or not at all.

1. A 70-year-old obese man attends his GP for a routine check up. Apart from the backache that he has suffered for many years, he is also complaining of increasing dyspnoea. On examination he is hypertensive, BP: 195/115. Urinalysis: blood + +, protein +. Subsequent investigation revealed: Hb 19.8 g/dl, CCa^{2+} 3.0 mmol/l.

2. A 'miserable-looking' 12-year-old boy is accompanied by his concerned mother to children's A&E with lethargy, joint pain and puffiness around the eyes. On examination, he has periorbital oedema. Two weeks prior, the child was given penicillin for a recurrent sore throat. Urinalysis: blood +, protein + + +.

3. A 65-year-old man with past medical history of recurrent urinary tract calculi attends his GP with a 6-month history of painless haematuria and recent weight loss. On examination, the patient looks thin and clinically anaemic. Urinalysis: blood + + +, protein trace, nitrite –ve. FBC: Hb 10.2 g/dl, WCC 9.0 × 10^9/l; U&Es: urea 7.2 mmol/l, Cr 90 μmol/l; PSA 2 nmol/l.

4. A 35-year-old woman visits her GP with a short history of painless haematuria. Three weeks before she was admitted to hospital for treatment of pulmonary embolism after spending a holiday in Australia. Examination was unremarkable. FBC: Hb 11.8 g/dl, WCC 8.9 × 10^9/l, U&Es: urea 3.2 mmol/l, Cr 59 μmol/l. Urinalysis: blood + +, protein trace, nitrate –ve.

13

5. A 33-year-old man presents with a short history of severe right-sided abdominal pain radiating to the groin. He is writhing around, unable to sit or lie still. He is shown to have microscopic haematuria but an abdominal radiograph is normal.

9. THEME: GENITAL TRACT INFECTIONS

A   Bacterial vaginosis
B   *Candida albicans*
C   *Chlamydia trachomatis*
D   *Haemophilus ducreyi*
E   Herpes simplex virus
F   Human papillomavirus
G   *Neisseria gonorrhoeae*
H   *Sarcoptes scabei*
I   *Treponema pallidum*
J   *Trichomonas vaginalis*

From the above list please choose the infection or infectious agent most likely to cause the clinical picture described. The items may be used once, more than once or not at all.

1. A 30-year-old woman presents with a grey–white offensive vaginal discharge. Microscopy of the discharge reveals 'clue cells' and the vaginal pH is raised.

2. A 28-year-old woman has a flu-like illness followed shortly after by several, painful vulval blisters. She has had no recent foreign travel. On examination she has tender, bilateral inguinal lymphadenopathy.

3. Following a vaginal delivery from an asymptomatic woman, a baby develops ophthalmia neonatorum. Gram staining of the ophthalmic discharge reveals Gram-negative intracellular diplococci.

4. A 27-year-old woman has lower abdominal pain and on examination has a temperature of 38°C and cervical excitation on vaginal examination. Her partner is currently under treatment for non-specific urethritis (NSU).

5. A 32-year-old woman presents with offensive, creamy-yellow vaginal discharge. Examination confirms this and microscopy of the discharge reveals motile, flagellated protozoa.

10. THEME: NEOPLASMS

✗ ✓ ✓ ✓✓

A Adenocarcinoma
B Adenoma
C Chondroma
D Fibroadenoma
E Lymphoma
F Malignant melanoma
G Malignant mesothelioma
H Meningioma
I Osteosarcoma
J Squamous cell carcinoma

From the above list, please select the neoplasm that each of the following patients is most likely to have. The items may be used once, more than once or not at all.

1. A 65-year-old man presents with a 6-week history of rectal bleeding and altered bowel habit. Investigations show a mass in the sigmoid colon. Biopsy of the mass shows a malignant tumour composed of glandular cells.

2. A 35-year-old woman attends for a routine cervical smear. This shows severely dyskaryotic cells and highly keratinised cells suspicious of malignancy. Colposcopy shows a 3 cm polypoid mass on the ectocervix which bleeds on contact. Biopsy confirms an invasive malignant tumour.

3. A 74-year-old man with Paget's disease of bone presents with a two-month history of pain around the left hip joint. Radiographs of the hip and pelvis show a partly calcified lytic lesion in the left pelvic bone.

4. A 72-year-old man who had worked in a shipyard as a young man presents with a six-month history of worsening dyspnoea. A radiograph and CT scan of the chest show a mass in the right pleural cavity. Biopsy shows a malignant biphasic tumour.

5. A 22-year-old woman presents with a 3 cm mobile breast lump which is solid and has well defined margins on ultrasound. Fine needle aspiration cytology (FNAC) shows benign cells.

11. THEME: RELATIONSHIPS IN THE MEDIASTINUM

✗ ✓ ✗ ✗ ✓

A   Aortic arch
B   Azygos vein
C   Body of the 4th thoracic vertebra
D   Body of the 7th thoracic vertebra
E   Descending thoracic aorta
F   Inferior vena cava
G   Left vagus nerve
H   Oesophagus
I   Right phrenic nerve
J   Superior vena cava

For each of the following descriptions, please choose the most appropriate structure from the above list. The items may be used once, more than once or not at all.

1. Lies at the level of the xiphisternal joint.

2. Lies wholly within the superior mediastinum.

3. Has a lateral relationship to the right atrium.

4. Passes through the diaphragm at the level of the 10th thoracic vertebra.

5. Lies in the groove between the trachea and the oesophagus.

12. THEME: CUTANEOUS INNERVATION OF THE UPPER LIMB

A   Anterior interosseous nerve
B   Axillary nerve
C   Lateral cutaneous nerve of forearm
D   Medial cutaneous nerve of forearm
E   Median nerve
F   Posterior cutaneous nerve of arm
G   Posterior cutaneous nerve of forearm
H   Posterior interosseous nerve
I   Radial nerve
J   Ulnar nerve

For each of the following cutaneous areas please choose the nerve that innervates it from the above list. The items may be used once, more than once or not at all.

1. Nail bed of the index finger. ☐

2. Skin over the distal attachment of the brachioradialis. ☐

3. Skin over the pisiform bone. ☐

4. Skin over the distal attachment of the deltoid muscle. ☐

5. Skin over the common flexor origin. ☐

Paper 1 answers

1. ANAEMIA

1. **E – Iron deficiency**
   This patient has been started on clopidogrel which is one of the newer antiplatelet treatments used in ischaemic heart and cerebrovascular disease. Like aspirin it causes upper gastrointestinal inflammation and subsequent occult or frank upper GI blood loss. The blood results show a microcytic anaemia compatible with iron deficiency secondary to the blood loss.

2. **B – Aplastic anaemia**
   This patient has developed aplastic anaemia secondary to his phenytoin therapy. It is thankfully a relatively uncommon side effect of a number of medications remembered by the fact that most are an 'ANTI' treatment. ANTIbiotic (sulphonamides and chloramphenicol), ANTIepileptic (phenytoin), ANTI-inflammatory (indomethacin and gold therapy), ANTIthyroid (propylthiouracil, carbimazole), ANTIemetic (prochlorperazine), as well as ANTIcancer (all chemotherapeutic agents), ANTIhyperglycaemics (chlorpropamide).

3. **G – Pancytopenia secondary to multiple myeloma**
   This patient has developed a pancytopenia secondary to her multiple myeloma. She also has renal failure, hypercalcaemia and a grossly elevated ESR in keeping with the diagnosis. Other investigations should include plasma electrophoresis, looking for monoclonal gammopathy with associated immunoparesis, urinary Bence Jones protein and skeletal radiographs (in this patient's case, of the lumbar spine) looking for lytic bone lesions. Note: lytic bone lesions do not show up on radioisotope bone scan.

4. **J – Thalassaemia trait**
   This patient has a microcytic anaemia but if one compares the MCV in this patient with that of the patient in case 1 we can see that there is a grossly reduced MCV in proportion to the degree of anaemia. This and the normal ferritin are highly suggestive of anaemia secondary to thalassaemia trait. The diagnosis should be confirmed on haemoglobin electrophoresis and the patient's relatives should also be screened.

5. **C – Autoimmune haemolytic anaemia**

    This woman has developed a Coomb's positive haemolytic anaemia secondary to her pneumonia, the most likely cause of which is an atypical infection such as *Mycoplasma*. Coomb's positive haemolytic anaemias are subdivided into 'warm' and 'cold' by whether the auto-antibodies produced attach to the red cells at body temperature (warm) or 4°C (cold). Warm antibodies are principally IgG and IgA and are often idiopathic. They may be associated with haematological malignancies such as lymphoma and leukaemia, carcinoma and classically with the antihypertensive methyldopa. Cold antibodies (IgM) may also be idiopathic but are produced in association with EBV and *Mycoplasma* infections as well as lymphomas.

2. RESPIRATORY FAILURE

1. **A – Asbestosis**
   This man has developed asbestosis secondary to his previous employment. The asbestos fibres cause an inflammatory response over the pleural, pericardial and diaphragmatic surfaces leading to asbestos 'plaques'. These are signs of asbestos exposure but not of asbestosis. Asbestosis is the pneumoconiosis associated with asbestos exposure causing a basal fibrosis, unlike the other pneumoconioses which predominantly cause an upper zone/apical fibrosis. They may all progress to cause overwhelming pulmonary fibrosis and 'honeycomb' lung. Initially patients develop a type I respiratory failure, as in this case, but later with more diffuse disease the patient may develop a type II picture. Other complications include the development of mesothelioma which may occur thirty or more years after the exposure.

2. **H – Pickwickian syndrome**
   This obese man with COPD has developed Pickwickian syndrome. His early morning headaches and daytime somnolence are a result of his nocturnal hypoventilation, hypercapnia and intermittent episodes of sleep apnoea and waking. Patients classically have episodes of snoring followed by episodes of upper airway obstruction and apnoea. They should be treated as with any patient with COPD but should be encouraged to lose weight and may benefit from non-invasive ventilation at night which maintains the patency of the upper airway and thus oxygenation, whilst avoiding the apnoea and hypercapnia.

3. **J – Pulmonary oedema**
   This woman has developed pulmonary oedema, as shown by the classic 'bat wing' appearance on the chest radiograph. Her ABGs reveal a type I respiratory failure and a metabolic acidosis secondary to a lactic acidosis due to tissue hypoxia. She should be treated with 60–100% oxygen, sat upright and given diuretics. If she remains hypotensive she will need intravenous inotrope support.

4. **F – *Legionella* pneumonia**
   This woman has developed a dry, non-productive cough, type I respiratory failure, hyponatraemia and mild renal impairment. This picture is highly suggestive of an atypical pneumonia and in particular *Legionella pneumophila* infection. This diagnosis is confirmed, as in this case, by the presence of urinary antigens.

5. **E – Idiopathic pulmonary fibrosis**
   This man has developed signs and symptoms suggestive of a fibrotic lung condition, in particular idiopathic pulmonary fibrosis or cryptogenic fibrosing alveolitis. This is a basal fibrotic disease which has no identifiable cause. A very similar condition is seen in rheumatoid arthritis and the connective tissue diseases. The patients have type I respiratory failure and a restrictive picture on their spirometry. They may develop a more diffuse fibrotic picture with time and subsequent type II failure.

3. ASCITES

1. F – Ovarian carcinoma

A middle-aged woman presenting with ascites, with no history of liver disease or alcohol excess should be assumed to have ovarian carcinoma until proven otherwise. The Ca-125 is a marker of ovarian carcinoma, although it is better employed as a treatment marker rather than as a diagnostic tool. The diagnosis may be confirmed by ascitic cytology, ultrasound scan of the pelvis or laparoscopy and biopsy.

2. E –Ischaemic cardiomyopathy

This chronic smoker (as evidenced by her tar stained fingers) has signs consistent with gross, primarily right sided heart failure. Her signs of right heart failure include her peripheral oedema, ascites, raised JVP and tricuspid regurgitation. Her ECG suggests an old anterior myocardial infarction. This is the clinical picture of chronic ischaemic cardiomyopathy.

3. H – Peritoneal mesothelioma

This retired docker has signs suggestive of peritoneal mesothelioma. Prolonged asbestos exposure may lead to pleural, pericardial and diaphragmatic plaques, pulmonary fibrosis (asbestosis) and pleural and peritoneal mesothelioma. This relatively rare malignancy has a poor prognosis and at present the only treatments are palliative.

4. I – Renal cell carcinoma

This man has night sweats, lethargy, a microcytic anaemia and cannonball metastases on his chest radiograph. The diagnosis of renal cell carcinoma may be confirmed on urine cytology, renal ultrasound scan or CT scan of the abdomen. Depending on the tumour stage and histology patients, if well enough, may be offered nephrectomy, chemotherapy and radiotherapy.

5. J – Tuberculosis

Caucasian people with this presentation and CT findings would be assumed to have Crohn's disease or backwash ileitis of ulcerative colitis. Asian people however, rarely get inflammatory bowel disease and this is a typical presentation of tuberculous ileitis and secondary peritoneal tuberculous infection. The patient should be treated with a 6-month course of antituberculous treatment and may need nutritional supplements, and more rarely bowel resection.

4. HEADACHE

1. F – Saggital sinus thrombosis

This patient has developed saggital sinus thrombosis secondary to her oral contraceptive pill. Similar in pathogenesis to deep vein thrombosis and pulmonary embolism, saggital sinus thrombosis may occur in females or males with thrombophilic tendencies. Risk factors include: dehydration, malignancy, the oral contraceptive pill (female), thrombocytosis and the congenital coagulopathies including antiphospholipid syndrome, factor V Leiden deficiency, Protein C & S deficiency and antithrombin III deficiency.

2. A – Benign intracranial hypertension

This obese woman has developed 'benign intracranial hypertension'. This is a diagnosis of exclusion and is *not* truly benign as it can lead to blindness. Patients should be encouraged to lose weight (if overweight) and often improve with diuretics.

3. E – Meningitis (viral)

This patient has developed viral meningitis as evidenced by the normal CSF glucose and protein and lymphocytosis. The clinical picture may be very similar to bacterial or tuberculous meningitis although it is rarely fatal and primarily requires symptomatic relief with analgesia, anti-emetics and intravenous fluids. Patients should be nursed in a quiet darkened side room until the diagnosis is confirmed.

4. I – Subdural haemorrhage

This man has left-sided frontoparietal subdural haemorrhage (SDH) with significant mass effect to the right. The haematoma has caused a similar clinical picture to a stroke with hemiparesis. The patient should be referred for urgent neurosurgical opinion and evacuation of the SDH.

5. C – Giant cell arteritis

This patient has frontal headaches associated with shoulder pains and an ESR = 110 mm/h. This is the typical picture of giant cell arteritis. The patient should immediately be started on steroids (prednisolone 30–40 mg Ó.d.) and an attempt to confirm the diagnosis should be made within 48 h of the initiation of steroids by temporal artery biopsy.

5. EPONYMOUS SIGNS

Despite the fact that

(i) eponymous disorders or signs were rarely described first by their namesake
(ii) they often have little clinical significance, and
(iii) they merely confuse the overstressed (and under-prepared) student.

we make no apologies for including a few historical facts about the eponymous signs in this question.

1. **A & J – Chvostek's and Trousseau's signs**
   This patient has developed osteomalacia and subsequent marked hypocalcaemia, confirmed by Chvostek's and Trousseau's signs.
   Franz Chvostek, Viennese physician (1835–1884). The sign is positive when the VIIth (facial) nerve is lightly tapped below the ear producing ipsilateral hemifacial spasm.
   Armand Trousseau, Parisian physician (1801–1867). The hand goes into a characteristic spasm (*main d'accoucher*) when a blood pressure cuff is inflated for several minutes above systolic blood pressure.

2. **B, C & G – de Musset's, Duroziez's and Quinke's signs**
   This patient has signs consistent with significant aortic regurgitation. There are multiple eponymous signs associated with this disorder many of which relate to the significant 'collapsing' wave of blood back through the regurgitant valve.
   Alfred De Musset: this relatively famous 19th century French poet had significant aortic regurgitation. His (less famous) brother, a physician, described the associated nodding or titubation of the head.
   Paul Duroziez, French physician (1826–1897). Duroziez's sign is the most significant clinical sign of aortic regurgitation. It is a diastolic and systolic bruit heard over the femoral pulse whilst attempting to occlude the pulse distally to the stethoscope with the fingers (thus attempting to stop the regurgitant wave travelling back towards the heart).
   Heinrich Quinke, German nuerologist (1842–1922). 'Lighthouse sign' – flashing of the capillary bed when the fingernail is pressed distally.

3. **I – Troisier's sign**
   This patient has signs of gastric carcinoma. This maybe associated with:

(i) Troisier's sign – left supraclavicular fossa lymph node. Charles Emile Troisier, Professor of Pathology, Paris, France (1844–1919): this node is eponymously known as Virchow's node.

(ii) Sister Joseph's nodule: described by Sister Joseph to Dr William Mayo (of Mayo Clinic and salad dressing fame). This is a metastatic deposit within the umbilicus.

4. **A, E & J – Cullen's, Grey Turner's and Trousseau's signs**

   This man has developed acute, severe pancreatitis. This is associated with signs of peritonism and more rarely Grey Turner's sign (bruising in the flanks – George Grey Turner, English surgeon) and Cullen's sign (periumbilical haematoma or 'umbilical blackeye') first described by Thomas Cullen (1869–1953, Professor of Obstetrics) in relation to a ruptured ectopic pregnancy. Severe, acute pancreatitis is also associated with hyopocalcaemia.

5. **F – Nikolsky's sign**

   Nikolsky's sign (Pyotr Nikolsky – born 1858 – worked in Russia and Poland, dermatologist) – commonly seen in pemphigus and other blistering conditions such as dermatitis herpetiformis and drug eruptions. Firm pressure is applied to 'apparently' normal skin which then shears away.

6. ILIAC FOSSAE MASSES

1. **A – Appendix mass**

   In a young male, appendix mass tops the list of likely diagnoses (tubo-ovarian causes are probably most common in females of this age). The history is characteristic for acute appendicitis, in this case complicated by mass formation. It is caused by adherence of omentum/other adjacent viscera to a severely inflamed or locally perforated appendix, and may have an abscess component. Depending on the clinical state of the patient, and to some extent the size of the mass, treatment may be surgical or conservative (intravenous antibiotics).

2. **C – Crohn's disease**

   The preceding history should alert you to this diagnosis in a patient that might otherwise have an acute history and findings compatible with a diagnosis of appendicitis. Management depends on the patient's overall clinical condition, but surgery should ideally be avoided and the acute Crohn's treated medically and the disease assessed further by appropriate imaging.

3. **E – Iliac lymphadenopathy**

   The history here suggests a diagnosis of lymphoma although TB might also be a possibility had there been a history of exposure. The patient has presented with inguinal lymph nodes but an iliac node mass is also present.

4. **F – Ovarian cancer**

   A mass of this size in a woman strongly suggests this diagnosis. Other symptoms can include weight loss, vaginal bleeding from hormone disturbance or endometrial invasion, and unilateral leg swelling from lymphatic or venous compression. In addition to palpating the mass, there may be ascites. The patient may also be anaemic and have lymphadenopathy. (The classification of ovarian tumours and their treatment is covered elsewhere.)

5. **B – Caecal carcinoma**

   With a microcytic anaemia in a patient of this age (ie an age in which cancer is prevalent) you should strongly consider bleeding into the gastrointestinal tract as a result of neoplasia to be a possibility (the urogenital tract being the other major contender). Of GI malignancies, caecal carcinoma is the commonest cause of asymptomatic anaemia because other more distal colonic sites of malignancy tend to cause other symptoms such as diarrhoea / bleeding PR, and gastric cancer is less common than colorectal cancer. Colonoscopy, ideally, or barium enema is indicated.

7. NIPPLE DISCHARGE

There are five common causes of nipple discharge: breast cancer, fibrocystic disease of the breast, intraduct papilloma, mammary duct ectasia and lactation. The main points in diagnosis to consider are whether discharge is unilateral or bilateral, and whether it is bloodstained.

1. **C – Intraduct papilloma**
   This should be suspected from the age of the patient (younger than carcinoma) and the solitary symptom of recurrent blood stained nipple discharge without the finding of a discrete lump. A true papilloma is usually single and occurs in a major duct in the subareolar area. The tumour consists of hyperplastic columnar epithelium with a rich blood supply (hence the presentation). They are entirely benign. Mammography may show a dilated duct behind the papilloma, although there is usually no visible abnormality. Treatment is to excise the involved duct (microdochectomy).

2. **E – Mammary duct ectasia**
   Symptomatic duct ectasia is best considered an aberration of normal breast involution. Duct ectasia principally affects older women and presents as a slit like retraction of the nipple or with nipple discharge (brown/green or cheese-like). No special treatment is required unless discharge becomes troublesome, when a microdochectomy (excision of one duct) or subareolar resection (multiple ducts) may be undertaken.

3. **H – Prolactinoma**
   Prolactinomas are benign tumours of the anterior pituitary. They are four times more common in women than in men and usually present in young women in their second and third decades with a history of amenorrhoea (fertility problems) and galactorrhoea (as in this case). Tumours < 1 cm in diameter are termed microadenoma and > 2 cm, macroadenomas. The latter may extend into the suprasellar region causing optic chiasmal compression and visual failure. Treatment is usually trans-sphenoidal resection.

4. **A – Carcinoma of the breast**
   In a patient of this age with unilateral bloodstained nipple discharge, this diagnosis should be considered before all others, regardless of other clinical findings.

5. **B – Fibrocystic disease of the breast (fibroadenosis)**
   The bilaterality and colour of discharge associated with mastalgia point to this diagnosis. This is a diffuse and painful benign condition of the breast in women aged 25–45 years. The condition is characterised by exacerbations and remissions that are usually cyclical with the menses. Aetiologically the disorder is probably one of abnormal expression of physiological proliferative and involutionary changes. There are four main pathological processes: adenosis, epitheliosis, fibrosis and cyst formation. The diagnosis is made by the history and examination (as above) and mammography/ultrasound with or without cyst aspiration (when present) and cytology.

8. HAEMATURIA

1. **H – Renal cell carcinoma**
   The textbook description of a 'classic triad' of findings in renal cell carcinoma (haematuria, loin pain and abdominal mass) can in practice be obscured in an obese, elderly patient with chronic back pain. However other less common but recognised paraneoplastic effects, hypertension, polycythaemia and hypercalcaemia (secondary to ectopic hormone production of renin, erythropoietin and parathyroid hormone respectively) and effects of lung secondaries (dyspnoea), should alert you to the possibility of this diagnosis. Genito-urinary tumours (renal, testicular and ovarian) commonly cause 'cannonball pulmonary metastases'.

2. **D – Glomerulonephritis**
   The patient has developed a post-streptococcal (and therefore usually proliferative) glomerulonephritis. This condition usually develops 2–3 weeks after the streptococcal infection and presents with features of the nephrotic syndrome (generalised oedema, hypoproteinaemia, proteinuria). Investigations include throat swab for microscopy, culture and sensitivity and ASOT serology. The mainstay of treatment is supportive with elimination of the streptococcus infection itself. The prognosis in terms of progression to renal failure is excellent.

3. **J – Transitional cell carcinoma of bladder**
   Painless haematuria in this age group should firstly be considered indicative of this diagnosis since it is more common than renal cell carcinoma. Whilst squamous cell carcinoma of bladder is weakly associated with chronic urolithiasis, this is still a very uncommon tumour in Western populations where schistosomiasis infection is not endemic.

4. **A – Anticoagulant therapy**
   Warfarin treatment is a common iatrogenic causes of haematuria (the other being urethral trauma from catheterisation). The INR (or PTT) should be checked and dose adjusted if required. Patients may still require cystoscopy to exclude a lesion from which the bleeding has originated.

5. **L – Urolithiasis**
   This patient has ureteric colic which is caused by calculus obstruction of the right ureter. The appearance of a patient unable to get comfortable in any position is classic of this condition which causes acute, very severe colicky pain which may be felt in the abdomen or loin and classically radiates to the groin or even the tip of the penis. The finding of blood in the urine in a male invariably indicates pathology and is consistent with this diagnosis. The abdominal radiograph is normal because a proportion of ureteric stones are radiolucent. The confirmatory investigation is an IVU provided this is not contraindicated (asthma/allergy).

9. GENITAL TRACT INFECTIONS

1. A – Bacterial vaginosis

Bacterial vaginosis (BV) is a polymicrobial disturbance of vaginal flora characterised by lack of lactobacilli and overgrowth of anaerobic bacteria. The vaginal discharge is homogenous, grey in colour and offensive (anaerobic by-products). Clue cells represent epithelial cells coated with anaerobes ('iron-filings') and raised vaginal pH (> 4.5) is likely to be the underlying cause of the bacterial imbalance – together with the clinical characteristic discharge they are part of the diagnostic criteria for BV (positive amine test with KOH is the other criterion). *Trichomonas* is the only other likely cause of offensive discharge but this does not have the other above criteria.

2. E – Herpes simplex virus

Primary HSV infection is characterised by viraemic symptoms followed by multiple painful vulval ulcers and tender lymphadenopathy. Syphilitic ulcers (chancres) are classically single and non-painful and do not usually have a preceding flu-like illness. *Haemophilus ducreyi* (chancroid) also tends to be single lesions without systemic upset, and foreign travel is nearly always involved.

3. G – *Neisseria gonorrhoeae*

Ophthalmia neonatorum is transmitted to the fetus via contact with infected endocervical secretions during vaginal delivery in women with asymptomatic *N. gonorrhoeae* or *C. trachomatis* (the majority). *N. gonorrhoeae* are Gram-negative intracellular diplococci commonly seen on Gram staining of infected secretions. Though intracellular, *C. trachomatis* are not visible on microscopy of Gram stains.

4. C – *Chlamydia trachomatis*

Acute PID is characterised by lower pelvic pain plus at least two of: temperature > 38°C, pulse > 90 bpm, peritonism, cervical excitation and adnexal tenderness and a raised WCC. PID is caused by *Chlamydia* commonly and *N. gonorrhoeae* less commonly. If her partner has NSU, this is an umbrella term for urethritis before a causative organism is found (or not), the commonest cause being *Chlamydia*. Male infection with symptomatic *N. gonorrhoeae* is usually picked up at the time of presentation with Gram staining of urethral discharge and would therefore be very unlikely to be labelled NSU.

5. J – *Trichomonas vaginalis*

T. vaginalis and BV both cause offensive vaginal discharge (see 1. above) but *Trichomonas* is a motile, flagellated protozoon which can be seen when discharge is placed in a spot of saline on a microscopy slide.

10. NEOPLASMS

1. **A – Adenocarcinoma**

   An adenocarcinoma is a malignant tumour originating in glandular epithelium; an adenoma is the benign counterpart. Adenocarcinoma is the most common malignant tumour of the large intestine and is increasing in frequency, accounting for up to 15% of cancer-related deaths in industrialised countries. Rectal bleeding and altered bowel habit are typical presenting features of adenocarcinomas arising on the left side of the colon, while caecal and right-sided tumours more frequently present with anaemia.

2. **J – Squamous cell carcinoma**

   The main differential diagnosis of a malignant tumour of the cervix lies between squamous cell carcinoma and adenocarcinoma. Squamous cell carcinomas are more common than adenocarcinomas, accounting for about 80% of all cervical malignancies. Well differentiated squamous cell carcinoma produces keratin and this can be seen on a cervical smear as atypical keratinised cells.

3. **I – Osteosarcoma**

   This is the typical presentation of an osteosarcoma arising on a background of Paget's disease of the bone. Osteosarcoma is a malignant tumour of osteoblasts (bone-forming cells) and has a bimodal age distribution. So-called primary osteosarcoma arises predominantly in teenage boys and occurs most commonly around the knee. Secondary osteosarcomas develop as a complication of Paget's disease of the bone and therefore occur in the elderly. In this setting the most common sites of origin are the pelvis, femur and humerus. The malignant osteoblasts produce varying amounts of osteoid, some of which becomes mineralised, and this can be seen radiologically.

4. **G – Malignant mesothelioma**

   Malignant mesothelioma is a tumour of mesothelial cells that arises most commonly in the visceral or parietal pleura. Approximately 50% of patients with malignant mesothelioma have a history of exposure to asbestos, usually related to their occupation. Shipyard workers, miners and insulators are at greatest risk. The latent period for developing this tumour is long, often 25 to 40 years after initial exposure. Malignant mesothelioma is a biphasic tumour with both sarcomatoid and epithelioid elements. In this scenario, the differential diagnosis lies between malignant mesothelioma, squamous cell carcinoma and adenocarcinoma. The location of the tumour in the pleural cavity is strongly suggestive of mesothelioma but it is only the fact that the tumour is biphasic that distinguishes it from a squamous cell or adenocarcinoma.

5. **D – Fibroadenoma**

   Fibroadenoma is the commonest benign tumour of the breast and occurs most frequently in young women. Fibroadenomas arise from the breast lobule and are mixed tumours containing both glandular epithelium and connective tissue stroma. Like areas of fibrocystic change, the epithelium of a fibroadenoma is hormonally responsive so that there may be a slight increase in size during the second half of the menstrual cycle. Unlike fibrocystic change, however, fibroadenomas are well circumscribed and solid with a lobulated appearance macroscopically. Fibroadenomas are not tethered to the surrounding breast tissue and this accounts for their mobility on palpation.

11. RELATIONSHIPS IN THE MEDIASTINUM

1. **C – Body of the 4th thoracic vertebra**
    The line from the sternal angle to the middle of the body of the 4th thoracic vertebra separates the superior mediastinum above from the anterior, middle and posterior mediastinum below. The sternal angle is also the marking for the 2nd costal cartilage and this is a useful marker when counting ribs.

2. **A – Aortic arch**
    The aortic arch is formed from the ascending aorta and becomes the descending aorta. It lies within the superior mediastinum, giving off its innominate, left common carotid and left subclavian arterial branches. It arches over the hilum of the left lung.

3. **I – Right phrenic nerve**
    The right phrenic is also a lateral relationship of the inferior and superior vena cavae. It pierces the central dome of the diaphragm and innervates the right half from its undersurface.

4. **H – Oesophagus**
    The oesophagus pierces the right crus of the diaphragm at this level. The inferior vena cava pierces the central tendon at the level of the 8th thoracic vertebra and the aorta passes between the right and left crura at the level of the body of the 12th thoracic vertebra.

5. **G – Left vagus nerve**
    The vagi contribute to the pulmonary and cardiac plexuses before uniting as the oesophageal plexus around the lower oesophagus. They then form the anterior and posterior vagal trunks that pass with the oesophagus into the abdomen as the anterior and posterior gastric nerves.

12. CUTANEOUS INNERVATION OF THE UPPER LIMB

1. **E – Median nerve**
   The median nerve supplies the lateral aspect of the palm, the palmar aspect of the thumb and adjacent 2½ fingers, and their nail beds.

2. **C – Lateral cutaneous nerve of forearm**
   The nerve is a continuation of the musculocutaneous nerve. The radial nerve overlaps its innervation over the snuffbox and also supplies a limited area over the dorsolateral aspect of the hand.

3. **J – Ulnar nerve**
   The ulnar nerve supplies the cutaneous innervation of the medial aspect of the palm and 1½ fingers through its palmar branch, and through its dorsal branch the dorsal surface of the medial 3½ fingers.

4. **B – Axillary nerve**
   This is through its upper lateral cutaneous nerve of arm branch and has important clinical implications since it is a convenient way to test the integrity of the axillary nerve after shoulder dislocation, pain making it difficult to confirm associated paralysis of the deltoid muscle.

5. **D – Medial cutaneous nerve of forearm**
   This nerve pierces the deep fascia in the mid-upper arm with the basilic vein. It supplies the skin over the medial aspect of the cubital fossa and forearm to the wrist.

PAPER 2

Paper 2 questions

✓ ✗ ✗ ✓ ✗

1. THEME: HEART SOUNDS

A   Early diastolic murmur
B   Early systolic murmur
C   Ejection systolic click
D   Fourth heart sound
E   Late systolic murmur
F   Mid diastolic murmur
G   Mid systolic click
H   Opening snap
I   Pansystolic murmur
J   Third heart sound

The following patients have all presented with added heart sounds on auscultation. Please choose the most appropriate options from the above list. The items may be used once, more than once, in combination or not at all.

1. A 64-year-old man presents in A&E with increasing angina and two episodes of collapse on exertion. Of note he has a BP = 110/100 and his ECG shows the voltage criteria of LVH.

2. A 71-year-old woman is admitted in A&E with acute shortness of breath. On examination she is cold and clammy with a BP= 80/40 and is tachycardic with a pulse rate of 120 bpm. No murmurs are heard. Her ECG confirms a large anterior myocardial infarction.

3. A 32-year-old Somalian woman is admitted to hospital with heart failure. On examination she is noted to have a collapsing pulse, De Musset's sign and a grossly displaced, hyperdynamic apex beat.

4. A 69-year-old man with a previous history of rheumatic fever is admitted for a valve replacement. He is noted to have a low volume radial pulse, atrial fibrillation, rate 70–80 bpm and BP = 120/70 and has a 'tapping', undisplaced apex beat.

5. A 19-year-old woman is reviewed by an anaesthetic SHO prior to her undergoing a wisdom tooth extraction. She notes her to have an 'innocent' murmur consistent with a floppy mitral valve. The ECG reveals anterolateral T-wave inversion.

2. THEME: CHEST PATHOLOGIES

A Empyema
B Haemothorax
C Lobar collapse
D Pleural effusion
E Pneumothorax
F Pulmonary consolidation
G Pulmonary embolism
H Pulmonary fibrosis
I Pulmonary oedema
J Tension pneumothorax

The following patients have all presented with chest 'problems'. Please choose the most appropriate cause from the above list. The items may be used once, more than once, or not at all.

1. A 23-year-old man represents 2 weeks after being admitted for a spontaneous pneumothorax. On examination he is unwell, tachypnoeic and pyrexial. On examination of his chest he has decreased expansion on the left (the side of his previous pneumothorax), there is dullness to percussion with reduced breath sounds and tactile vocal fremitus on the left.

2. A 47-year-old man being investigated for weight loss and haemoptysis is admitted with increasing exertional dyspnoea. On examination he has a right sided Horner's syndrome and on examination of his chest he has dullness to percussion extending up to the midzone on the right associated with quiet breath sounds and reduced tactile vocal fremitus. Whispering pectriloquy is also reduced.

3. A 57-year-old previous pipe lagger and boiler fitter presents to his GP with a 6-month history of increasing exertional dyspnoea. On examination he has clubbing of the fingernails and marked fine inspiratory basal crepitations which are unchanged with coughing. His chest radiograph shows multiple pleural and diaphragmatic shadows.

4. A 29-year-old woman presents in A&E with acute shortness of breath. On examination she is obviously distressed and tachypnoeic. She is apyrexial and her oxygen saturation is 98% on air. Examination of her chest reveals her trachea to be in the midline, hyper-resonant percussion note on the right associated with markedly reduced breath sounds and vocal fremitus.

5. A previously fit and well 21-year-old man presents in A&E with a 4-day history of increasing shortness of breath, pleuritic chest pain and a productive cough. On examination he looks unwell, he is tachypnoeic and pyrexial. Examination of his chest reveals reduced expansion on the right secondary to pain and dullness to percussion associated with bronchial breathing and increased vocal fremitus in the right axilla.

3. THEME: ORAL AND GLOSSAL LESIONS

A   Aphthous ulceration
B   Atrophic glossitis
C   Candidiasis
D   Geographic tongue
E   Kaposi's sarcoma
F   Lichen planus
G   Perifollicular haemorrhages
H   Oral hairy leukoplakia
I   Snail track ulceration
J   Tonsillitis

The following patients have all presented with oral and/or glossal lesions. Please choose the most appropriate cause from the above list. The items may be used once, more than once, in combination or not at all.

1. A 29-year-old Malawian man presents in A&E with weight loss and a 4-day history of confusion and left sided paresis. On examination he is noted to have multiple violaceous lesions over his chest and palate.

2. A 34-year-old HIV-positive man is admitted to hospital with *Pneumocystis carinii* pneumonia (PCP). On examination he is obviously unwell and is noted to have white plaque-like lesions covering the right more than left border of his tongue. These do not scrape away with a tongue spatula.

3. A 21-year-old woman is admitted to hospital for investigation of 6-months of increasing weight loss and steatorrhoea. Examination is remarkable only for the fact she is thin and clinically anaemic. She is clinically euthyroid and has no lymphadenopathy. The diagnosis is confirmed with positive anti-endomysial antibodies and subtotal villus atrophy on duodenal biopsy.

4. A 31-year-old man on visiting his dentist is incidentally noted to have bilateral white papular lesions over the buccal mucosa and the dorsum of the tongue. He tells the dentist that these have been present for more than eighteen months and cause him no associated symptoms.

5. A 48-year-old homeless woman is brought into A&E by the police having been found unconscious. On examination she is dishevelled and pyrexial and has signs of a right lower lobe pneumonia. Amongst other nutritional deficiencies she is confirmed to have vitamin A and C deficiency.

4. THEME: GAIT DISTURBANCE

A Antalgic gait
B Cerebellar ataxia
C Festinating gait
D Hemiparetic/circumducting gait
E Hysterical gait
F Scissoring gait
G Sensory ataxia
H Spastic gait
I Trendelenburg gait
J Waddling gait

The following patients have all presented with an abnormal gait. Please choose the most appropriate cause from the above list. The items may be used once, more than once, in combination or not at all.

1. A 69-year-old woman with osteoarthritis of both hips for 4–5 years is referred to an orthopaedic outpatient department by her GP with increasing pain and immobility. On examination she has severely decreased abduction, internal and external rotation of both hips, the right worse than the left, and her gait shows her left hip 'giving way'. When asked to stand only on her right leg, her left hip is seen to 'sag down'.

2. A 64-year-old man with Dupuytren's contracture and gynaecomastia is seen in the outpatient department with falls. On examination has dysdiadochokinesia and past pointing.

3. A 37-year-old woman presents to her GP with falls. On examination she has a high stepping gait and is clinically anaemic.

4. A 64-year-old man presents to his GP with increasing instability and falls. On examination he has a resting tremor, cogwheel rigidity and 'mask-like facies'.

5. A 61-year-old woman on long-term steroids presents to her GP with increasing falls and 'weakness'. On examination she has difficulty standing from a sitting position and the GP finds she is unable to maintain her arms in abduction when he pushes lightly down on them.

5. THEME: LYMPHADENOPATHY X √√√//

A   Acute lymphoid leukaemia
B   Cytomegalovirus
C   Epstein–Barr virus
D   HIV
E   Hodgkin's lymphoma
F   Non-Hodgkin's lymphoma
G   Sarcoidosis
H   Syphilis
I   Toxoplasmosis
J   Tuberculosis

The following patients have all presented with lymphadenopathy. Please choose the most appropriate cause from the above list. The items may be used once, more than once or not at all.

1.   A 17-year-old schoolboy attend his GP with fevers, severe malaise and increasingly tender cervical lymphadenopathy. A Paul–Bunnell test is negative but an IgM immunofluorescent antibody test (IgM-IEA) confirms the diagnosis.

2.   A 24-year-old woman presents to her GP with increasing shortness of breath on exertion associated with a rash over her anterior shins. Apart from the rash, examination is relatively unremarkable but her chest radiograph shows bilateral hilar lymphadenopathy and her serum ACE and CCa^{2+} are elevated.

3.   A 29-year-old woman presents to her GP with increasing malaise and predominantly right sided 'massive cervical lymphadenopathy'. On examination she is noted to have firm 'rubbery' lymph nodes in the neck, axillae and inguinal regions. Her chest radiograph confirms bilateral hilar lymphadenopathy. The diagnosis is confirmed on lymph node biopsy which shows 'large abnormal predominant B-cell lymphocytes'.

4.   A 15-year-old girl presents to her GP with 'flu-like illness' for 2 weeks associated with pharyngitis and tender cervical lymph nodes. Her peripheral blood film shows atypical monocytes and the diagnosis is confirmed by increasing titres of specific IgM.

5.   A 31-year-old black Zimbabwian woman presents in A&E with a non-productive cough, fever and weight loss. Of note she looks very ill, has widespread lymphadenopathy and florid oral candidiasis. Routine investigations reveal a relatively normal chest radiograph but her peripheral blood film shows 'marked lymphopenia with atypical lymphocytes and thrombocytopenia'.

6. THEME: NAUSEA AND VOMITING

A   Appendicitis
B   Central neuronal causes
C   Cholecystitis
D   Drug therapy
E   Infective gastroenteritis
F   Metabolic
G   Obstruction: gastric outflow
H   Obstruction: large intestine
I   Obstruction: small intestine
J   Pancreatitis

The following patients have all presented with vomiting. Please select the most appropriate cause from the above list. The items may be used once, more than once or not at all.

1. A 67-year-old woman with a several month history of dyspepsia, nausea, early satiety and weight loss is admitted with a 4-day history of vomiting followed by an episode of coffee grounds. On examination the patient is anaemic, severely dehydrated and has a distended abdomen with a succussion splash. FBC: Hb 9.7 g/dl, WCC 10.8 × 10^9/l, Plt 368 × 10^9/l; U&Es: Na^+ 135 mmol/l, K^+ 2.9 mmol/l, urea 17.7 mmol/l, Cr 180 μmol/l.

2. A 25-year-old man returns from holiday with a 24 hour history of severe lower abdominal cramp-like pain with passage of watery brown offensive diarrhoea. He has felt generally unwell with flu-like symptoms for the preceding 2–3 days and is now vomiting. On examination he is clinically dehydrated and febrile (38.2°C), pulse 100 bpm. Hb 15.4 g/dl, WCC 14.8 × 10^9/l.

3. A 92-year-old lady presents with a 3-day history of colicky central abdominal pain and bilious vomiting. On examination the abdomen is distended and tympanic but non-tender. However, there is a small swelling in the groin which is tender.

4. An 80-year-old man is brought to A&E with confusion. He has been found at home lying in a pool of vomit which his son describes as brown and smelling of faeces. On examination he has a GCS of 14/15 and is clinically severely dehydrated. The abdomen is hugely distended, tympanic but not obviously tender. He has no surgical incisions and there are no herniae. His son adds that his father has had several months of abdominal pain, reduced appetite and weight loss.

5. A 38-year-old man with a history of attending the A&E department with injuries sustained whilst drunk presents with a 2-day history of increasing epigastric/left-sided upper abdominal pain radiating to the back. He is retching continuously in the department and is clinically dehydrated. There is upper abdominal tenderness and guarding.

7. THEME: AUDITORY CONDITIONS

A   Acoustic neuroma
B   Acute middle ear effusion
C   Acute suppurative otitis media
D   Cholesteotoma
E   Chronic serous middle ear effusion
F   Foreign body in the ear
G   Meniere's disease
H   Otitis externa
I   Otosclerosis
J   Referred pain
K   Wax

The following patients have all presented with otalgia, discharge from the ear or deafness. Please select the most appropriate diagnosis from the above list. The items may be used once, more than once or not at all.

1. A 59-year-old woman presents with a 1-year history of progressive hearing loss and ringing in her right ear. On examination she has an absent right corneal reflex and a partial, lower motor neurone facial nerve palsy. Audiometry demonstrates a right sensorineural deafness.

2. A 3-year-old child presents to his GP with a history of bilateral otalgia and poor speech development. On examination both eardrums are dull and indrawn. Acoustic impedance testing gives a flat trace.

3. A 40-year-old man presents with unilateral loss of hearing for 6 weeks. On examination the tympanic membrane is indrawn and dull. Acoustic impedance testing shows a flat trace. Audiometry demonstrates conductive deafness. On examination there is cervical lympadenopathy in the upper posterior triangle and examination of the postnasal space shows an ulcerated infected lesion.

4. A 25-year-old man is referred by his GP with recurrent right-sided otalgia without deafness or discharge. He has been treated unsuccessfully on several occasions for otitis media. On examination the external canal and tympanic membranes are normal but there is tenderness on palpation over the angle of the mandible. Dental examination shows that the right lower third molar tooth is not present. An orthopantomogram of the mandible shows an unerupted and impacted lower third molar (wisdom tooth).

5. A 55-year-old man is referred with an episode of acute vertigo associated with nausea and vomiting that gradually subsided over 24 hours. This left him 'unsteady' for 3 weeks. On direct questioning he had noticed hearing loss and tinnitus in his left ear before the vertigo, of which the tinnitus had increased shortly before the attack. After the attack he noticed that his hearing had also worsened. On examination the only abnormal finding is a left-sided sensorineural hearing loss, confirmed on audiometry.

8. THEME: HEAD INJURY AND GCS

A GCS 3
B GCS 4
C GCS 5
E GCS 7
F GCS 8
G GCS 10
H GCS 11
I GCS 12
J GCS 13
K GCS 14
L GCS 15

The following patients have all sustained head injuries. Please select the appropriate Glasgow Coma Scale (GCS) from the above list. The items may be used once, more than once, or not at all.

1. A 34-year-old man is hit on the vertex of the skull with a hammer by a mugger who steals his mobile phone. There is a large boggy swelling over the left high parietal region. There was a momentary loss of consciousness but he is now alert and orientated.

2. A 33-year-old builder falls from a low scaffolding hitting his head. At the scene, he was alert and orientated. On arrival in A&E he has a localised right temporoparietal boggy swelling. Approximately 1 hour later whilst waiting for further assessment he suddenly collapses in the waiting room. At this time his speech is confused, he has eye opening to and localisation of pain.

3. An 18-year-old French student is hit by a bus after looking the wrong way before crossing a road. He has severe external injuries to the scalp and facial skeleton and other internal injuries. He has no eye opening, verbal or motor responses. After appropriate sustained resuscitation a CT head scan demonstrates multiple vault and facial fractures and loss of the brain sulcal pattern with poor grey–white differentiation. There are small brain contusions but no focal space occupying lesion.

4. A 19-year-old girl falls from a height sustaining multiple injuries including blunt injury to the head. She is deeply unconscious on arrival in A&E and there are no responses other than extension to pain on the right-hand side.

5. A 24-year-old is attacked whilst leaving his bar one night after closing. On examination he has multiple facial injuries and scalp lacerations, bilateral black eyes and a left sub-conjuctival haemorrhage. Blood mixed with a clear fluid is leaking from his nose. He has eye opening to verbal commands, obeys some commands but is only mumbling occasional inappropriate words.

9. THEME: INFERTILITY

A Azoospermia
B Endometriosis
C Genital tract agenesis/dysgenesis
D Hypothalamic dysfunction
E Oligospermia
F Pelvic adhesions
G Pelvic inflammatory disease (PID)
H Polycystic ovary syndrome (PCOS)
I Prolactinoma
J Sexual dysfunction

The couples below have all recently been diagnosed with primary infertility by their GP. From the above list please choose the condition most likely to cause the clinical picture described. The items may be used once, more than once, in combination or not at all.

1. A 30-year-old woman has a long history of oligomenorrhoea and hirsutism. Her 29-year-old partner has no medical history of note. On examination she has a BMI of 32 and some male pattern hair distribution. Her routine investigations reveal FSH 3.1 u/litre, LH 8.7 u/litre, Testosterone is high-normal and SHBG is reduced.

2. A married couple are seen by their GP. The husband has no medical history of note and routine examination and investigations are all normal. His 26-year-old wife has secondary amenorrhoea but no other gynaecological or medical history of note. Her BMI is 17 but examination is otherwise unremarkable. Investigations reveal FSH 1.3 u/litre, LH 1.2 u/litre, testosterone and SHBG are normal and prolactin is 375 mu/litre. Her pelvic ultrasound is also normal.

3. A 36-year-old woman has a regular menstrual cycle but describes severe dysmenorrhoea and deep dyspareunia. She has no other gynaecological, medical or surgical history of note. On examination she has a fixed, retroverted uterus. Her 35-year-old partner has no medical history of note.

4. A 20-year-old woman has primary amenorrhoea, short stature, a webbed neck and appears 'young' for her age. Her LH and FSH are found to be grossly elevated and her oestradiol levels very low. Testosterone and SHBG are normal and prolactin is 275 mu/litre. Her 22-year-old partner has no medical history of note.

5. A couple with infertility are seen by their GP. The 36-year-old woman has regular cycles with no other gynaecological or medical history of note.

Her hormone profile and pelvic ultrasound are normal. Her 45-year-old partner has long-standing type 1 diabetes mellitus and has evidence of systemic vasculopathy and neuropathy. He is reluctant to provide a semen sample when requested.

10. THEME: PATHOGENS IN THE IMMUNOCOMPROMISED PATIENT

A   *Aspergillus flavus*
B   *Candida albicans*
C   *Cryptococcus neoformans*
D   *Cryptosporidium parvum*
E   Cytomegalovirus
F   Human papillomavirus
G   *Leishmania donovani*
H   *Mycobacterium avium intracellulare*
I   *Pneumocystis carinii*
J   *Toxoplasma gondii*

From the above list, please select the pathogen with which each of the following patients is most likely to be infected. The items may be used once, more than once or not at all.

1. A 32-year-old man who is receiving chemotherapy for high grade lymphoma presents with a 2-week history of dysphagia. Endoscopy shows white plaques on the oesophageal mucosa. Biopsy of the plaques shows fungal hyphae and yeast forms on the mucosal surface.

2. A 35-year-old HIV-positive woman develops shortness of breath accompanied by a dry cough. Chest radiograph shows bilateral reticulonodular shadowing. Sputum culture is negative. Transbronchial biopsy shows alveoli filled with a foamy eosinophilic material and numerous boat-shaped organisms staining positively with a silver stain.

3. A 40-year-old man with established AIDS develops abdominal pain, bloody diarrhoea and low-grade pyrexia. Sigmoidoscopy shows a friable ulcerated mucosa. Rectal biopsies show severe active chronic proctitis with 'owl's eye' intranuclear inclusions in endothelial and epithelial cells.

4. A 54-year-old woman who had a renal transplant 3 years previously presents with several warty nodules on both hands. On examination she has two similar lesions on the ectocervix. Excision biopsy of one of the cervical lesions shows a condyloma acuminatum with intraepithelial neoplasia grade 2 (CIN 2).

5. A 36-year-old HIV-positive man presents with severe watery diarrhoea, anorexia and malabsorption. Duodenal biopsy shows numerous small cysts adherent to the surface epithelium.

11. THEME: PATHOLOGICAL PROCESSES

A   Apoptosis
B   Atrophy
C   Dysplasia
D   Embolism
E   Fibrosis
F   Hyperplasia
G   Hypertrophy
H   Infarction
I   Metaplasia
J   Thrombosis

From the above list, please select the pathological process occurring in each of the following scenarios. The items may be used once, more than once, or not at all.

1.   A 75-year-old woman who is taking tamoxifen for breast carcinoma develops post-menopausal vaginal bleeding. An endometrial aspirate shows closely packed glands with obvious proliferative activity.

2.   A 45-year-old man who has been a heavy smoker for 30 years develops haemoptysis. His chest radiograph is suggestive of a bronchial neoplasm. Biopsies of the suspicious area taken at bronchoscopy show stratified squamous epithelium lining the bronchial wall.

3.   A 35-year-old woman suffers complications following a colectomy for toxic megacolon and is bed-bound on the intensive care unit for several weeks. On recovery, her legs are weak and both quadriceps are visibly wasted.

4.   A 72-year-old man suffers a right-sided 'stroke'. A CT scan shows a necrotic lesion with associated oedema in the left cerebral hemisphere.

5.   A 65-year-old man with long-standing emphysema develops right-sided cardiac failure. An echocardiogram shows a thickened right ventricular free wall.

12. THEME: INNERVATION OF THE MUSCLES OF THE UPPER LIMB

A   Anterior interosseous nerve
B   Axillary nerve
C   Long thoracic nerve
D   Lower subscapular nerve
E   Medial cutaneous nerve of forearm
F   Median nerve
G   Musculocutaneous nerve
H   Posterior interosseous nerve
I   Radial nerve
J   Ulnar nerve

For each of the following muscles please choose the nerve that innervates it from the above list. The items may be used once, more than once or not at all.

1. Serratus anterior.

2. Biceps.

3. Extensor carpi radialis longus.

4. Pronator teres.

5. Flexor carpi ulnaris.

Paper 2 answers

1. HEART SOUNDS

1. **B, C and D – Early systolic murmur, ejection systolic click and fourth heart sound**

    This man has presented with symptoms and signs suggestive of significant aortic stenosis. He has worsening angina due to obstruction of the coronary sinuses and exertional collapses. He has a narrow pulse pressure and a slow rising pulse. The murmur of aortic stenosis (ejection systolic or 'crescendo–decrescendo' murmur) may or may not be preceded by an ejection click and associated with a fourth heart sound, occurring in late diastole. A fourth heart sound reveals the pressure overload being experienced by the left ventricle. Other causes of a fourth heart sound include severe systemic hypertension, coarctation of the aorta and ischaemic heart disease leading to a poorly compliant left ventricle.

2. **D and J – Fourth and third heart sounds**

    This woman has developed acute cardiogenic shock associated with heart failure secondary to her anterior myocardial infarction. Such infarcts may be associated with a loud systolic murmur due to acute rupture of the mitral valve's chordae or the ventricular septum producing acute mitral regurgitation or a ventricular septal defect. No murmurs are heard in this case and so auscultation reveals the normal heart sounds plus a third and possible fourth heart sound. The early diastolic, third heart sound signifies 'volume overload' of the left ventricle leading to a 'gallop' rhythm. A fourth heart sound occurs late in diastole and is caused by the poorly compliant left ventricle associated with an acute infarct. It is more commonly associated with 'pressure overload' of the ventricle when the ventricle has to contract against increased resistance.

3. **A and F – Early diastolic murmur and mid diastolic murmur**

    This woman has signs consistent with significant aortic regurgitation. The murmur of aortic regurgitation is an early diastolic murmur heard loudest at the left sternal edge with the patient sitting forward in expiration. There may be an associated mid diastolic murmur, eponymously known as the 'Austin Flint' murmur. This murmur is supposedly caused by the 'regurgitant jet' of blood hitting the mitral valve in diastole.

4. **F and H – Mid diastolic murmur and opening snap**

    This man has signs consistent with significant mitral stenosis as evidenced by his low volume pulse in atrial fibrillation and the tapping, undisplaced apex beat. Mitral stenosis is a low rumbling mid diastolic murmur best heard at the apex using the bell of the stethoscope (L of beLL, L of Low rumbling murmur). It may be preceded by an early diastolic opening snap. The time duration between the second heart sound and the opening snap determines the significance of the mitral stenosis, the closer the two sounds the more significant the lesion.

5. **E and G – Late systolic murmur and mid systolic click**

    This patient has a floppy mitral valve which is characterised by a mid systolic click and a late systolic murmur. If the prolapse of the valve leaflets becomes significant there may be associated regurgitation, cardiac failure and this may require valve replacement. As with this patient, all patients identified as having a floppy valve require endocarditis prophylaxis when undergoing any procedure associated with a significant bacteraemia.

2. CHEST PATHOLOGIES

1. A – Empyema
This man has developed an empyema secondary to the insertion of a chest drain for his spontaneous pneumothorax. The signs are similar to that of a pleural effusion or haemothorax but the history and the pyrexial illness are more suggestive of the empyema. Treatment should include aspiration and/or drainage of the empyema, intravenous broad spectrum antibiotics, which should include an agent to cover staphylococcus, appropriate analgesia and antipyretics.

2. D – Pleural effusion
This man has signs and symptoms suggestive of a malignancy in the chest. He has now developed a malignant pleural effusion and a Horner's syndrome suggesting an apical tumour. He should have the effusion drained and fluid sent for cytology to confirm the diagnosis. He may also require a bronchoscopy and staging CT scan of the chest and abdomen. Treatment will depend on the histology, the stage of the tumour and the patient's wishes.

3. H – Pulmonary fibrosis
This man has developed basal pulmonary fibrosis due to asbestosis. The fine inspiratory crepitations that are 'fixed', ie do not change with coughing, are very typical of this disorder. The chest radiograph confirms asbestos exposure by the presence of the pleural and diaphragmatic plaques but it is only when the patient has signs confirmed radiologically and by respiratory function tests that one may infer fibrotic lung disease, ie asbestosis. Other complications of asbestos exposure include pleural and peritoneal mesothelioma.

4. E – Pneumothorax
This patient has developed a right-sided pneumothorax. The diagnosis should be confirmed on chest radiograph and treated by initial attempts to aspirate the free air using a large syringe, needle and three-way tap. If this fails to re-inflate the affected lung one should site an intercostal chest drain in the fifth intercostal space in the mid axillary line.

5. F – Pulmonary consolidation
This young man has developed right middle lobe consolidation as evidenced by the dullness to percussion, bronchial breathing and increased vocal fremitus in the right axilla. The radiological sign for this clinical problem is loss of the right heart border due to overlying consolidation. The patient should be treated with analgesia and intravenous amoxycillin or cefuroxime and clarithromycin.

3. ORAL AND GLOSSAL LESIONS

1. E – Kaposi's sarcoma
This man has developed AIDS-related illness with an intracranial lesion due possibly to toxoplasmosis, non-Hodgkin's lymphoma or an abscess. The violaceous lesions are consistent with Kaposi's sarcoma, which may produce lesions over the upper chest, back, palate, face, intrapulmonary and within the gastrointestinal tract.

2. H – Oral hairy leukoplakia
This man has developed white, plaque-like lesions over the border of his tongue which do not scrape away with a spatula. In view of his HIV disease this is most likely to be to oral hairy leukoplakia (OHL). Any part of the oral mucosa and tongue can be involved and there may be malignant transformation. In the absence of HIV-related disease it may be related to viral infection or smoking.

3. A & B – Aphthous ulceration and atrophic glossitis
This young woman has signs, symptoms and investigations suggestive of coeliac disease. This may be associated with aphthous ulceration and atrophic glossitis due to the associated malabsorption of vitamin B12 and folate.

4. F – Lichen planus
This patient has developed lichen planus which characteristically forms white linear lesions at areas of trauma. In the mouth this trauma occurs in the bite areas around the inner cheek and produces the classical white, lacy pattern that does not scrape away. Other commonly affected areas include the ankles and wrists and to a lesser extent the scalp, nails and genitalia. It is one of the skin conditions which exhibits 'Koebner's phenomenon'.

5. B & G – Atrophic glossitis and perifollicular haemorrhages
This malnourished patient has developed scurvy due to vitamin C deficiency, and, with the associated vitamin K deficiency, has severe bleeding of the gums. With this degree of malnutrition she will almost certainly have vitamin B12 and folate deficiency leading to atrophic glossitis.

4. GAIT DISTURBANCE

1. **A & I – Antalgic gait and Trendelenburg gait**

   This patient has developed a Trendelenburg gait due to her severe osteoarthritis around the hips. The abductors of the hip weaken with the chronic arthritis and this leads to the hip 'giving way' when standing on the affected side. If asked to stand only on the affected leg, the abductors are unable to hold the contralateral hip up and thus the raised leg 'drops down' – known as a positive Trendelenburg test. She may also have an antalgic gait.

2. **B – Cerebellar ataxia**

   This gentleman has signs of chronic liver disease and cerebellar disease as evidenced by the dysdiadochokinesia and past pointing. Patients classically have a wide-based ataxic gait.

3. **G – Sensory ataxia**

   This patient has developed a high stepping gait consistent with sensory ataxia due to peripheral sensory neuropathy. The patient is described as anaemic which suggests possible B12 deficiency with associated sensory neuropathy or subacute combined degeneration of the cord (SACD).

4. **C – Festinating gait**

   This patient has Parkinsonism with associated festinating gait. The most likely cause is idiopathic Parkinson's disease but secondary causes including vascular Parkinson's, iatrogenic-induced Parkinsonism and the Parkinsonism plus syndromes may also present in a similar manner.

5. **J – Waddling gait**

   This patient has been on long-term steroids which has caused secondary Cushing's and proximal myopathy as evidenced by the weakness of the upper limbs in abduction and being unable to stand from a sitting position. Proximal myopathy produces a 'waddling' gait.

5. LYMPHADENOPATHY

1. I – Toxoplasmosis
This young man has developed toxoplasmosis, which clinically may present in a very similar manner to EBV and CMV infections in the immunocompetent patient. It is caused by an intracellular protozoan, *Toxoplasma gondii* and may be congenital, or acquired by the ingestion of the cysts through infected lamb or pork meat or foods infected by cat faeces. The major clinical disorders associated with this illness cause lymphadenopathy, fever and may be associated with meningism, rashes, hepatosplenomegaly, eye problems and myocarditis. In most cases the disorder is a mild condition and is self-limiting, requiring no active treatment.

2. G – Sarcoidosis
This young woman has developed pulmonary sarcoid, as evidenced by the respiratory symptoms, probable erythema nodosum, bilateral hilar lymphadenopathy on her chest radiograph and raised serum ACE and hypercalcaemia. The diagnosis may be confirmed by bronchoscopy and bronchoalveolar lavage (BAL) which shows inflammatory cells with T-helper cells.

3. F – Non-Hodgkin's lymphoma
This patient has developed non-Hodgkin's lymphoma (NHL) as evidenced by the non-tender, firm, rubbery lymphadenopathy. The classification of this disorder is based on its division into high grade and low grade tumours. High grade tumours are characterised by rapidly dividing 'highly malignant' blast cells. Both types of tumour may also be subdivided into B-cell and T-cell lines although most non-Hodgkin's lymphoma tumours are B-cell in origin.

4. C – Epstein–Barr virus
This young girl has developed an EBV infection, or infectious mononucleosis, characterised by tender lymphadenopathy, pharyngitis, malaise, fever and lethargy. In the peripheral blood there are atypical mononuclear cells (hence its name) and specific EBV IgM antibodies. These are responsible for the diagnostic Paul–Bunnell reaction.

5. D – HIV
This patient has presented with widespread or generalised non-tender lymphadenopathy, a dry cough, fever, oral candidiasis and looks unwell. Her peripheral blood film shows lymphopenia with typical lymphocytes in keeping with new onset HIV infection. After counselling an HIV test should be performed along with a CD4 count and viral load estimation.

6. NAUSEA AND VOMITING

A complete overview of *all* the causes of vomiting (not possible in one EMQ: one recent review listed 150!) should broadly include: (1) central (intracranial and labyrinthine), (2) metabolic and endocrine (e.g. uraemia, pregnancy, diabetes), (3) iatrogenic (e.g. cancer chemotherapy, digoxin, opiates), (4) obstructive (any level – see above), and (5) mucosal (e.g. appendicitis, gastritis, cholecystitis).

1. **G – Gastric outflow obstruction**
   Gastric outflow obstruction, in this case is most probably caused by pyloric carcinoma of the stomach (the differential in this age group is pyloric obstruction secondary to peptic inflammation). Treatment includes resuscitation with correction of electrolyte disturbances, NG drainage then surgery (either palliative bypass or curative resection).

2. **E – Infective gastroenteritis**
   This can be caused by bacteria, enteroviruses and parasites. This patient probably has bacterial enteritis as evidenced by the history of foreign travel and symptoms and signs. A preceding flu-like 'prodrome' is also common before diarrhoea and vomiting ensue. Common causative infective agents include *E. coli* strains, *Salmonella*, *Shigella* and *Campylobacter*. Commoner causes of vomiting predominant enteritis are *Staphylococcus aureus* and *Bacillus cereus* food poisoning.

3. **I – Obstruction: small intestine**
   This is the classic clinical description of a patient presenting with small bowel obstruction: colicky central abdominal pain, distension, nausea and vomiting (eventually bile-stained). In this woman's case, the cause is probably a femoral hernia.

4. **H – Obstruction: large intestine**
   In this case it is probably caused by an obstructing colonic carcinoma. It should be noted that faeculant vomiting as described is not vomiting of faeces (which only occurs in rare cases of gastrocolic fistula) but small intestinal content which has stagnated and been altered by bacteria. This can thus also occur with distal small bowel obstruction but in this case no common cause for this is suggested in the vignette (adhesions/hernia).

5. **J – Pancreatitis**
   This is evidenced by the history of alcoholism and the clinical presentation. The differential would be alcoholic gastritis but the severe abdominal pain is more characteristic of pancreatitis. The diagnosis could be confirmed by blood biochemistry.

7. AUDITORY CONDITIONS

1. A – Acoustic neuroma

These represent 80% of cerebellopontine angle tumours and 8% of all intracranial tumours. They arise from the neurilemmal cells of a cranial nerve virtually always in the internal auditory meatus. They are slow-growing benign tumours but exert their effects by pressure on surrounding structures in the fixed space imposed by the bony cranium. The history of progressive loss of hearing and tinnitus (VIII nerve compression) should always prompt consideration of this diagnosis. The accompanying finding of adjacent cranial nerve dysfunction (ophthalmic branch of V) and of facial nerve (VII) is pathognomonic. Large tumours can also cause cerebellar signs and rising intracranial pressure.

2. E – Chronic serous middle ear effusion (glue ear)

This very common condition occurs in one in five children between the ages of 1 and 7 years. The aetiology is chronic obstruction of the eustachian tube and the condition is therefore often associated with adenoid enlargement, and is commoner in children with allergic rhinitis. If left untreated, 50% of cases resolve spontaneously within 6 months. Surgical intervention is drainage followed by grommet insertion. Adenoidectomy decreases the likelihood of recurrence.

3. B – Acute middle ear effusion

This patient has an acute middle ear effusion caused by blockage of the eustachian tube at its opening in the nasopharynx. Acute middle ear effusions usually follow flu and upper respiratory tract infections when mucosal oedema causes the obstruction. In children, acute suppurative otitis media may occur. In such cases the tympanic membrane may bulge outwards. However, in all other middle ear effusions (acute and chronic) the drum is retracted. In an adult (as in this case) a nasopharyngeal carcinoma must *always* be excluded by examination.

4. J – Referred pain

Dental and temporomandibular joint dysfunction are common causes of pain referred to the ear (mandibular branch of the V nerve). For this reason, any patient in which no intrinsic auditory cause of otalgia can be found should undergo oral and dental examination, not least because carcinomas of the oropharynx can present in this way.

5. G – Meniere's disease

Prosper Meniere (1799–1862) was a French ENT specialist, assistant of Baron Dupuytren, and friend of Balzac and Victor Hugo. The condition he described is characterised by **d**eafness, **d**izziness and tinnitus (**d**in) = **the 3 Ds** (as in this patient). All patients presenting with vertigo should have imaging to exclude an acoustic neuroma and testing for syphilis, as neurosyphilis may present in this way and should be treated.

8. HEAD INJURY AND GCS

BMR = **Best Motor Response**
BVR = **Best Vocal Response**
BER = **Best Eye Response**
EO = **Eyes Open**

1. **L – GCS = 15**

   This patient has a probable depressed skull fracture (by causative weapon and clinical findings) and despite his intact GCS should have a CT head scan to exclude brain injury (400 times the risk of a patient without skull fracture!) and to further assess the fracture morphology.

2. **H – GCS = 11**

   [BER = EO to pain = 2, BMR = localisation = 5, BVR = confused speech = 4]. This patient probably also has an extradural haematoma based on the description of a 'lucid interval' before a rapid decline in neurological status due to cerebral compression from arterial bleeding. The so-called 'talk and die' scenario.

3. **A – GCS = 3**

   There are no responses. The CT findings are those of diffuse axonal injury (the most severe type of diffuse brain injury, less severe being defined as mild concussion and cerebral concussion).

4. **B – GCS = 4**

   [BER = 1, BMR = 2, BVR = 1]. In many ways this is the worst GCS to have since it almost always implies severe brain injury with decerebration / decortication (a GCS of 3 can also be due to drugs, alcohol, hypoxia and fitting).

5. **I – GCS = 12**

   [BER = EO to speech = 3, BMR = obeys commands = 6, BVR = inappropriate words = 3]. The patient also probably has a base of skull fracture as evidenced by some of the characteristic clinical signs listed. These may include 'panda or racoon eyes', subconjuctival haemorrhage, otorrhoea or blood in the external auditory meatus and CSF rhinnorhoea.

9. INFERTILITY

1. **H – Polycystic ovary syndrome (PCOS)**
   The commonest cause of oligomenorrhoea and hirsutism, by far, is PCOS. It is diagnosed by PCO morphology on ultrasound *plus* clinical features including obesity (BMI > 30), hirsutism and acne, oligo/amenorrhoea and sometimes hypertension and type 2 diabetes. LH/FSH ratios are classically around 3/1 but can vary enormously. Testosterone levels are usually at the top end of the normal range but SHBG is low, meaning that the free androgen fraction is raised.

2. **D – Hypothalamic dysfunction**
   Secondary amenorrhoea has multiple causes. Her very low BMI suggests that PCOS is unlikely as the patients are usually obese (but need not be so). Her prolactin level is normal ruling out prolactinoma. With a very low BMI anorexia nervosa or excessive exercising is most likely which tends to switch off hypothalamic GnRH production leading to switching off of the Hypothalamic-Pituitary-Ovarian (H-P-O) axis (hence low FSH and LH) and therefore secondary amenorrhoea.

3. **B – Endometriosis**
   Her symptoms of severe dysmenorrhoea and deep dyspareunia suggest intrapelvic pathology. Her fixed, retroverted uterus and age (30–40 years) are the classic presentation of endometriosis. PID is more common under 30 years old and pelvic adhesions will often result from previous pelvic surgery of which she has no history. Though pelvic adhesions will often be present in someone with endometriosis and pelvic rigidity it is a secondary phenomenon and resultant upon the original disease (i.e. endometriosis).

4. **C – Genital tract agenesis/dysgenesis**
   Primary amenorrhoea has multiple causes and this woman has a classic description of Turner's syndrome (XO). In Turner's syndrome there is only rudimentary development of the ovaries (streak ovaries). Sometimes menarche is possible (secondary amenorrhoea is inevitable) but it commonly presents with primary amenorrhoea. As a result the hormonal profile is the same as menopausal ovarian function – low oestradiol and high gonadotrophins to try and stimulate the non-functioning ovaries.

5. **J – Sexual dysfunction**
   The regular cycles and lack of gynaecological symptoms give no obvious indication of anovulation or gynaecological disease though it cannot be completely ruled out. Men with long-standing type 1 diabetes mellitus can develop neurovascular impotence, which is commonly not talked about due to embarrassment. The semen characteristics are unlikely to be abnormal with type 1 diabetes mellitus alone.

10. PATHOGENS IN THE IMMUNOCOMPROMISED PATIENT

1. **B** – *Candida albicans*
    The finding of fungal hyphae in this patient's biopsy is diagnostic of fungal oesophagitis. The differential diagnosis lies between aspergillosis, caused by *Aspergillus* species, and candidiasis caused by *Candida* species, usually *Candida albicans*. The fact that yeast forms were also present rules out *Aspergillus* as this is not a yeast-forming fungus. In addition, the endoscopic appearance of white plaques on the mucosal surface is typical of candidiasis. This disease is common in immunosuppressed patients such as those on chemotherapy or with AIDS.

2. **I** – *Pneumocystis carinii*
    Pneumocystis carinii is an ubiquitous organism, now classified as a fungus. It does not cause disease in normal individuals but may cause a severe pneumonia in immunosuppressed patients. The organism cannot be grown in culture, so diagnosis requires cytological or histological identification. Useful cytological preparations include bronchial washings or lavage. Transbronchial biopsy shows foamy eosinophilic material in the alveolar spaces. On both cytology and histology, silver stain outlines the boat-shaped or cup-shaped organisms.

3. **E** – **Cytomegalovirus**
    The 'owl's eye' intranuclear inclusions are characteristic of cytomegalovirus (CMV) infection. Infected cells are strikingly enlarged and show intranuclear basophilic inclusions that are separated from the nuclear membrane by a clear halo. Over 50% of the adult population have serological evidence of infection with CMV, though infection is usually asymptomatic. As with other herpesviruses, CMV persists for life, becoming latent in leukocytes, which are the major reservoir. In patients with HIV and AIDS, the latent virus becomes reactivated and can be a cause of considerable morbidity, particularly in the later stages of the disease. The major problems encountered are colitis, retinitis, oesophageal ulceration, pneumonitis and encephalitis.

4. **F** – **Human papillomavirus**
    Warts are benign tumours of squamous epithelium known as squamous cell papillomas. They arise not only in keratinised squamous epithelium, such as the skin, but also in non-keratinised squamous epithelium such as that lining the ectocervix, where they are termed condyloma acuminatum. All warts are caused by human papillomavirus (HPV), of which there are many serotypes. Genital warts are sexually transmitted and are caused by HPV types 6 and 11. Other serotypes, notably 16, 18 and 31, have been implicated in the development of high grade cervical intraepithelial neoplasia (CIN) and invasive cervical carcinoma. In immunosuppressed patients HPV-associated warts are slow to respond to treatment, recur repeatedly and progress to dysplasia and malignancy more rapidly than in normal individuals.

5. **D – *Cryptosporidium parvum***

The two organisms on this list that commonly cause diarrhoea are cytomegalovirus and *Cryptosporidium parvum*. The typical features of CMV infection have been described above. *Cryptosporidium parvum* causes a self-limiting acute diarrhoea in normal individuals but in HIV infected patients it causes severe progressive watery diarrhoea associated with anorexia, nausea, vomiting and abdominal pain. Cysts attach to the surface epithelium of the small intestine causing malabsorption and secretion of fluid into the intestinal lumen. The cysts are readily identified on duodenal biopsy and can also be seen on stool microscopy using a special stain.

11. PATHOLOGICAL PROCESSES

1. F – Hyperplasia

Hyperplasia is an increase in the *number* of cells in a given cell population. In contrast, hypertrophy is an increase in *size* of cells without an increase in number. Hyperplasia is usually hormonally driven while hypertrophy occurs in response to an increased workload. The decrease in oestrogen levels that results from the menopause causes atrophy of the post-menopausal endometrium with widely spaced glands that lack mitotic activity. In contrast, this patient's endometrium has closely packed glands with obvious proliferation, indicating hyperplasia. Hyperplasias of the endometrium occur in response to excess oestrogen. This can be endogenous (from an oestrogen-secreting ovarian tumour, for example) or exogenous as a result of oestrogen therapy. In the breast, tamoxifen is an oestrogen antagonist, hence its widespread use in the treatment of breast carcinoma, but in the endometrium it acts as a partial oestrogen agonist. Hence, endometrial hyperplasia is common in women on tamoxifen.

2. I – Metaplasia

Metaplasia is a change in cell type from one fully differentiated form to another fully differentiated form. It is usually a protective response to chronic irritation or cell damage, the new cell type being more able to withstand the irritating agent than the original. The respiratory tract is normally lined by ciliated pseudostratified columnar epithelum. This type of epithelium cannot easily withstand the injury caused by cigarette smoke so metaplasia occurs to stratified squamous epithelium, which is better able to bear the damage. Like many other metaplastic conditions, squamous metaplasia of the bronchus is prone to developing dysplasia and hence is associated with an increased risk of malignancy.

3. B – Atrophy

Atrophy is a decrease in the size of cells, tissues or organs, often leading to a loss of function. Lack of use of striated muscles, as often occurs in patients who are bed-bound, leads to shrinkage in the size of myocytes and to loss of muscle bulk. This is known as disuse atrophy.

4. H – Infarction

A stroke is defined as a neurological deficit that lasts more than 24 hours. Infarction is defined as necrosis of tissue caused by interruption of its blood supply. The vast majority of strokes are caused by either cerebral infarction or cerebral haemorrhage. In this patient's case, there is a necrotic lesion in the left hemisphere, and although the CT appearances are not pathognomonic, of the options available, a cerebral infarct is the most likely.

5. **G – Hypertrophy**

As described in answer 1, hypertrophy is an increase in *size* of cells without an increase in number and usually occurs in response to an increased workload. In patients with chronic lung disease, the right ventricle has to pump against increased vascular resistance and its workload is therefore increased. The consequent increase in size of the cardiac myocytes leads to right ventricular hypertrophy and eventually right-sided heart failure. Right ventricular hypertrophy as a consequence of chronic lung disease is termed *cor pulmonale*.

12. INNERVATION OF THE MUSCLES OF THE UPPER LIMB

1. **C – Long thoracic nerve**
   The nerve arises from the 5th, 6th and 7th roots of the brachial plexus and passes downwards behind the trunks and vessels, to reach the medial wall of the axilla and supply the muscle.

2. **G – Musculocutaneous nerve**
   The nerve is a terminal branch of the lateral cord of the brachial plexus. It passes laterally to supply coracobrachialis, biceps and brachialis, and emerges lateral to these muscles to pierce the deep fascia in front of the elbow and become the lateral cutaneous nerve of the forearm.

3. **I – Radial nerve**
   The nerve is the continuation of the posterior cord of the brachial plexus. It passes obliquely over the spiral groove of the humerus in the posterior compartment of the arm. It supplies triceps, brachioradialis and extensor carpi radialis longus. Its posterior interosseous branch supplies the muscles arising from the common extensor origin and from the extensor aspect of the forearm.

4. **F – Median nerve**
   The median nerve passes between the heads of the pronator teres and deep to the flexor digitorum superficialis in the forearm supplying both of these muscles together with the flexor carpi radialis, palmaris longus, thenar muscles except adductor longus, lateral two lumbricals and, through its anterior interosseous branch, the flexor pollicis longus, pronator quadratus and the lateral half of the flexor digitorum profundus.

5. **J – Ulnar nerve**
   The ulnar nerve enters the forearm between the heads of the flexor carpi ulnaris and supplies it and the medial half of the flexor digitorum profundus, the hypothenar and interosseous muscles, the medial two lumbricals and the adductor pollicis muscle.

PAPER 3

Paper 3 questions

1. THEME: CARDIAC THERAPIES

A   Abciximab
B   Aspirin
C   Atenolol
D   Bisoprolol
E   Clopidogrel
F   Insulin
G   Isosorbide mononitrate
H   Nicorandil
I   Streptokinase
J   tPA

The following patients have all presented with cardiac disease. Please choose the NEXT most appropriate therapeutic intervention from the above list. The items may be used once, more than once or not at all.

1. A 61-year-old man with long-standing ischaemic heart disease is re-referred to the cardiology outpatient clinic with a 3-month history of worsening shortness of breath on exertion and occasional episodes of angina lasting no longer than 2–3 min and always relieved with GTN spray. His echocardiogram shows mild to moderate LV dysfunction. He is on clopidogrel (he could not tolerate aspirin) and GTN spray prn.

2. A 79-year-old woman presents in A&E with angina-like chest pain for the previous 3 hours, which is now resolving. She is haemodynamically stable but her ECG shows ST depression in leads V_1–V_4. She is admitted and placed on aspirin and metoprolol. Her subsequent troponin I is negative.

3. A 44-year-old man who is awaiting transfer for coronary stenting develops further angina pain that persists despite low-molecular-weight heparin, a nitrate infusion and maximal oral antianginal therapy.

4. A 38-year-old man with a strong family history of IHD presents in A&E with a 90-minute history of severe central chest pain. On examination in the resuscitation area he is tachycardic, hypotensive and looks distressed and unwell. His ECG confirms ST elevation in leads V_1–V_4. He was given aspirin by the paramedics and has received some diamorphine and anti-emetic for the pain.

5. A 64-year-old man presents to his GP with a 3-month history of worsening angina. He is placed on a β blocker and aspirin and is told to use a GTN spray if and when he gets any further pain. Six months later he returns complaining of worsening pains. He is referred to the cardiology clinic for further assessment.

2. THEME: BACK PAIN

A   Acute disc prolapse
B   Ankylosing spondylitis
C   Lytic metastases
D   Multiple myeloma
E   Osteoarthritis
F   Osteoporotic collapse
G   Paget's bone disease
H   Pott's disease of the spine
I   Retroperitoneal haematoma
J   Sclerotic metastases

The following patients have all presented with back pain. Please choose the most appropriate cause from the above list. The items may be used once, more than once, in combination or not at all.

1. A 25-year-old man presents to his GP with a 4-month history of increasing pain in his lumbar spine radiating into his buttocks and down the backs of his lower limbs. He has also had red painful eyes over the last few weeks. Radiographs of his lumbar spine and pelvis reveal erosions of his sacroiliac joints.

2. A 67-year-old man presents to his GP with increasing pain in his lower back, malaise and lethargy. On examination he is clinically anaemic and has marked purpura over his forearms. He has hepatosplenomegaly but no associated lymphadenopathy and is tender over L3–L4. Routine investigations show FBC: Hb 6.1 g/dl, MCV 89 fl, WCC 3.2 × 10⁹/l, Plt 21 × 10⁹/l; ESR 117 mm/h.

3. A 39-year-old homeless man is admitted to hospital with severe mid-thoracic back pain. On examination he is unwell, pyrexial and is very tender over T8–T9. The radiograph of his thoracic spine shows loss of the intervertebral space between T8–T9 and erosion of the two vertebral bodies.

4. A 47-year-old woman presents to her GP with a 5-month history of change in bowel habit and weight loss. Subsequent colonoscopy reveals a large polypoid tumour at 37 cm from the anal margin which is surgically excised. Four months later she returns to the GP with severe lumbar back pain.

5. A 74-year-old man presents to his GP with severe lower back, hip and pelvic pain. Radiographs of his pelvis show 'increased trabecular pattern with cortical thickening'.

3. THEME: CAUSES OF ABDOMINAL PAIN

A   Acute intermittent porphyria
B   Acute pancreatitis
C   Diabetes mellitus
D   Diverticulitis
E   Gallstones
F   Incarcerated femoral hernia
G   Mesenteric ischaemia
H   Peptic ulcer
I   Splenic infarct
J   Spontaneous bacterial peritonitis

The following patients have all presented with abdominal pain. Please choose the most appropriate cause from the above list. The items may be used once, more than once or not at all.

1. A 29-year-old man presents in A&E with severe generalised abdominal pain and vomiting after a night of celebrating his birthday. On examination he is tachycardic, hypertensive and is obviously ethanolic. FBC: Hb 13.9 g/dl , MCV 86 fl, WCC 11.9 × 10^9/l, Plt 299 × 10^9/l; U&Es: Na$^+$ 134 mmol/l, K$^+$ 3.9 mmol/l, urea 6.6 mmol/l, Cr 84 μmol/l, amylase 67 iu/l; LFTs: Tbil 29 μmol/l, AST 54 iu/l, Alk phos 127 iu/l, Alb 39 g/l.

2. A 34-year-old overweight woman presents to her GP with severe upper abdominal pain and vomiting. On examination she is unwell, jaundiced and pyrexial. She has a positive Murphy's sign. She is admitted to hospital and improves with intravenous cefuroxime and metronidazole. FBC: Hb13.9 g/dl, WCC 23.5 × 10^9/l , Plt 322 × 10^9/l; LFTs: Tbil 41 μmol/l, AST 39 iu/l, Alk phos 347 iu/l, Alb 37 g/l, γGT 184 iu/l, amylase 210 iu/l.

3. A 91-year-old woman is admitted to hospital with severe left lower quadrant pain. On examination she is unwell, distressed and has obvious left lower quadrant rebound and tenderness. The SHO documents there is *no* hernia but the abdominal radiograph reveals dilated loops of small bowel consistent with obstruction.

4. A 42-year-old man with a long history of alcohol excess presents with severe general abdominal pain. He is encephalopathic, jaundiced and has clinical ascites. He has severe, general abdominal tenderness. An ascitic tap reveals > 250 WCC/mm^3.

5. A 47-year-old smoker presents to his GP with recurrent upper abdominal pain associated with meals. Of note he has had two previous myocardial infarctions and experiences intermittent claudication in the calves, right more than the left. Routine blood tests including FBC, U&Es, LFTs and amylase are normal and OGD shows mild gastritis with a negative CLO test.

4. THEME: DELIRIUM

A   Atypical pneumonia
B   Encephalopathy
C   Hypercalcaemia
D   Hypercapnia
E   Hypoglycaemia
F   Hyponatraemia
G   Meningitis
H   Opiate narcosis
I   Subdural haemorrhage
J   Uraemia

The following patients have all presented with delirium. Please choose the most appropriate cause from the above list. The items may be used once, more than once or not at all.

1. An 83-year-old woman is found at home by her son, she is very confused and is dragging her left leg. He takes her to the local hospital and tells the admitting doctor that she has been deteriorating for the past 10 days since falling down a flight of steps whilst out on a coach trip with her friends.

2. A 92-year-old previously fit and well woman is admitted to hospital with diarrhoea, faecal incontinence and increasing confusion. Routine investigations reveal FBC: Hb 12.2 g/dl, MCV 85 fl, WCC 7.8 × 10⁹/l (with a relative lymphopenia), Plt 377 × 10⁹/l; U&Es: Na⁺ 127 mmol/l, K⁺ 4.3 mmol/l, urea 9.7 mmol/l, Cr 107 μmol/l. She is noted to have type I respiratory failure despite a relatively normal chest radiograph.

3. A 78-year-old woman is placed on paroxetine by her GP following the death of her son in a motorbike accident. Three weeks later the GP is called out by the patient's youngest son who is concerned that she has become increasingly confused. The GP can find no abnormalities on examination, urinalysis and BM. The son does not want her admitted to hospital, so the GP stops the paroxetine and sends some routine blood tests. She improves over the next week as do her abnormal tests.

4. A 79-year-old woman with known hypertension and ischaemic heart disease is started on ramipril by a SHO in outpatients. Her other medications include bendrofluazide and spironolactone. Six weeks later she is admitted to hospital with increasing confusion and is noted to have hiccups and 'twitches'.

5. A 79-year-old woman is started on chlorpropamide in Pakistan after being admitted to hospital with chest pains and high blood glucose. Several months after her return to the UK she is found at home by her daughter very clammy and confused. She improves with some glucagon administered by the paramedics at the scene.

5. THEME: SKIN RASHES

A   Contact dermatitis
B   Discoid lupus
C   Erythema multiforme
D   Erythema nodosum
E   Lupus vulgaris
F   Pemphigoid
G   Pemphigus
H   Psoriasis
I   Pyoderma gangrenosum
J   Rosacea

The following patients have all presented with a skin rash. Please choose the most appropriate cause from the above list. The items may be used once, more than once or not at all.

1. A 17-year-old woman who has recently been started on the oral contraceptive pill presents to her GP with a painful rash over her anterior shins. On examination the GP notes the lesions have coalesced and are tender to palpation.

2. A previously fit and well 27-year-old man is referred to the 'leg-ulcer' clinic with an ulcerating lesion on the left anterior shin. He describes the lesion as starting several weeks ago as an area of pustules which 'joined' to form the bigger ulcer.

3. A 69-year-old woman is admitted to hospital with delirium secondary to a urinary tract infection. She is started on trimethoprim but 2 days later develops a severe blistering rash over her limbs, back, chest and abdomen. The SpR comments on the presence of 'target lesions'.

4. A 77-year-old man presents in A&E with a severe blistering rash involving 'most areas of his skin'. The PRHO notes the blisters are 'completely popped and raw' and involve his face and oral mucosa. He improves slowly with oral prednisolone.

5. A 21-year-old Asian man is seen admitted to hospital with a severe pneumonia, haemoptysis and fever. The SHO notes a scaling plaque like lesion over his anterior shin. A biopsy confirms 'granulomatous infiltration with positive staining for AAFBs'.

6. THEME: RECTAL BLEEDING

A   Anal carcinoma
B   Anal fissure
C   Angiodysplasia
D   Colonic carcinoma
E   Colonic polyp
F   Crohn's disease
G   Diverticular disease
H   Haemorrhoids
I   Infective colitis
J   Ischaemic colitis
K   Ulcerative colitis

The following patients have all presented with rectal bleeding. Please select the most appropriate diagnosis from the above list. The items may be used once, more than once or not at all.

1. An 18-year-old mother presents with a 1-week history of bright red rectal bleeding and severe anal pain on defaecation. Her symptoms started post-partum. On examination rectal examination is impossible because of discomfort but no obvious abnormality is seen.

2. A 32-year-old man presents with a 3-week history of lower abdominal colicky pain, diarrhoea (bowels open 6–10 times per day) and passage of blood mixed with the stool. FBC: Hb 9.8 g/dl, WCC 12.1 × 10^9/l, MCV 78.6 fl; ESR: 62 mm/h.

3. A 76-year-old woman with a 10-year history of intermittent constipation and left-sided abdominal pain presents in A&E with a 48-hour history of dark-red rectal bleeding. Rectal examination is unremarkable, sigmoidoscopy demonstrates blood in the lumen. She had a similar episode investigated 1 year previously with no site of bleeding found.

4. A 37-year-old homosexual presents with a 3-month history of episodes of bright red rectal bleeding associated with soreness and pruritis ani. On examination he has widespread excoriations perianally, and an area of ulceration at the anal verge with an everted irregular edge.

5. A 92-year-old woman presents with painless bright red rectal bleeding with no other associated symptoms. She has a normal barium enema and is sent back to the nursing home. One week later she rebleeds and returns to A&E. Again the bleeding settles and after re-transfusion she undergoes a gastroscopy and colonoscopy. No abnormality is found and she is referred for mesenteric angiography.

7. THEME: COMMON FRACTURE EPONYMS

A   Barton's fracture
B   Bennet's fracture
C   Colles' fracture
D   Galleazzi fracture
E   Garden II fracture
F   Garden IV fracture
G   Monteggia fracture
H   Pott's fracture
I   Salter Harris' fracture
J   Smith's fracture

The following are descriptions of fractures. Please select the most appropriate fracture eponym from the above list. These are all commonly used in current clinical practice (and thus remain important). The items may be used once, more than once or not at all.

1. An injury in which the upper half of the ulna is fractured and the radial head is dislocated.

2. An injury in a child involving the growth plate (physis).

3. An injury in which the fibula and tibia are fractured at the ankle.

4. A complete but undisplaced fracture of the neck of femur.

5. A fracture-subluxation of the first metacarpal.

8. THEME: SALIVARY GLAND DISEASE

A Adenoid cystic carcinoma
B Bacterial sialadenitis
C HIV-associated sialadenitis
D Lymphoma
E Pleomorphic adenoma
F Sjögren's syndrome
G Sialolithiasis
H Viral parotitis
I Warthin's tumour

The following are descriptions of patients with salivary gland disorders. Please select the most appropriate descriptive term from the above list. The items may be used once, more than once or not at all.

1. A 67-year-old man with progressive dysphagia and cachexia is nil by mouth for an endoscopy. You are called to see him on the ward where on examination he is dehydrated, pyrexial and has a left parotid swelling which is hot and tender.

2. A 21-year-old man presents in an ophthalmology clinic with dry eyes and recurrent conjunctivitis. On direct questioning he admits to dry mouth. On examination there is swelling of his salivary glands and cervical lymphadenopathy. There is no history of polyarthritis and a full auto-antibody screen is negative.

3. A 32-year-old man presents with a short history of acute left submandibular pain and swelling immediately (1 minute) after eating.

4. A 44-year-old woman is referred to surgical clinic by her GP with a small 3 cm swelling in the region of the right parotid gland. The swelling is smooth and non-tender. There is no lymphadenopathy. Facial nerve function is intact.

5. An 80-year-old man has a long-standing swelling of the left parotid gland which he declined to have removed because of ill health. Recently, the mass has grown markedly causing pain. Of note he has a lower motor neurone facial nerve palsy.

9. THEME: INTRAPARTUM COMPLICATIONS

A   Cephalopelvic disproportion (CPD)
B   Chorioamnionitis
C   Cord prolapse
D   Malposition of the occiput
E   Meconium-stained liquor
F   Placental abruption
G   Ruptured uterus
H   Shoulder dystocia
I   Uterine hyperstimulation
J   Uterine inertia

From the above list please choose the item most likely to have caused the clinical picture described. The items may be used once, more than once or not at all.

1. A 30-year-old primiparous woman is being induced at 42 weeks' gestation for prolonged pregnancy. Her antenatal period has been complicated by idiopathic polyhydramnios. The presenting part (cephalic) is 5/5th palpable. Immediately after a controlled ARM there is a fetal bradycardia to 60 bpm. There is no PV bleeding and the uterus is soft and non-tender. After a vaginal examination the registrar positions the woman on all fours with elbows to knees and head down before taking her straight for emergency Caesarean section.

2. A 30-year-old primiparous woman is in spontaneous labour at term. Her antenatal period has been uneventful. She is 5 cm dilated at 6am. At her next vaginal examination at 10am she is still 5 cm dilated.

3. A 30-year-old primiparous low-risk woman is in spontaneous labour at term. Her antenatal period has been uneventful. She is 5 cm dilated at 6am and is being monitored by intermittent auscultation. After spontaneous rupture of membranes (SROM), the registrar recommends continuous cardiotocography (CTG) monitoring with a quick recourse to fetal blood sampling (FBS) in the presence of CTG abnormalities.

4. A 30-year-old primiparous low-risk woman is in spontaneous labour at term. Her antenatal period has been uneventful. She is on a syntocinon infusion for slow progress and is contracting 5–6 in 10 min strongly. The CTG shows repeated late decelerations. The registrar attends and stops the syntocinon infusion and awaits events over the next few minutes.

5. A 30-year-old multiparous low-risk woman is in spontaneous labour at term. Her antenatal period has been uneventful. Her labour has progressed well to 8 cm dilatation but after a further 2 hours she is still 8 cm dilated. She is contracting 3 in 10 strongly. The registrar examines her vaginally and is unwilling to use syntocinon, preferring to reassess her in 1 hour.

10. THEME: BACTERIAL INFECTIONS

A   *Campylobacter jejuni*
B   *Clostridium difficile*
C   *Clostridium perfringens*
D   *Escherichia coli*
E   *Helicobacter pylori*
F   *Neisseria meningitidis*
G   *Salmonella typhi*
H   *Staphylococcus aureus*
I   *Streptococcus pneumoniae*
J   *Streptococcus pyogenes*

From the above list, please select the bacterium that each of the following descriptions applies to. You may use each once, more than once or not at all.

1. A Gram-negative, lactose-fermenting bacillus that is a common cause of urinary tract infection. ☐

2. A Gram-negative coccus that is a common cause of meningitis in adults. ☐

3. A Gram-positive, α-haemolytic diplococcus that causes lobar pneumonia. ☐

4. A Gram-positive, cytotoxin-producing bacillus that causes pseudomembranous colitis. ☐

5. An S-shaped urease-positive bacillus that is the major cause of chronic gastritis and peptic ulcer disease. The organism stains poorly with Gram stain. ☐

11. THEME: CRANIAL NERVES

A   Abducent nerve
B   Accessory nerve
C   Facial nerve
D   Glossopharyngeal nerve
E   Hypoglossal nerve
F   Oculomotor nerve
G   Trigeminal nerve
H   Trochlear nerve
I   Vagus nerve
J   Vestibular nerve

For each of the following descriptions, please choose the most appropriate nerve from the above list. The items may be used once, more than once or not at all.

1. Has a branch passing through the foramen rotundum.

2. Provides secretomotor fibres to the parotid gland.

3. Innervates lateral gaze.

4. Innervates the cricothyroid muscle.

5. Transmits the taste fibres from the anterior two-thirds of the tongue to the tractus solitarius.

12. THEME: MUSCLES CONCERNED WITH MASTICATION

A Anterior belly of digastric
B Buccinator
C Genioglossus
D Hyoglossus
E Lateral pterygoid
F Masseter
G Medial pterygoid
H Mylohyoid
I Palatoglossus
J Temporalis

For each of the following descriptions, please choose the most appropriate muscle from the above list. The items may be used once, more than once or not at all.

1. Supplied by the facial nerve.

2. Attached to the body of the hyoid bone.

3. Has the submandibular duct as a lateral relation.

4. Is attached to the lower border of the anterior two-thirds of the zygomatic arch.

5. Is attached to the intra-articular disc of the temporomandibular joint.

Paper 3 answers

1. CARDIAC THERAPIES

1. **D – Bisoprolol**

    This patient has unstable angina and symptoms suggestive of the mild to moderate heart failure seen on the echocardiogram. Recent cardiology studies have contradicted previous thinking on the use of β blockers in cardiac failure and have shown improvements in both morbidity and mortality, particularly with the use of the cardioselective β blockers such as bisoprolol, carvidelol and metoprolol. In this case the β blocker effects will also improve his anginal symptoms.

2. **E – Clopidogrel**

    This woman has developed an acute coronary syndrome, her subsequent troponin I suggests that no significant myocardial damage has been sustained. She has been placed on aspirin and metoprolol and the recent 'Clopidogrel in Unstable angina to prevent Recurrent Events' (CURE) study suggests such patients should also be placed on clopidogrel. The benefits of this combination of antiplatelet therapy must be balanced against the increased risk of upper GI bleeds particularly in the elderly.

3. **A – Abciximab**

    This patient has unstable angina and is awaiting a definitive procedure. He is on maximal antianginal therapy and low molecular weight heparin and until he can be transferred for his stenting he should be placed on abciximab, the GIIb/IIIa receptor antagonist. This class of drugs has been licensed for non-ST elevation MIs (Non-STEMIs) but are principally used in patients awaiting coronary investigation and procedures. The glycoprotein GIIb/IIIa receptor is a platelet receptor, which when blocked stops platelet and fibrinogen binding thus stopping clot formation.

4. **J – tPA**

    This young man presents with hypotension, tachycardia and ECG changes suggestive of an acute anterior MI. He has received analgesia and aspirin and should now have thrombolysis. He has presented with the four criteria for administering tPA rather than streptokinase which are he is young, male, presenting early (within 4 hours) and has an acute anterior MI. However, the principal reason for administering tPA rather than streptokinase is his hypotension. Streptokinase can cause hypotension and so is contraindicated in this case.

5. H – Nicorandil

This man has ongoing unstable angina despite the β blocker and aspirin he is on. He should have his anti-anginal therapy increased, secondary risk factors addressed such as smoking, hyperlipidaemia and hyperglycaemia, and he may require coronary angiography. The recent IONA study has suggested the K^+ gate agonist, nicorandil, should be considered as the second-line therapy to β blockade, rather than calcium channel blockers or nitrates. Side effects are similar to those for nitrates, including headaches, flushing and hypotension.

2. BACK PAIN

1. **B – Ankylosing spondylitis**
   This patient has developed ankylosing spondylitis with associated iritis. It principally affects young men and presents with low back pain and stiffness. It has a genetic association with HLA B27. The classic pain of sacroilitis is felt in the buttocks and radiates down the back of the legs. Diagnosis is confirmed by radiographic evidence of sacroiliac erosion. Later in the disease the sacroiliac joints fuse and the lumbar vertebrae develop outgrowths known as syndesmophytes which cause the classical appearance of the 'bamboo spine', as it resembles a stem of bamboo.

2. **D – Multiple myeloma**
   This man has developed signs and symptoms of a pancytopenia secondary to multiple myeloma. He has myelomatous lytic lesions in the spine causing the back pain. He has a grossly elevated ESR and may also have renal impairment, a monoclonal gammopathy and urinary Bence Jones proteins. Older patients presenting with anaemia and back pain should have myeloma and metastatic disease excluded.

3. **H – Pott's disease of the spine**
   This man has developed tuberculosis which has caused osteomyelitis of the thoracic vertebrae and subsequent tuberculous abscess, eponymously called Pott's disease of the spine. Patients may present with severe local back pain and fever, pulmonary and other systemic features of tuberculosis. If the abscess is left unchecked it may also cause 'long tract' signs in the limbs with paraplegia associated with 'absolute' constipation and urinary retention. Treatment includes decompression and drainage if there are cord symptoms, antituberculous therapy including rifampicin, isoniazid, (pyridoxine) and pyrizinamide for at least 2 months with rifampicin and isoniazid continued for a further 4 months.

4. **C – Lytic metastases**
   This patient has developed bony metastases from her colonic carcinoma. Breast, lung, thyroid and kidney usually cause lytic lesions whilst prostate may cause both lytic and osteosclerotic lesions.

5. **G – Paget's bone disease**
   This man has developed Paget's bone disease as evidenced by the radiographic findings and the raised alkaline phosphatase in the presence of normal liver function tests and serum calcium. Complications of Paget's include local pain, pathological fractures and rarely osteosarcoma. It may also cause deafness due to otosclerosis and nerve compression, and brainstem and high cervical cord signs due to invagination at the skull base, known as platybasia.

3. CAUSES OF ABDOMINAL PAIN

1. A – Acute intermittent porphyria

This man has acute intermittent porphyria (AIP) precipitated by his 'alcoholic' celebrations. Patients present with severe abdominal pain but their initial investigations including FBC, U&Es, glucose and amylase are often unremarkable other than a slight leukocytosis. Other common acute precipitants include drugs.

2. E – Gallstones

This woman has developed acute cholecystitis secondary to her gallstones. These may also cause acute pancreatitis. The diagnosis should be confirmed on ultrasound scan of the liver and biliary tree and if dilatation of the biliary tract is seen an ERCP should be undertaken.

3. F – Incarcerated femoral hernia

Older women often present with incarcerated femoral rather than inguinal herniae and these may often be missed by the inexperienced clinician. The patient if otherwise well requires urgent operative intervention otherwise the incarcerated bowel will become ischaemic and perforate.

4. J – Spontaneous bacterial peritonitis

This patient with alcohol-related chronic liver disease has developed spontaneous bacterial peritonitis which has in turn led to encephalopathy and acute hepatic decompensation. The peritonitis is thought to be due to bacteria crossing the bowel mucosa into the already present ascites, leading to an acute infection. This is confirmed by the high white cell count in the ascites. Treatment includes intravenous cefuroxime and metronidazole, intravenous fluids and good nursing care whilst the patient remains encephalopathic.

5. G – Mesenteric ischaemia

This man has mesenteric ischaemia or 'abdominal angina'. The patient classically gets ischaemic-type pain with or after meals. They are, as with this man, invariably arteriopaths. The diagnosis may be confirmed with mesenteric angiography and by-pass or revascularisation procedures may be undertaken. The classic presentation is 'food fear' (due to the pain), diarrhoea and weight loss. Often there is a delay in making this diagnosis as the presentation may mimic many other abdominal conditions. The patient may have several other investigations and labels prior to the diagnosis actually being confirmed.

4. DELIRIUM

1. **I – Subdural haemorrhage**
   This patient's fall down some stairs has led to a subdural haemorrhage and subsequent right-sided space-occupying effects including a left monoparesis and confusion suggestive of raised intracranial pressure. The diagnosis should be confirmed on CT head scan which shows a hyperdense concave rim around the right cortex. Early subdural haematomas appear as white (fresh blood) or hypodense areas. Subdurals at approximately 10 days may be difficult to define as they are isodense to the underlying brain tissue. This patient needs urgent neurosurgical evacuation of the subdural which should reverse her monoparesis and confusion.

2. **A – Atypical pneumonia**
   This previously fit and well elderly patient has presented with atypical symptoms (confusion and diarrhoea), atypical investigation findings (normal white cell count with relative lymphopenia and hyponatraemia) and improves rapidly with cefuroxime and clarithromycin. These are the features of an atypical pneumonia, possibly Legionella pneumophila. The diagnosis may be confirmed using rising antibody titres and urinary Legionella antigen.

3. **F – Hyponatraemia**
   This scenario implies that this older patient has developed significant hyponatraemia secondary to her SSRI treatment. Examination is unremarkable and she rapidly improves with withdrawal of the paroxetine. The diagnosis is confirmed by a set of U&Es but a second set must be sent, even with rapid clinical resolution of the symptoms, to exclude ongoing hyponatraemia. If this is the case SIADH should be excluded with paired urinary and serum osmolalities.

4. **J – Uraemia**
   This woman has developed signs of uraemia as evidenced by the confusion, hiccups and 'twitches'. The combination of ramipril (ACEI), spironolactone and bendrofluazide has caused progressive renal impairment and led to frank uraemia. The combination of spironolactone and an ACEI may also lead to hyperkalaemia and a careful monitoring of such patients is advisable.

5. **E – Hypoglycaemia**
   This older woman has been placed on chlorpropamide, which is relatively contra-indicated in the older patient. This sulphonylurea has a relatively long half life and will cause hypoglycaemia due to the overlapping effect of two consecutive doses. The patient should be changed to either a shorter acting sulphonylurea such as gliclazide or the biguanide metformin. All diabetics need expert multidisciplinary care and follow up in dedicated specialist clinics.

5. SKIN RASHES

1. D – Erythema nodosum

This young woman has developed erythema nodosum (EN) secondary to her oral contraceptive pill. EN is a tender red plaque like or nodular rash which classically occurs over the anterior shin. It may rarely affect the upper limbs as well. Common causes in the UK include IBD, sarcoid, TB, streptococcal infection and drugs such as the OCP and antibiotics. 50% of cases are idiopathic.

2. I – Pyoderma gangrenosum

This man has developed pyoderma gangrenosum, a violaceous, ulcerating lesion which also commonly occurs over the shins. The lesion often begins as pustules and these coalesce and form a large necrotic ulcerating lesion. Fifty percent of cases are idiopathic but common associations include IBD, rheumatoid and the seronegative arthropathies, and the haematological malignancies, particularly the paraproteinaemias and acute leukaemias.

3. C – Erythema multiforme

This patient has developed a severe blistering rash secondary to her trimethoprim treatment. It is characterised by the presence of the annular 'target lesion'. Erythema multiforme is a relatively common side effect of several classes of drugs particularly antibiotics, infections such as herpes simplex, *Mycoplasma pneumoniae*, *Streptococcus* and TB, and more rarely the systemic arthritides and malignancy. A more malignant form of the condition which involves the mucous membranes, genitalia and eyes, known as Stevens–Johnson syndrome, may cause a severe systemic illness and may be fatal, particularly in the elderly.

4. G – Pemphigus

Pemphigus and pemphigoid are severe autoimmune, blistering conditions which occur in late middle age and the elderly. PemphiguS forms Superficial blisters which typically Sheer and leave large raw areas, commonly in a generalised distribution and involving the mucous membranes. Nikolsky's sign is positive in apparent normal areas of skin. The antibody is found in the epidermiS and is typically an IgG. PemphigoiD is a Deeper lesion which forms large tense blisters over localised areas of the skin eg a limb or the back. The antibody is an IgG and attaches to at the level of the basement membrane in the Dermis. Both conditions require steroid treatment for a prolonged period and this should be accompanied by a bone-sparing agent.

5. E – Lupus vulgaris

Lupus vulgaris is a TB associated skin condition caused by direct infiltration of the skin by the acid fast bacilli, usually through haematogenous spread. The chronic lesion may take on a bitten, gnarled appearance hence its name lupus meaning 'wolf like'. The patient often has evidence of pulmonary or systemic TB infection and should be treated with antituberculous therapy for at least 6 months. TB may also be associated with erythema nodosum and erythema multiforme.

6. RECTAL BLEEDING

1. **B – Anal fissure**
    The presentation (acute pain and bleeding) is typical of this condition which can be precipitated by constipation, acute diarrhoea, pregnancy or childbirth. The condition can be acute (as in this case) or chronic. Treatment is medical (GTN 0.2% ointment heals 50–75% in 8 weeks) or surgical with lateral sphincterotomy, although this carries a risk of incontinence.

2. **K – Ulcerative colitis**
    This is the commonest diagnosis in a young patient with a long history of bloody diarrhoea. The microcytic anaemia reflects chronic blood loss, and the WCC and ESR reflect the underlying inflammatory condition.

3. **G – Diverticular disease**
    The long history of characteristic symptoms in a female of this age indicates this as the most likely diagnosis. A carcinoma could present similarly but she has presumably had negative investigations for this the year before.

4. **A – Anal carcinoma**
    Whilst this condition is relatively rare, it has an increased incidence in homosexual men due to anal infection with HPV. Lesions are of epithelial origin and are most commonly squamous. Historical treatment was by radical surgery (abdominoperineal excision of rectum, but long-course chemoradiotherapy is now the preferred first line in most specialist centres).

5. **C – Angiodysplasia**
    This is a type of arteriovenous malformation and is one of the common causes of significant lower GI bleeding in the elderly population. As in this case it is notoriously difficult to pinpoint the offending vessel. Where direct vision fails, mesenteric angiography or radionuclide scans can sometimes be of diagnostic use but often also yield negative results if the vessel is not actively bleeding at the time of investigation. Treatment sometimes therefore occasions total colectomy as a life-saving measure.

7. COMMON FRACTURE EPONYMS

1. G – Monteggia fracture dislocation

There are two common fracture dislocations of the forearm best known by their Italian eponyms. The other (also in the above list) is Galeazzi and describes an injury in which the lower half of the radius is fractured and the inferior radioulnar joint is dislocated.

2. I – Salter Harris' fracture

Injuries involving the growth plate (syn. physeal injuries) are common in children and are a special problem because of the risk of abnormal subsequent bone growth. Salter and Harris' classification of such injuries is useful and defines five types depending on the exact morphology of injury. Types 1 and 2 are milder forms with a good prognosis but types 3–5 can often result in arrested, slowed or asymmetric growth.

3. H – Pott's fracture

Fractures and fracture dislocations of the ankle were first described by Percival Pott in 1768. Modern classification is that of Danis–Weber which defines three types of injury (A, B and C) depending on level of the fibula fracture and resultant instability. These are however still grouped together for convenience as Pott's fractures. The student should note that Pott was not a man whose discoveries were limited to one body region. His name is given to Pott's disease of the spine (TB of the vertebrae), and to Pott's puffy tumour (osteomyelitis of the frontal bone of the skull). He is perhaps best remembered however for his description of the first occupational cancer – that of scrotal carcinoma in chimney sweeps in 1775.

4. E – Garden II fracture

Garden's classification is perhaps the best known and most commonly used of all fracture classifications. It defines four types: stage I: incomplete, impacted; stage II: complete, undisplaced; stage III: complete with moderate displacement; and stage IV: severely displaced.

5. B – Bennet's fracture

Bennet described a special case of metacarpal fracture involving the base of the thumb in which an oblique fracture extends into the first metacarpal joint producing an unstable fracture-subluxation.

8. SALIVARY GLAND DISEASE

1. **B – Bacterial sialadenitis**
    This is a typical description of this uncommon condition which used to classically occur in cases such as that described when salivary flow is reduced. With better attention to in-patient oral hygiene and nutrition, it is now seen equally commonly in patients without any obvious predisposition. Pain is made worse on eating and pus may occasionally be expressed from the duct. Treatment is with antibacterial therapy against the causative staphylococcal and streptococcal organisms.

2. **C – HIV-associated sialadenitis**
    The presentation is one of keratoconjunctivitis sicca (dry eyes) and xerostomia (dry mouth). The differential is one of primary (alone) or secondary (in association with connective tissue disease) Sjögren's syndrome or HIV. The latter is indistinguishable in presentation from Sjögren's but autoantibody screen is negative. In addition, Sjögren's is much less common in males (ratio F:M = 10:1).

3. **G – Sialolithiasis (salivary duct stones)**
    The typical history gives the diagnosis. The submandibular gland is most commonly affected (80%) and 80% are radiopaque. The diagnosis can be confirmed by a contrast sialogram and treatment is largely surgical (stone extraction from Wharton's duct).

4. **E – Pleomorphic adenoma**
    This is the most common benign salivary gland tumour (75% of parotid tumours). They can occur at any age (mean age 42) and occur equally in both sexes. Whilst benign histologically, they require complete excision (usually superficial, conservative parotidectomy) to prevent recurrence and the long-term risk of malignant change.

5. **A – Adenoid cystic carcinoma**
    There are a number of variants of epidermoid tumours in the salivary gland (squamous, adenosquamous, adenoid cystic, adenocarcinoma) of which this is the most common. In this case, the tumour has arisen from a long-standing pleomorphic adenoma in the parotid (the most common site of malignant as well as benign tumours). Invasion is direct with a propensity to perineural spread causing palsies and eventually CNS destruction and by metastasis to the lung. Prognosis is usually poor. Treatment can involve surgery (radical total parotidectomy) and sometimes radiotherapy.

9. INTRAPARTUM COMPLICATIONS

1. **C – Cord prolapse**
   Polyhydramnios and a high head are risk factors for cord prolapse at the time of ARM. If the cord prolapses into the vagina, the change in temperature can cause vasospasm in the umbilical vessels leading to a fetal bradycardia and fetal death if not delivered urgently. The manoeuvre described aims to take any pressure off the cord by the presenting part. In this context a placental abruption, which is also more common at the time of ARM with polyhydramnios, is much less likely as there is no revealed bleeding or abdominal signs present.

2. **J – Uterine inertia**
   From the list there are only three possible choices for slow progress in labour: uterine inertia ('**powers**'), malposition of the occiput ('**passenger**') and CPD ('**passages and passenger**'). True CPD is very rare and is usually due to an abnormal pelvis, eg previous pelvic fracture. In primiparous women up to 50% (higher in some series) need augmentation due to uterine inertia (inadequate or incoordinate contractions). Multiparous women who have laboured before rarely have this problem as their uterine action is more efficient. It is in the multiparous group where malpositions of the occiput are most common.

3. **E – Meconium-stained liquor**
   Intermittent auscultation is recommended for all low-risk women in labour, as CTG monitoring doubles the CS rate with no reduction in perinatal morbidity or mortality. Risk status can however change to high risk due to the dynamic nature of labour, eg meconium-stained liquor, which is only recognised after SROM. In the presence of meconium stained liquor CTG monitoring is recommended and this should be backed up with FBS in the presence of CTG abnormalities.

4. **I – Uterine hyperstimulation**
   Syntocinon is a synthetic oxytocin used to augment or induce labour. It should be titrated against the strength and frequency of uterine contractions aiming for not more than 4 in 10 mins: more frequent contractions are uterine hyperstimulation. If there is insufficient time for relaxation fetal hypoxia can occur relatively rapidly manifesting as an abnormal CTG. The timing of the contractions and the fact that the infusion was switched off to see if the situation improved indicates that this is the most likely cause. Cord prolapse and abruption are possible, but much less likely.

5. **D – Malposition of the occiput**
   From the list there are only three possible choices for slow progress in labour – uterine inertia ('**powers**'), malposition of the occiput ('**passenger**') and CPD ('**passages and passenger**'). Multiparous women who have laboured before rarely have a problem with uterine action as it is more efficient than in primips. Her contractions are also described as 3 in 10 strong. It is in the multip group where malpositions of the occiput especially occipito-posterior (OP) are the most

common cause of slow progress in labour. Therefore Syntocinon should never be used in multips if there is any clinical suspicion of obstructed labour. True CPD is very rare and is usually due to an abnormal pelvis e.g. previous pelvic fracture. In primiparous women up to 50% (higher in some series) will need augmentation due to uterine inertia (inadequate or incoordinate contractions).

10. BACTERIAL INFECTIONS

1. **D – *Escherichia coli***
   Escherichia coli is the cause of 60–90% of urinary tract infections. It is a Gram-negative, lactose-fermenting bacillus that is a normal commensal of the large intestine. Transfer to the urinary tract may be via the bloodstream, via lymphatics or by direct extension (e.g. from a vesicocolic fistula) but is most frequently via the ascending transurethral route, particularly in women.

2. **F and I – *Neisseria meningitidis* and *Streptococcus pneumoniae***
   The two most likely causes of meningitis from the list are *Neisseria meningitidis* (meningococcus) and *Streptococcus pneumoniae* (pneumococcus). Both organisms are cocci but the former is Gram-negative while the latter is Gram-positive. Diagnosis depends on identifying the organism in CSF or blood culture.

3. **I – *Streptococcus pneumoniae***
   In about 90% of cases of lobar pneumonia the causative organism is *Streptococcus pneumoniae*. This organism is a Gram-positive diplococcus that shows alpha-haemolysis on blood agar. The colonies are typically described as draughtsman-shaped on account of their sunken centre. Vagrants and alcoholics who have poor social and medical care are particularly prone to lobar pneumonia.

4. **B – *Clostridium difficile***
   The organism that causes pseudomembranous colitis is a toxigenic strain of *Clostridium difficile*, an anaerobic Gram-positive bacillus. *Clostridium difficile* produces two toxins: Toxin A is an enterotoxin responsible for the gut symptoms, Toxin B is a cytotoxin that has a cytopathic effect in cell cultures.

5. **E – *Helicobacter pylori***
   Helicobacter pylori is an S-shaped, urease-producing, flagellate bacillus that colonises the gastric antrum. In some parts of the third world the prevalence of infection exceeds 80%, and even in industrialised countries the prevalence has been estimated to be 40–50%. Up to 85% of cases of chronic gastritis and 90% of cases of duodenal ulcer are caused by *H. pylori*. The organism has also been implicated in the development of gastric adenocarcinoma and primary gastric lymphoma. *H. pylori* infection can be diagnosed by non-invasive methods such as serology for IgG antibodies or the ^{13}C or ^{14}C urea breath test. Invasive methods of detection require endoscopy and include the rapid urease test, microbiological culture of the organism and histological identification in gastric biopsies. *H. pylori* is found in greatest numbers in the mucus layer on the surface epithelium or in gastric pits. The organism stains poorly with Gram stain and is best visualised using a modified Giemsa stain.

11. CRANIAL NERVES

1. **G – Trigeminal nerve**
   The maxillary division of the trigeminal nerve passes through the foramen rotundum into the pterygopalatine fossa. Here it gives off sensory fibres to the pterygopalatine ganglion that pass without synapsing to the nose, palate and nasopharynx.

2. **D – Glossopharyngeal nerve**
   These parasympathetic secretomotor fibres synapse in the otic ganglion before passing in the auriculotemporal nerve to the parotid gland. The glossopharyngeal nerve also supplies taste fibres to the posterior third of the tongue and innervates the carotid baro- and chemoreceptors.

3. **A – Abducent nerve**
   The lateral rectus nerve is supplied by the abducent nerve; the superior oblique is supplied by the trochlear nerve (LR_6SO_4) and the other extraocular muscles by the oculomotor nerve.

4. **I – Vagus nerve**
   All laryngeal muscles are supplied by the vagus nerve, the cricothyroid by the external laryngeal nerve and the remainder through the recurrent laryngeal nerve.

5. **C – Facial nerve**
   Taste fibres from the tongue, mouth and pharynx are carried in the facial, glossopharyngeal and vagus nerves to the nucleus of the tractus solitarius in the floor of the 4th ventricle. Fibres from the anterior two-thirds of the tongue pass via the chorda tympani to the 7th nerve.

12. MUSCLES CONCERNED WITH MASTICATION

1. **B – Buccinator**
   The buccinator from the outside, and the muscles of the tongue and floor of the mouth from the inside, retain food between the teeth for chewing.

2. **H – Mylohyoid**
   The two mylohyoid muscles meet as a midline raphe, and are attached laterally to the mylohyoid line on the medial aspect of the body of the mandible. The mylohyoid, and the anterior belly of the digastric, are supplied by the inferior alveolar branch of the mandibular nerve.

3. **D – Hyoglossus**
   Other lateral relationships are the styloglossus, lingual nerve, submandibular ganglion, submandibular gland and hypoglossal nerve. The last supplies this muscle, genioglossus, styloglossus and all the intrinsic muscles of the tongue.

4. **F – Masseter**
   The mandibular attachment is to the lateral surface of the ramus and angle of the mandible. A similar area gives attachment to the medial pterygoid muscle on the medial surface of the mandible. Both the pterygoids, and the masseter and temporalis muscles are supplied by the mandibular branch of the 5th nerve.

5. **E – Lateral pterygoid**
   This attachment is also to the neck of the mandible and the joint capsule. The two heads of the lateral pterygoid are attached to the inferior temporal surface of the greater wing of the sphenoid and the lateral surface of the pterygoid plate. The latter is embraced by the two heads of the medial pterygoid.

PAPER 4

Paper 4 questions

1. THEME: CARDIAC CHEST PAIN

A   Acute anterior myocardial infarction
B   Acute inferior myocardial infarction
C   Decubitus angina
D   Dissecting thoracic aortic aneurysm
E   Myocarditis
F   Non-Q wave myocardial infarction
G   Pericarditis
H   Prinzmetal's angina
I   Syndrome X
J   True posterior myocardial infarction

The following patients have all presented with cardiac chest pains. Please choose the most appropriate cause from the above list. The items may be used once, more than once or not at all.

1. A 39-year-old woman with a strong family history of ischaemic heart disease presents in A&E with a 4-hour history of severe central chest pain radiating to the left shoulder and the neck associated with nausea, sweating and shortness of breath. Examination is unremarkable as are her initial blood tests, including CK. Her subsequent troponin I is normal. Her ECG shows sinus tachycardia with normal axis and flattening of the T-waves in leads II, III and aVF. Her exercise stress test shows 'pseudonormalisation'of the T-waves but her coronary angiography is totally unremarkable.

2. A 48-year-old man who has smoked since the age of 8 presents in A&E with a 2-hour history of severe angina like chest pain associated with sweating and feeling faint and dizzy. His pain is poorly relieved with GTN and oxygen. His ECG shows deep ST depression in leads V_1–V_3 associated with dominant R-waves in leads V_1 and V_2. His CK is 567 iu/l.

3. A 27-year-old male smoker presents in A&E with central chest pain which he tells the medical SHO is worse when he moves around on the trolley but seems to be eased a little if he leans forward over the trolley bars. His ECG shows saddle-shaped ST elevation in leads V_1, V_5, V_6, aVL, I and II. His CK is 567 iu/l and troponin 6.9 ng/ml

4. A 61-year-old diabetic woman is admitted to hospital with an 8–10-hour history of dull central chest pain and shortness of breath. Her ECG shows T-wave inversion in leads V_4–V_6, I and aVL and subsequent troponin I is 7.6 ng/ml and CK 1099 iu/l.

5. A 76-year-old woman with known hypertension and diabetes mellitus presents in A&E with severe epigastric and low chest pains radiating to her shoulders. Her ECG shows ST elevation in leads II, III and aVF. Her CK is 397 iu/l and troponin is 4.9 ng/ml.

2. THEME: MONOARTHRITIS

A Brucellosis
B Charcot's joint
C Gonococcal arthritis
D Haemophilia A-induced haemarthrosis
E Haemophilia B-induced haemarthrosis
F Osteoarthritis
G Reiter's syndrome
H Pyrophosphate arthropathy
I Syphilitic arthropathy
J Tuberculous arthritis

The following patients have all presented with a monoarthritis. Please choose the most appropriate cause from the above list. The items may be used once, more than once or not at all.

1. A 26-year-old HIV-positive man attends his GP with 3 days of increasing pain and swelling in his left knee, two weeks after a febrile illness and dysuria. Aspiration of the joint shows no organisms or crystals but a urethral swab shows Gram-negative intracellular diplococcus.

2. A 29-year-old alcohol abuser is admitted to hospital acutely unwell with fever and rigors. On examination he has signs of a left apical pneumonia and a hot, swollen right knee.

3. A 31-year-old HIV-positive man is seen in the GUM clinic with a swollen hot left ankle associated with dysuria and conjunctivitis. This is similar to a previous episode 3 months earlier secondary to a *Chlamydia* infection.

4. A 79-year-old man presents in A&E with a 3-day history of pain and swelling in the left knee despite having been placed on allopurinol 2 months earlier by his GP for a similar event. Microscopy of the joint aspirate confirms weakly positive bifringent crystals under polarised light. No organisms are seen.

5. A 17-year-old man presents to his GP with a badly swollen left knee 2 days after a rugby match. Subsequent investigation reveals a normal INR, bleeding time and prothrombin time with reduced factor VIII:C levels, 85% of normal.

3. THEME: GASTROINTESTINAL BLOOD LOSS

A   Barret's oesophagus
B   Colonic carcinoma
C   Crohn's disease
D   Diverticular disease
E   Duodenal ulcer
F   Gastric ulcer
G   Gastro-oesophageal reflux disease
H   Meckel's diverticulum
I   Oesophageal varices
J   Ulcerative colitis

The following patients have all presented with occult or frank gastrointestinal blood loss. Please choose the most appropriate cause from the above list. The items may be used once, more than once, in combination or not at all.

1. A 41-year-old man presents to his GP with upper abdominal pain, which is worse before meals and occasionally radiates through to his back. The pain comes and goes and is associated with 'burping' and dyspepsia. Routine investigations reveal FBC: Hb 8.2 g/dl, MCV 74 fl, WCC 9.2 × 10^9/l, Plt 412 × 10^9/l. He declines an OGD but a C^{14} breath test is positive.

2. A 64-year-old woman presents to her GP with weight loss and constipation. Investigations reveal FBC: Hb 7.9 g/dl, MCV 69 fl, WCC 5.9 × 10^9/l, Plt 513 × 10^9/l; ESR 78 mm/h; CCa^{2+} 2.27; LFTs: Tbil 32 µmol/l, AST 44 iu/l, ALT 51 iu/l, Alk phos 449 iu/l, Alb 32 g/l. Her ultrasound scan of her abdomen confirms 'multiple hypoechogenic lesions in the liver'.

3. A 39-year-old-man presents to his GP with lethargy and jaundice. Routine investigations reveal FBC: Hb 9.2 g/dl, MCV 104 fl, WCC 4.4 × 10^9/l, Plt 61 × 10^9/l; LFTs: Tbil 42 µmol/l, AST 314 iu/l, ALT 211 iu/l, Alk phos 565 iu/l, Alb 26 g/l, γGT 207 iu/l. INR 1.8. He is referred to gastroenterology outpatients but prior to his appointment he is admitted with a large fresh haemetemesis.

4. A 67-year-old woman presents in A&E with severe left iliac fossa pain. On examination she is obviously distressed, is vomiting and is pyrexial with a temperature of 39.5°C. She is very tender in the left iliac fossa with guarding but no signs of peritonism. Investigations show FBC: Hb 7.4 g/dl, MCV 71 fl, WCC 29.2 × 10^9/l, Plt 445 × 10^9/l; U&Es: Na$^+$ 156 mmol/l, K$^+$ 4.9 mmol/l, urea 29.7 mmol/l, Cr 288 µmol/l. Blood cultures confirm an *E. coli* bacteraemia.

5. A 54-year-old man is referred to gastroenterology outpatients with a microcytic anaemia. He denies any upper or lower gastroenterological symptoms. Subsequent upper and lower GI endoscopy are unremarkable but a 'special scan' confirms the diagnosis, showing an ileal lesion at 50–60 cm from the ileocaecal valve.

4. THEME: STROKE

A   Cerebellar
B   Cervical
C   Frontal
D   Medullary
E   Mid brain
F   Occipital
G   Parietal
H   Pontine
I   Temporal
J   Thalamic

The following patients have all presented with signs of a stroke. Please choose the most appropriate site of their lesion from the above list. The items may be used once, more than once, in combination or not at all.

1. A 64-year-old left-handed man with known hypertension presents in A&E with an episode of collapse. On examination he is well but his BP = 210/135. He is noted by the SHO to have marked nystagmus to the right, right-sided dysdiadochokinesia and past pointing.

2. A 67-year-old right-handed woman calls out her GP because of sudden difficulty with her speech. On arrival she finds the patient has no obvious limb weakness but has marked dysarthria. Her pupils and eye movements are normal but her palate deviates to the left when asked to say 'aaagh' and her tongue deviates to the right on protrusion.

3. An 84-year-old right-handed woman with a previous history of stroke presents in A&E with a collapse. On examination she has signs of her old right hemiparesis but has a new right homonymous hemianopia.

4. A 59-year-old man is brought to A&E with a GCS = 3. He has bilateral pupillary constriction which does not improve with several doses of naloxone. CT head scan fails to demonstrate any abnormalities and remarkably he makes some improvement. The diagnosis is confirmed on MRI scan.

5. A 78-year-old right-handed woman is admitted to hospital with a right hemisphere stroke. On the stroke rehabilitation ward she complains of shooting pains down her left arm and leg which improve somewhat with gabapentin.

5. THEME: GENITAL ULCERATION

A   Behçet's syndrome
B   Chancroid
C   Donovanosis
D   Herpes simplex
E   Herpes zoster
F   Lymphogranuloma venereum
G   Pemphigus
H   Stevens Johnson syndrome
I   Syphilitic chancre
J   Syphilitic gumma

The following patients have all presented with genital ulceration. Please choose the most appropriate cause from the above list. The items may be used once, more than once or not at all.

1. A 29-year-old Asian man presents in GUM clinic 10 days after unprotected sexual intercourse on holiday in India. On examination he has a painless ulcerating papular rash over the glans penis. He has experienced no urethral discharge. Diagnosis is confirmed on cell culture showing an obligate intracellular organism. Both gonococcal and VDRL tests are negative. He improves with doxycycline.

2. A 24-year-old known HIV-positive African woman presents in the GUM clinic with a 2-week history of an ulcerating lesion extending over her labia and perineum. The ulcerated area is friable and exhibits contact bleeding. It is very painful. The Gram stain taken from swabs show a characteristic coccobacillus.

3. A 37-year-old Afro-Caribbean man presents in the GUM clinic 2 weeks after unprotected sexual intercourse at a party in Jamaica. On examination he has a 'heaped' ulcerated lesion on his glans but no discharge. Gonococcal and chlamydia investigations are negative as are HSV and VDRL. A short encapsulated Gram-negative bacillus is grown on culture.

4. A 18-year-old woman presents to her GP with painful multiple ulcerating lesions over her vulva. She has fever and feels 'achey' all over. VDRL is negative, as are gonococcal and bacterial screen. Culture confirms presence of an icosahedral virus.

5. A 24-year-old homosexual man is seen by his GP with a 4-week history of a painless ulcerating lesion over the glans penis 6 weeks after unprotected sex. Subsequent investigations identify a motile spirochaete under dark ground microscopy.

6. THEME: COMPLICATIONS OF GALLSTONE DISEASE

A   Acute cholecystitis
B   Acute pancreatitis
C   Ascending cholangitis
D   Biliary colic
E   Bilioenteric fistula
F   Chronic cholecystitis
G   Empyema of the gallbladder
H   Gallstone ileus
I   Mucocele
J   Perforated gallbladder
K   Obstructive jaundice

The following are descriptions of patients with complications of gallstone disease. Please select the most appropriate diagnosis from the above list. The items may be used once, more than once or not at all.

1. A 58-year-old man presents in A&E with sudden onset of severe upper abdominal pain with exacerbations and associated nausea. On examination there is tenderness and guarding, maximal in the right upper quadrant. LFTs: Tbil 35 μmol/l, AST 18 iu/l, ALT 22 iu/l, Alk phos 180 iu/l, Alb 41 g/l.

2. A 45-year-old woman attends her GP with a 6-month history of episodic indigestion. Attacks commonly occur after eating. On direct questioning she also admits to postprandial belching. On examination there is no jaundice, and abdominal examination is unremarkable other than mild obesity and previous hysterectomy scar. Her LFTs are normal.

3. A 75-year-old woman presents in A&E with a 1-day history of colicky central and right-sided abdominal pain, bileous vomiting and distension. On examination she is dehydrated but not jaundiced. The abdomen is distended and tympanic with obstructed bowel sounds. Her LFTs are normal.

4. A 68-year-old man presents in A&E with a 12-hour history of severe upper abdominal pain radiating to the back, associated with nausea and vomiting. On examination he is dehydrated and tachycardic with tenderness and guarding in the epigastrium and left hypochondrium. LFTs: Tbil 32 μmol/l, AST 40 iu/l, ALT 27 iu/l, Alk phos 155 iu/l, Alb 39 g/l. LDH 610 iu/l, amylase 2150 U/l.

5. A 72-year-old woman presents in A&E with a 2-day history of severe right hypochondrial pain, nausea and vomiting and fever. On examination, she is distressed, dehydrated but not jaundiced. There is guarding and rebound in the right upper quadrant with suspicion of an underlying mass extending from beneath the costal margin. WCC: 27.6×10^9/l; LFTs: Tbil 32 μmol/l, AST 85 iu/l, ALT 95 iu/l, Alk phos 175 iu/l, Alb 38 g/l.

7. THEME: CHEST TRAUMA

A   Cardiac tamponade
B   Diaphragmatic rupture
C   Flail chest
D   Haemothorax
E   Massive haemothorax
F   Myocardial contusion
G   Open pneumothorax
H   Pulmonary contusion
I   Simple pneumothorax
J   Tension pneumothorax
K   Tracheobronchial disruption
L   Traumatic aortic disruption

The following patients have all had thoracic injuries. Please select the most appropriate diagnosis from the above list. The items may be used once, more than once or not at all.

1. A 19-year-old man is brought to A&E following a stab wound to the right side of the chest. He is shocked (pulse 115 bpm, BP = 90/50) and slightly dyspnoeic. Examination of the chest some decreased breath sounds and dullness to percussion of the left side. A chest radiograph demonstrates a moderate pleural effusion on the right side and a chest drain is inserted which drains 500 ml of blood.

2. A 26-year-old pedestrian is brought to A&E after being hit by a car travelling at approximately 50 mph. He has serious lower extemity injuries and a minor head injury. Shortly after arrival he becomes acutely dyspnoeic, cyanotic, tachycardic and hypotensive. Examination of the chest demonstrates reduced breath sounds and increased resonance to percussion on the left side. The neck veins are distended.

3. A 45-year-old man is brought to A&E having been hit by a train. Although he was thrown clear of the track, he has serious chest and abdominal injuries. He is dyspnoeic and in considerable distress. Examination reveals evidence of blunt injury to both sides of the chest. On the right side there is paradoxical movement of the chest wall with inspiration and expiration.

4. A 21-year-old man is brought to hospital following an isolated stab wound to the left side of the chest. There is little external haemorrhage and a chest radiograph demonstrates a simple small pneumothorax which is treated by chest drain insertion. In A&E he rapidly becomes severely hypotensive (BP = 70/30). Re-examination of the chest shows bilateral, equal breath sounds and expansion and the chest drain is swinging but not draining any significant blood (100 ml total). His neck veins are distended.

5. A 52-year-old unrestrained driver hits a tree at 50 mph. She has some bruising over the sternum and tenderness on palpation. There is no evidence of shock. A chest radiograph demonstrates widening of the mediastinum.

8. THEME: SURGICAL INCISIONS

A Gridiron/McBurney's
B Kocher's
C Lanz
D Long midline
E Lower midline
F Paramedian
G Pfannenstiel
H Rooftop/Gable
I Rutherford Morrison
J Upper midline

The following are descriptions of patients requiring operations. Please select the most appropriate/commonly-used surgical incision from the above list. The items may be used once, more than once or not at all.

1. A 24-year-old man is brought to A&E following a major road traffic accident. He is cardiovascularly shocked despite fluid resuscitation and has a blunt abdominal injury. He is taken for emergency laparotomy.

2. A 65-year-old woman with symptomatic gallstone disease has had two previous laparotomies for adhesional small bowel obstruction following a hysterectomy aged 50. She requires cholecystectomy.

3. A 34-year-old woman has a complicated second stage of labour. She requires an emergency caesarean section.

4. A 65-year-old man is to undergo cadaveric liver transplantation for cirrhosis and hepatic failure.

5. A 72-year-old woman requires a sigmoid colectomy for colorectal carcinoma.

9. THEME: GYNAECOLOGICAL THERAPEUTIC AGENTS

A   Combined oral contraceptive pill (COCP)
B   Cyproterone acetate
C   Danazol
D   Goserelin (GnRH analogue)
E   Medroxyprogesterone acetate
F   Mefanamic acid
G   Oestrogen-only HRT
H   Oestrogen–progesterone HRT
I   Tamoxifen
J   Tranexamic acid

From the above list please choose the agent most likely to be used for the clinical picture described. The items may be used once, more than once, in combination or not at all.

1. This agent is used to down-regulate the hypothalamo-pituitary axis, prior to IVF cycles. It is taken non-orally and commonly has the side effects of hot flushes and night sweats. ☐

2. This agent is commonly used for menorrhagia and dysmenorrhoea. It is taken orally and is relatively contraindicated in patients with asthma. ☐

3. This oral agent has some beneficial effects including a reduction in ovarian and endometrial cancer with long-term use. ☐

4. This oral agent is known to reduce hirsutism and acne with long-term use. It needs to be given with oestrogen to prevent feminisation of a male fetus if the patient becomes pregnant. ☐

5. This agent may commonly be used in women post-hysterectomy, to prevent or treat hot flushes and night sweats. ☐

10. THEME: PATHOGENIC VIRUSES

A   Coronavirus
B   Cytomegalovirus
C   Epstein–Barr virus
D   Hepatitis C virus
E   Herpes simplex virus type 2
F   Human papillomavirus
G   Measles virus
H   Rhinovirus
I   Rotavirus
J   Varicella zoster virus

From the above list, please select the virus that is the most likely cause of each of the following diseases. The items may be used once, more than once or not at all.

1. Cirrhosis of the liver.

2. Severe acute respiratory syndrome (SARS).

3. Shingles.

4. Verruca vulgaris.

5. Infectious mononucleosis.

11. THEME: PHARYNGEAL MUSCLES

A Inferior constrictor
B Levator palatini
C Middle constrictor
D Palatoglossus
E Palatopharyngeus
F Pharyngobasilar fascia
G Salpingopharyngeus
H Stylopharyngeus
I Superior constrictor
J Tensor palatini

For each of the following descriptions, please choose the most appropriate structure from the above list. The items may be used once, more than once or not at all.

1. Is attached to the lateral aspect of the cricoid cartilage.

2. Underlies the anterior pillar of the fauces.

3. Is attached to the upper border of the greater horn of the hyoid bone.

4. Encircles the opening of the eustachian tube.

5. Is innervated by the trigeminal nerve.

12. THEME: MUSCLE ATTACHMENTS IN THE UPPER LIMB

A Biceps
B Brachialis
C Deltoid
D Extensor carpi radialis longus
E Flexor carpi ulnaris
F Flexor digitorum profundus
G Flexor digitorum superficialis
H Flexor pollicis longus
I Pronator teres
J Triceps

For each of the following attachments please choose the most appropriate muscle from the above list. The items may be used once, more than once or not at all.

1. Along the upper border of the radial groove of the humerus.

2. Anterior aspect of the lower humerus.

3. Lateral supracondylar ridge on the humerus.

4. Lateral aspect of the mid-radius.

5. Anterior aspect of the base of the distal phalanx of the middle finger.

Paper 4 answers

1. CARDIAC CHEST PAIN

1. **I – Syndrome X**

   This patient has a strong family history of ischaemic heart disease, a history highly suggestive of angina and an abnormal ECG. She has no rise in her cardiac enzymes but her exercise tolerance test shows 'pseudonormalisation' of her inverted T waves. This change occurs when patients' ECGs show permanent T wave inversion and 'right' themselves on exertion. However despite these changes her subsequent coronary arteriogram is normal. This suggests she either has another cause for her pain, e.g. oesophageal spasm, or has cardiac syndrome X, microvascular angina. This diagnosis of exclusion is more common in females. They may present with angina like chest pain, ECG changes and a positive exercise stress test but coronary angiography is normal. Such patients should still have their macrovascular risk factors addressed and receive symptomatic treatment with calcium channel blockers. There is no proof that the addition of antiplatelet therapy is of benefit.

2. **J – True posterior myocardial infarction**

   This middle-aged man has the historical features of an acute coronary syndrome and his ECG confirms a true posterior myocardial infarction as evidenced by the deep ST depression in the anterior leads associated with the dominant R waves in leads V_1 and V_2. He should be treated as if he were having a ST elevation myocardial infarction (STEMI) with aspirin, thrombolysis and other prognostic changing drugs such as insulin, β blockers, statins and ACE inhibitors. Symptomatic relievers such as nitrates, diuretics, calcium channel blockers and nicorandil may also be required.

3. **G – Pericarditis**

   This young man has the historical features and ECG changes of acute pericarditis. He has sharp chest pain that is eased on leaning forward and 'saddle' ST elevation in a non-anatomical distribution. He should be treated symptomatically with NSAIDs and rest. The most likely cause in an otherwise well individual is viral. Other causes such as IHD, uraemia, malignant invasion and sepsis (TB) should be excluded.

4. **F – Non-Q wave myocardial infarction**

    Recently, patients presenting with unstable chest pain (increased in frequency, severity and/or duration) have been classified as having an acute coronary syndrome (ACS). Patients are then subdivided by their ECG changes and cardiac enzyme results into (1) patients with ST elevation MIs (STEMI) and (2) those with non-ST elevation MIs and unstable angina. Both groups should have macrovascular risk factors addressed and receive aspirin, β blockers and other prognostic changing drugs (see above). Group 1 should receive thrombolysis and Group 2 should receive LMW heparin and/or abciximab. Group 2 patients should have an early exercise stress test, whereas Group 1 patients may require early coronary angiography and intervention.

5. **B – Acute inferior myocardial infarction**

    This patient has presented with an acute coronary syndrome with ECG changes suggestive of an acute inferior STEMI (leads II, III and aVF). She requires thrombolysis, her secondary risk factors addressed and the addition of prognostic changing drugs.

2. MONOARTHRITIS

1. C – Gonococcal arthritis

This patient has developed a gonococcal arthritis. This condition is usually a flitting polyarthritis or arthralgia primarily affecting the large joints of the upper and lower limbs. There may be associated effusions and tenosynovitis but it does not cause progressive joint destruction. Diagnosis may be confirmed from synovial fluid or blood cultures but it is usually made from anal or genital swabs. The treatment as with all gonococcal infection is penicillin, cotrimoxazole or in resistant cases ciprofloxacin.

2. J – Tuberculous arthritis

This patient has a left lower lobe pneumonia and an associated acute arthritis of the right knee. As with most systemic involvement this is due to direct haematogenous spread from the primary pulmonary infection. The diagnosis may be confirmed on microscopy of joint aspiration, sputum sample and blood cultures. Treatment is with standard antituberculous therapy for at least 6 months.

3. G – Reiter's syndrome

This patient has developed Reiter's syndrome secondary to his *Chlamydia* infection. He has the classic triad of arthritis, urethritis and conjunctivitis. Other features include keratoderma blennorrhagica, plantar fascitis, Achilles tendonitis, circinate balanitis (in males) and sacroilitis.

4. H – Pyrophosphate arthropathy

This older man has developed a monoarthritis of the knee associated with weakly positive bifringent crystals. Pyrophosphate arthropathy or 'pseudogout' is commoner in older people presenting as a 'new' arthritis, compared to gout which starts in late middle age. Aspiration of the joint and microscopy is important to confirm or exclude one or both of these diagnoses. Analgesia *without* long-term gout prophylaxis (allopurinol) is given to patients with pyrophsphate arthropathy.

5. D – Haemophilia A-induced haemarthrosis

This young man has a haemarthrosis secondary to haemophilia A. This is an autosomal recessive disorder characterised by a low factor VIII:C. The severity of presentation depends on the residual levels of the factor. Levels more than 5% of normal produce a mild disorder (as in this case) with later onset of symptoms discovered often only by excessive bleeding after trauma. Levels between 1–5% of normal produce occasional spontaneous bleeds, e.g. haemarthrosis, but at 3–4% are often discovered after trauma. Levels less than 1% of normal present in neonates and early childhood with spontaneous bleeding into joints, muscles and even intracranially. The treatment is with factor VIII:C replacement.

3. GASTROINTESTINAL BLOOD LOSS

1. E – Duodenal ulcer
This man has developed a peptic ulcer which is most likely to be duodenal. He has 'hunger' pains associated with dyspepsia and upper GI flatulence which are suggestive of duodenal rather than gastric ulceration. His C^{14} breath test confirms the presence of *Helicobacter pylori* which is found in 90–95% of duodenal ulcers but only 60% of gastric ulcers. He should be treated with a week's course of eradication therapy using a proton pump inhibitor: e.g. lansoprazole, esomeprazole or pantoprazole combined with two antibiotics such as amoxycillin, clarithromycin or metronidazole.

2. B – Colonic carcinoma
This woman has developed colonic carcinoma with hepatic metastases. Her investigations show a microcytic anaemia, deranged liver function tests and her ultrasound scan confirms the presence of multiple metastases. She may need surgical resection, adjuvant chemo- and radiotherapy.

3. I – Oesophageal varices
This man's investigations confirm he has a hepatitic jaundice and a macrocytic anaemia associated with a raised INR and thrombocytopenia. This combination of results is highly suggestive of alcohol excess. His subsequent presentation with a large upper GI bleed is most likely to be due to oesophageal varices. He will need urgent transfusion and once haemodynamically stable (if possible) urgent upper GI endoscopy. If varices are confirmed these should be injected with a sclerosant agent or banded.

4. D – Diverticular disease
This woman has presented with the classical picture of acute diverticulitis. She has left iliac fossa pain (diverticulitis is commonly called 'left-sided appendicitis'), vomiting, pyrexia and severe left iliac fossa tenderness. She should be treated with intravenous fluids, antibiotics (cefuroxime and metronidazole) and she should be made 'Nil by mouth'. She should have an erect chest and an abdominal radiograph to exclude perforation or obstruction. Diverticular disease is a common complication of a low-fibre diet seen in the Western world and patients must be encouraged to increase roughage in their diet and avoid prolonged episodes of constipation.

5. H – Meckel's diverticulum
This man has a Meckel's diverticulum, which most commonly is an asymptomatic lesion found within the ileum, classically 60 cm from the ileocaecal valve. In adults it is a 'diagnosis of exclusion' when more common causes of upper and lower GI blood loss have been excluded. It is demonstrated radiologically using a radionuclide scan, injecting technetium-99, which concentrates in gastric mucosa. The ectopic mucosa within the diverticulum shows up using a gamma camera.

4. STROKE

1. **A – Cerebellar**
   This man has suffered a right-sided cerebellar stroke as evidenced by the nystagmus to the right, right sided dysdiadochokinesia and past pointing. Posterior fossa strokes may not be visualised on CT head scan because of the artefact caused by the closely surrounding bone. CT head scan is still the radiological investigation of choice in most hospitals as it will exclude large cerebellar bleeds or space occupying lesions which represent neurosurgical emergencies and require urgent intervention.

2. **D – Medullary**
   This woman has a right vagus nerve palsy, causing the palate to deviate to the left on asking the patient to say 'aaagh' and a right-sided hypoglossal nerve palsy causing the tongue to deviate to the right on protrusion. These lesions produce a dysarthria and are consistent with a medullary or bulbar stroke (the medulla is known as the bulb). She will invariably have swallowing difficulties and will need Speech and Language therapy.

3. **F – Occipital**
   This patient has developed a new right homonymous hemianopia which localises the lesion to the left optic tract, radiation or occipital cortex, i.e. the left optic pathways distal to the optic chiasma.

4. **H – Pontine**
   This man presents with pupillary constriction and a GCS of 3/15. As with all unconscious patients one should follow the simple rules of Airway, Breathing, Circulation (A,B,C) and in the patient with bilaterally constricted pupils one should try intravenous naloxone to exclude opiate toxicity. Pontine strokes will cause constricted pupils, whereas midbrain strokes will often affect both the sympathetic (dilatation) and parasympathetic (constriction) leading to an unresponsive mid-dilated pupil.

5. **J – Thalamic**
   It is not uncommon for patients to complain of burning or shooting pains down their affected hemiparetic limbs following a stroke. This is said to be thalamic in origin and should be treated as with other causes of neuropathic pain with gabapentin or carbamazepine.

5. GENITAL ULCERATION

1. **F – Lymphogranuloma venereum**
    This patient has developed lymphogranuloma venereum (LGV) which is caused by *Chlamydia trachomatis*. The primary lesion is a *painless* ulcerating lesion over the genitalia. This heals followed by *painful* lymphadenopathy (local), which may become buboes and rupture. In a rectal infection a proctitis occurs with associated abscess formation.

2. **B – Chancroid**
    This patient has developed chancroid sexually transmitted disease caused by *Haemophilus ducreyi*. This ulcerating condition may be difficult to differentiate clinically from other sexually transmitted diseases such as LGV and HSV infection and the diagnosis should be confirmed from swabs of the ulcerated areas or pus from the resulting abscesses. The lesion initially starts as a small papule which ulcerates to form a painful necrotic lesion. Multiple ulcers often coalesce to form a single, painful ulcer with associated local lymphadenopathy.

3. **C – Donovanosis**
    This patient has developed Donovanosis or granuloma inguinale. This is an endemic infection in the Caribbean, south-east Asia and southern India and is caused by the Gram-negative bacillus *Calymmatobacterium granulomata*. This infection causes a characteristic 'heaped' ulcerating lesion on the skin contact areas. The primary infection then spreads to the local lymph nodes causing the characteristic 'pseudo-buboes'.

4. **D – Herpes simplex**
    This patient has developed genital herpes infection caused predominantly by HSV2. In women the infection may be asymptomatic if intravaginal but classically causes painful genital ulceration with associated dysuria and regional lymphadenopathy. The virus invades the sacral ganglia where it lies dormant until episodically causing secondary infections with associated genital ulceration, pain in the buttocks, thighs and inguinal regions.

5. **I – Syphilitic chancre**
    This patient has developed a syphilitic chancre, a *painless* ulcerating lesion which is associated with primary syphilis infection. The chancre which develops at the primary site of contact, i.e. penis, labia, anus or even mouth is associated with *painless* lymphadenopathy (local) and heals within a few weeks of forming. Syphilitic gummas are ulcerating lesions occurring in tertiary syphilis.

6. COMPLICATIONS OF GALLSTONE DISEASE

1. D – Biliary colic

The characteristic history, especially sudden onset of severe pain, gives the diagnosis in this case. Whilst described as a colic, patients typically have pain even in between exacerbations. The pain is caused by a stone impacted in the cystic duct and spasm of the gallbladder in an attempt to force it distally. Approximately 20% of patients will develop clinical jaundice, however a larger proportion have subclinically deranged LFTs as in this case.

2. F – Chronic cholecystitis

This lady has the characteristic symptoms of 'flatulent dyspepsia'. Classically pain is said to start some 15–30 minutes after eating and usually lasts 30–90 minutes. It is often worse after fatty foods. The diagnosis is usually based on the history and the finding of gallstones on ultrasound (and exclusion of other causes). Treatment is elective surgery with laparoscopic cholecystectomy (provided there are no contraindications).

3. H – Gallstone ileus

The symptoms are those of small bowel obstruction. Gallstones are a relatively rare cause of intestinal obstruction (well down the list compared with adhesions and hernias) and gallstone ileus is a rare complication of gallstone disease (2%). A large gallstone enters the duodenum usually by means of a bilioenteric fistula and typically impacts in the narrower terminal ileum where it causes acute obstruction. This rarely resolves spontaneously, and requires emergency laparotomy.

4. B – Acute pancreatitis

The patient has the classical clinical presentation of this disorder which is further suggested by the raised LDH and confirmed by the raised amylase. In Western populations, gallstones and alcohol are the two commonest causes. Gallstone pancreatitis typically occurs in the patient over the age of 60 and can be severe with serious subsequent complications. Initial management is that of pancreatitis (starting with resuscitation and fluid management) with subsequent treatment of the cause.

5. G – Empyema of the gallbladder

The presentation is that of acute cholecystitis, but the finding of a palpable distended gallbladder especially with the accompanying severity of symptoms and marked leukocytosis suggests empyema of the gallbladder. The mildly deranged LFTs (mixed picture) reflect local inflammation. This is a relatively uncommon complication of acute cholecystitis in which obstructed bile in the gallbladder becomes infected and replaced eventually by pus. Treatment is resuscitation and prompt surgery (drainage or cholecystectomy). The other two complications of severe acute cholecystitis are perforation and gangrene.

7. CHEST TRAUMA

1. **D – Haemothorax**
   This is caused by a laceration of the lung or intercostal vessel. It is best treated by a large calibre chest drain and is usually self limiting unless bleeding continues in which case thoracotomy may be required. It is distinguished from massive haemothorax which is defined as a rapid accumulation of more than 1.5 litres of blood in the chest cavity with subsequent respiratory compromise.

2. **J – Tension pneumothorax**
   This develops when a 'one-way valve' air leak occurs either from the lung or the chest wall. Air is forced into the thoracic cavity without any means of escape, completely collapsing the affected lung. The mediastinum is displaced to the opposite side, decreasing venous return and compressing the opposite lung. The commonest cause of tension pneumothorax is mechanical (positive pressure) ventilation in the patient with a visceral pleural injury. Rapid decompression is required (needle then chest drain) to prevent rapid death.

3. **C – Flail chest**
   This occurs when a segment of chest wall has no bony continuity with the rest of the thoracic cage. There are multiple rib fractures with fractures in two places (usually front and back) as a result of a significant force, usually a crush injury. Whilst the flail segment moves paradoxically and compromises respiration slightly, it is the underlying severe pulmonary contusion that is the main source of morbidity and mortality. Treatment is positive pressure ventilation/oxygen therapy, surgical fixation not usually being required.

4. **A – Cardiac tamponade**
   The pericardium can fill with blood from the heart, especially following penetrating injuries. Only a small amount of pericardial blood is required to restrict cardiac activity and prevent filling. The diagnosis of cardiac tamponade can be difficult. The classic diagnostic Beck's triad consists of increased CVP, decreased BP and muffled heart sounds, but muffled heart sounds are difficult to assess in a trauma care scenario and distended neck veins difficult to assess with a hard collar in place. In general, marked hypotension or cardiac arrest with pulseless electrical activity (PEA) in the absence of hypovolaemia or tension pneumothorax should prompt consideration of this diagnosis. Treatment is with needle pericardiocentesis and/or thoracotomy. (The definition of pericardiocentesis is two very anxious people joined by a large needle!)

5. **L – Traumatic aortic disruption**

This is usually a cause of sudden death at scene after a RTA or a fall from a height; however, a proportion of patients have a small laceration that becomes contained by a mediastinal haematoma (at least for a while). The diagnosis is suggested by the mechanism of injury (blunt force to the sternum) and should be strongly suspected after the findings of a sternal fracture. The chest radiographic findings of a widened mediastinum in this context are almost confirmatory and should prompt urgent arteriography and surgery.

8. SURGICAL INCISIONS

1. **D – Long midline**

   In such cases there may be multiple visceral injuries requiring attention. This incision allows adequate exposure of all the abdominal contents. It may extend from xiphisternum to the symphysis pubis.

2. **B – Kocher's**

   Before the advent of laparoscopic cholecystectomy, this was the most commonly employed incision for open gallbladder surgery. It is an oblique right subcostal incision extending for approximately 15 cm, parallel to the costal margin. In this patient, a laparoscopic cholecystectomy would probably be contraindicated because of adhesions and risk of small bowel injury.

3. **G – Pfannenstiel**

   This is a suprapubic transverse incision, separating the rectus abdominal muscles. The lower segment uterine incision is almost universally employed. This can be performed via a lower midline incision, but is best and most commonly performed by a Pfannenstiel incision.

4. **H – Rooftop/Gable**

   This incision is formed by bilateral oblique subcostal incisions which meet in the middle giving an inverted 'V' appearance. It gives excellent exposure for major, especially hepatobiliary, surgery in the upper abdomen. To gain even greater exposure, a vertical extension can be added from the midpoint to the xiphisternum (often called a Mercedes incision – because of its similarity to the car emblem).

5. **E – Lower midline**

   This is the commonly employed incision for surgery to the sigmoid colon and rectum including sigmoid colectomy, anterior resection, abdominoperineal resection, and in general describes a midline incision from just above the umbilicus to the symphysis pubis. If difficulty is encountered, and especially if the splenic flexure requires mobilisation, this incision may be extended upwards into a longer midline incision.

9. GYNAECOLOGICAL THERAPEUTIC AGENTS

1. **D – Goserelin (GnRH analogue)**

   GnRH analogues can not be given orally as they are small peptides which are broken down quickly if swallowed. They act by initial stimulation of the hypothalamus and pituitary GnRH receptors followed quickly by competitive blockade of the receptor sites. They effectively switch off the H-P-O axis (temporary medical menopause, hence the side effects due to hypo-oestrogenism) so that stimulated cycles in IVF start from a basal level. Tamoxifen can cause similar side effects but is taken orally and acts as an ovulation induction agent, not a down-regulator.

2. **F – Mefanamic acid**

   COCP, mefanamic acid, tranexamic acid, medroxyprogesterone acetate, GnRH analogues (non-oral) and even danazol (rarely nowadays) are all used for menorrhagia. COCP and mefanamic acid are also used extensively for dysmenorrhoea. Mefanamic acid is a NSAID which alters prostaglandin balance and therefore menstrual flow and pain. Due to its action on PGs it can induce bronchospasm in asthmatics so is relatively contraindicated. COCP has no such effects and is therefore safe in asthmatics.

3. **A – Combined oral contraceptive pill (COCP)**

   COCP stops ovulation and endometrial proliferation and significantly reduces the user's risk of both endometrial and ovarian cancer with long-term use (5–10 years). However, there is a slight increased incidence of breast and cervical cancers. Tamoxifen increases the risk of endometrial cancer and HRT (either oestrogen only or combined) shows no reduction in endometrial cancer (and possibly a slight, non-significant increase). The evidence about long-term progestagens is confusing but should be considered to have no effect on the incidence of these cancers. GnRH analogues are not given alone long-term due to a deleterious effect on bone mineral density.

4. **B – Cyproterone acetate**

   COCP, GnRH analogues and cyproterone acetate are the only agents that have an anti-androgenic effect reducing hirsutism and acne. GnRH analogues are not given alone long-term due to a deleterious effect on bone mineral density. Cyproterone acetate is a competitive blocker of androgen action. It is usually given as part of Dianette, a form of COCP. COCP already contains oestrogen by definition and does not cause feminisation of male fetuses if pregnancy occurs while taking it.

5.   G – Oestrogen-only HRT

Oestrogen-only HRT is all that is required post-hysterectomy and is highly effective at preventing or treating vasomotor symptoms of the menopause. If the patient still has a uterus then combined oestrogen–progesterone HRT is required to prevent endometrial stimulation. COCP already contains oestrogen and progesterone by definition and therefore is inappropriate. Medroxyprogesterone acetate (as Depo Provera) can be effective in the management of vasomotor symptoms but is only given to patients in whom oestrogen is contraindicated or best avoided (i.e. it is not commonly used).

10. PATHOGENIC VIRUSES

1.　D – Hepatitis C virus
Hepatitis C is an RNA virus belonging to the flavivirus family. The major routes of infection are through blood transfusion and intravenous inoculation, but the incidence of transmission by both these routes is falling. At least 75% of patients infected with hepatitis C eventually develop chronic liver disease. Cirrhosis is seen in up to 20% of patients and of these, 7–15% will go on to develop hepatocellular carcinoma. Fulminant hepatitis is rare. Patients who are infected after the age of 40 years, particularly men, and patients infected with genotypes 1 and 4 have more rapid progression of fibrosis.

2.　A – Coronavirus
Severe acute respiratory syndrome (SARS) is a condition first described in the Far East and Canada in early 2003. It is characterised by a prodromal fever followed by dry cough, dyspnoea and hypoxia. In 10–20% of patients, the disease is severe enough to require mechanical ventilation. The mortality is in the region of 5%. The responsible virus is a novel coronavirus, an RNA virus named after its halo (corona)-like appearance on electron microscopy. Before it came to prominence as the cause of SARS, coronavirus was known as one of the viruses causing the common cold.

3.　J – Varicella zoster virus
Varicella zoster virus is a DNA virus of the α-herpes virus family. It causes two distinct diseases, varicella (chicken pox) and herpes zoster (shingles). Varicella is the primary infection and usually occurs in children. Shingles can occur at all ages but is most common in the elderly. It produces vesicular skin lesions similar to chicken pox, usually in the distribution of a single dermatome. The lesions are often preceded by severe dermatomal pain, indicating the involvement of sensory nerves. Shingles never occurs as a primary infection but results from reactivation of latent virus from dorsal root and/or cranial nerve ganglia.

4.　F – Human papillomavirus
Verrucae or warts are benign tumours of squamous epithelium known as squamous cell papillomas. They arise not only in keratinised squamous epithelium, such as the skin, but also in non-keratinised squamous epithelium such as that lining the ectocervix. All warts are caused by human papillomavirus (HPV), a DNA virus belonging to the papovavirus family. There are almost 50 different serotypes of HPV. Genital warts are usually caused by HPV types 6 and 11. Other serotypes, notably 16, 18 and 31, have been implicated in the development of high grade cervical intraepithelial neoplasia (CIN) and invasive cervical carcinoma.

5. C – Epstein–Barr virus

Infectious mononucleosis is a multisystem disorder caused by Epstein–Barr virus (EBV). This is a DNA virus belonging to the herpesvirus family. Diagnosis of infectious mononucleosis is made by finding heterophil antibodies to sheep erythrocytes in the patient's serum. As well as causing infectious mononucleosis, EBV has a strong association with certain human malignancies, particularly Burkitt's lymphoma and nasopharyngeal carcinoma.

11. PHARYNGEAL MUSCLES

1.   A – Inferior constrictor

A further component of the muscle is attached to the oblique line on the thyroid cartilage. Between the crico- and thyro-pharyngeal components, there is a potential weakness (the dehiscence of Killian), this being the site of protrusion of a pharyngeal pouch.

2.   D – Palatoglossus

The posterior pillar is underlain by the palatopharyngeus. The palatine tonsil lies between the anterior and posterior pillars on the superior constrictor, which separates it from the facial artery and the carotid sheath.

3.   C – Middle constrictor

The anterior attachment is also from the stylohyoid ligament. Posteriorly, the three constrictors meet in the midline raphe, the superior being within the middle, which is within the inferior constrictor muscle.

4.   F – Pharyngobasilar fascia

The fascia completes the pharyngeal wall superolaterally being continuous with the superior constrictor and attached to the skull base. The eustachian (auditory) tube passes from the lateral wall of the pharynx to the anterior wall of the middle ear. Its medial two-thirds is cartilaginous but it passes laterally into the petrous temporal bone.

5.   J – Tensor palatini

The stylopharyngeus is supplied by the glossopharyngeal nerve. The remainder of the muscles in the option list are supplied by the vagus through the pharyngeal plexus.

12. MUSCLE ATTACHMENTS IN THE UPPER LIMB

1. **J – Triceps**
    The description is that of the attachment of the lateral head of the triceps. The medial head comes from the posterior aspect to the humerus below the radial groove, the long head is attached proximally to the infraglenoid aspect of the scapula. The three heads are attached distally to the olecranon process of the ulna. The muscle is a powerful extensor of the forearm.

2. **B – Brachialis**
    From its extensive humeral attachment, the tendon is attached to the coronoid process of the ulna. The muscle is a powerful flexor of the forearm.

3. **D – Extensor carpi radialis longus**
    The ridge also gives rise to the brachioradialis muscle. Extensor carpi radialis brevis arises from the common extensor origin on the lateral epicondyle of the humerus; distally the tendons are attached to the base of the 2nd and 3rd metacarpal bones; they extend the wrist and have a weak action across the elbow.

4. **I – Pronator teres**
    Proximally the muscle has two heads, one just above the common flexor origin on the humerus and the second from the medial side of the coronoid process on the ulna. The muscle is a pronator of the forearm and forms the medial border of the cubital fossa.

5. **F – Flexor digitorum profundus**
    These are long flexor tendons passing deep to the flexor retinaculum, deep to the flexor digitorum superficialis. They gain attachment to the palmar surface of the base of the terminal phalanx of the fingers, and they also give attachment to the lumbrical muscles in the palm. The tendons of the flexor digitorum superficialis split over the proximal phalanx, each half encircling the corresponding tendon of the flexor digitorum profundus, and after partial decussation, the tendon is attached to the sides of the middle phalanx. These two muscles flex the wrist and phalanges.

PAPER 5

Paper 5 questions

1. THEME: HEART FAILURE

A   Alcoholic cardiomyopathy
B   Aortic regurgitation
C   Aortic stenosis
D   Beri-beri
E   Cardiac tamponade
F   COPD
G   Ischaemic cardiomyopathy
H   Mitral regurgitation
I   Mitral stenosis
J   Pulmonary fibrosis

The following patients have all presented with heart failure. Please choose the most appropriate cause from the above list. The items may be used once, more than once, in combination or not at all.

1. A 59-year-old diabetic man presents in A&E with a 4-day increasing shortness of breath and ankle oedema. On examination he is unwell with signs of biventricular failure. Cardiac enzymes are within normal limits, ECG: sinus tachycardia, 120 bpm; left axis deviation and poor anterior 'R wave' progression with a partial left bundle branch block.

2. A 29-year-old man is recovering in hospital after a severe pneumonia for which he has been on intravenous antibiotics for 1 week. He becomes acutely unwell with pyrexia and shortness of breath. On examination he has several splinter haemorrhages and signs of left ventricular failure. There is a loud early diastolic murmur heard primarily at the left sternal edge. An old intravenous cannula is noted in the left antecubital fossa.

3. A 71-year-old woman is seen in the medical outpatient department for her 6-monthly check-up. She has been increasingly unwell with shortness of breath on exercise, PND, orthopnoea and leg oedema. On examination she has signs of biventricular failure and a low volume pulse in atrial fibrillation. Auscultation reveals a soft mid diastolic murmur at the apex with a loud pansystolic murmur at the left sternal edge.

4. A 19-year-old Somalian man is admitted to hospital with suspected pulmonary tuberculosis. The SpR notes he has positive Kussmaul's sign and his heart sounds are difficult to hear. His ECG confirms low voltage complexes.

5. A 72-year-old man is admitted to hospital with worsening oedema and shortness of breath. On examination he is short of breath at rest and his oxygen saturation is 84% on air. He has marked clubbing of the fingernails and fixed inspiratory bibasal crepitations, as well as signs of biventricular failure.

2. THEME: DEFINITIVE UROLOGICAL INVESTIGATIONS

A   Anti-dsDNA antibody
B   Anti-GBM antibody
C   Blood glucose
D   cANCA
E   Plasma electrophoresis
F   PSA
G   Renal angiogram
H   Renal biopsy
I   Urine cytology
J   Ultrasound scan of the renal tract

The following patients have all presented with urological problems. Please choose the most definitive investigation to confirm the diagnosis in each case from the above list. The items may be used once, more than once or not at all.

1. A 61-year-old man presents to his GP with increasing problems passing urine. He has hesitancy, poor stream and terminal dribbling. Examination is unremarkable other than PR which reveals a smoothly enlarged prostate gland. Subsequent investigations including FBC, U&Es, CCa^{2+} and chest radiograph are all within normal limits.

2. A 27-year-old woman presents in A&E with increasing peripheral and facial oedema. On examination she is noted to have a malar rash as well as marked ascites and facial and ankle oedema. Urinalysis confirms protein+++ and microscopy shows the presence of renal casts. FBC: Hb 9.2 g/dl, MCV 88 fl, WCC 4.2 × 10^9/l, Plt 191 × 10^9/l; U&Es: Na$^+$ 132 mmol/l, K$^+$ 6.9 mmol/l, urea 34.7 mmol/l, Cr 553 μmol/l.

3. A 59-year-old man presents in A&E with a 10-day history of a flu-like illness associated with myalgia, arthralgia and shortness of breath, episodic haemoptysis and two day history of oliguria and ankle oedema. Investigations show U&Es: Na$^+$ 133 mmol/l, K$^+$ 5.8 mmol/l, urea 17.1 mmol/l, Cr 303 μmol/l; his chest radiograph shows hazy shadowing throughout both lung fields.

4. A 24-year-old woman presents in A&E with vague abdominal pains and haematuria. Of note she has a strong family history of 'kidney problems' and her grandmother and aunt both died suddenly of 'brain haemorrhages'. Urinalysis confirms blood + + +, protein++, nitrites −. Microscopy: no organisms or renal casts seen. FBC: Hb 16.7 g/dl, Hct 54.8, WCC 14.2 × 10^9/l, Plt 553 × 10^9/l; U&Es: Na$^+$ 129 mmol/l, K$^+$ 5.7 mmol/l, urea 25.8 mmol/l, Cr 401 μmol/l.

5. An 87-year-old woman presents with severe back pain and general malaise. Routine investigations reveal FBC: Hb 5.9 g/dl, MCV 93 fl, WCC 2.8 × 10^9/l, Plt 33 × 10^9/l; U&Es: Na$^+$ 131 mmol/l, K$^+$ 6.2 mmol/l, urea 18.0 mmol/l, Cr 322 μmol/l; CCa^{2+} 3.43 mmol/l; ESR 110 mm/h.

3. THEME: DYSPHAGIA

A   Achalasia
B   External oesophageal compression
C   Motor neurone disease
D   Oesophageal candidiasis
E   Oesophageal carcinoma
F   Oesophageal diverticulum
G   Oesophageal peptic stricture
H   Pharyngeal pouch
I   Presbyoesophagus
J   Systemic sclerosis

The following patients have all presented with difficulty in swallowing (dysphagia). Please choose the most appropriate cause from the above list. The items may be used once, more than once, or not at all.

1. A 62-year-old woman presents in medical outpatients with a 3-month history of worsening 'high level' dysphagia associated with nasal regurgitation. She has now developed speech problems and increasing limb weakness.

2. A 49-year-old man who has been in hospital for several weeks with a severe infective exacerbation of COPD requiring several courses of antibiotics and steroids complains to the PRHO of worsening retrosternal pain and dysphagia to solids. OGD shows circumferential erosions and ulceration with linear white plaques.

3. A 91-year-old woman presents in the Health Care of the Older Person outpatient department with a 6-month history of worsening dysphagia to solids and liquids. Barium swallow reveals no intrinsic lesion but shows severe 'corkscrew' dysmotility.

4. A 54-year-old Hong Kong Chinese man presents with dysphagia to solids and liquids. Barium swallow confirms a long, irregular stricture extending over several centimetres.

5. A 31-year-old man presents to his GP with an 8-month history of worsening dysphagia to solids, with occasional regurgitation of unaltered food. The dysphagia is not as bad if he eats small amounts and washes everything down with lots of fluids. The diagnosis is confirmed on barium swallow which shows a 'bird's beak' deformity in the lower oesophagus.

4. THEME: WEAKNESS

A   Alcoholic myopathy
B   Amyotrophy
C   Cervical myelopathy
D   Demyelination
E   Duchenne muscular dystrophy
F   Guillain–Barré syndrome
G   Hypokalaemia
H   Motor neurone disease
I   Paraneoplastic motor neuropathy
J   Thyrotoxic proximal myopathy

The following patients have all presented with muscle weakness. Please choose the most appropriate cause from the above list. The items may be used once, more than once or not at all.

1. A 73-year-old man presents to his GP with increasing weakness in all four limbs associated with nasal regurgitation of fluids and speech difficulties. Initial investigations, including FBC, U&Es, RBG, LFTs, CCa^{2+}, chest radiograph, ECG and CT head scan, are normal.

2. A 64-year-old woman is admitted to A&E with severe generalised weakness. She was recently started on metolazone and frusemide for peripheral oedema which had begun after she was placed on nifedipine for hypertension.

3. A 19-year-old woman is seen by her GP with increasing difficulty water ski-ing. On examination she is thin, peripherally vasodilated, tachycardic and tremulous.

4. A 34-year-old man is admitted to hospital with a 10-day history of an upper respiratory tract infection followed by increasing difficulty walking associated with pins and needles and numbness in his feet. Two days after admission he has to be electively ventilated due to a decreasing FEV_1 and FVC.

5. A 63-year-old man on gliclazide for type II diabetes sees his GP with increasing pain and weakness in his thighs. His symptoms improve with insulin.

5. THEME: NEW THERAPEUTIC INTERVENTIONS

A   Abciximab
B   Aldesleukin
C   Alemtuzumab
D   α interferon
E   Basiliximab
F   β interferon
G   Granulocyte colony-stimulating factor (GCSF)
H   Infliximab
I   Rituximab
J   Trastazumab

The following patients have all presented with disorders requiring one of the newer therapeutic interventions. Please choose the most appropriate intervention from the above list. The items may be used once, more than once, in combination or not at all.

1. A 39-year-old woman is admitted to her local hospital under the consultant neurologist with her third relapse of her multiple sclerosis in the past 18 months. He has discussed starting a new therapy which may help prevent these frequent relapses.

2. A 29-year-old man with severe Crohn's disease is re-admitted to hospital with a further acute flare up of his colitis. The surgical registrar notes he has an infected anal fistula which has been resistant to treatment in the past.

3. A 63-year-old man with known IHD is re-admitted to hospital with a prolonged episode of angina like chest pain. His troponin I is significantly raised but his ECG shows only T wave inversion through the anterolateral leads. He continues to experience angina pains on minimal exertion and is referred for inpatient angiography at the local cardiology centre.

4. A 25-year-old previous intravenous drug user is seen in the hepatology clinic to be told his recent blood tests have confirmed he has active hepatitis C virus (HCV) infection. The consultant discusses the possibility of starting him on a relatively new treatment but on review of his notes tells him he is unfortunately not eligible because of a recent episode of severe depression and attempted suicide.

5. A 31-year-old woman undergoing her third course of chemotherapy for metastatic breast cancer is given a new drug which she is told may stop her getting the infections related to her blood cells becoming very low with the chemotherapy.

6. THEME: JAUNDICE

A   Acute viral hepatitis
B   Ascending cholangitis
C   Carcinoma of the gallbladder
D   Cholangiocarcinoma
E   Cirrhosis
F   Gallstones
G   Hepatocellular carcinoma
H   Multiple hepatic metastases
I   Pancreatic carcinoma
J   Sclerosing cholangitis

The following are descriptions of patients with jaundice. Please select the most appropriate diagnosis from the above list. The items may be used once, more than once or not at all.

1. A 78-year-old woman is seen in A&E with a 2-week history of progressive jaundice and pruritis. On direct questioning, she has a 3-month history of anorexia and weight loss. On examination she is cachectic, deeply icteric with a palpable gallbladder but no hepatomegaly. LFTs: Tbil 262 μmol/l, AST 62 iu/l, ALT 56 iu/l, Alk phos 695 iu/l, Alb 31 g/l.

2. A 65-year-old woman attends her GP with a 3-day history of increasing jaundice, nausea and upper abdominal pain. She has had several previous bouts of acute abdominal pain and a long history of dyspeptic symptoms. Examination reveals jaundice and slight tenderness in the right hypochondrium but no masses. LFTs: Tbil 90 μmol/l, AST 37 iu/l, ALT 23 iu/l, Alk phos 312 iu/l, Alb 39 g/l.

3. A 39-year-old man with known ulcerative colitis presents to his GP with a 2-week history of painless worsening jaundice. He is admitted to hospital where an abdominal ultrasound scan demonstrates dilated intrahepatic ducts but a normal diameter common bile duct.

4. A 43-year-old man presents in A&E with acute jaundice, nausea, vomiting and upper abdominal pain. On examination he is unwell, pyrexial and there is tender hepatomegaly. LFTs: Tbil 96 μmol/l, AST 435 iu/l, ALT 570 iu/l, Alk phos 212 iu/l, Alb 42 g/l.

5. A 49-year-old woman presents with recent onset of jaundice. On further questioning she has noticed bouts of pruritis and dark urine for several months. LFTs: Tbil 63 μmol/l, AST 40 iu/l, ALT 27 iu/l, Alk phos 509 iu/l, Alb 36 g/l. An autoantibody screen demonstrates a positive titre (> 1/80) for antimitochondrial antibodies.

7. THEME: INTESTINAL OBSTRUCTION

A   Adhesions
B   Bezoar
C   Colonic carcinoma
D   Crohn's stricture
E   Diverticular stricture
F   Gallstones
G   Hernia
H   Intussusception
I   Small bowel lymphoma
J   Tuberculous stricture
K   Volvulus

The following patients have all presented with intestinal (large or small bowel) obstruction. Please select the most appropriate diagnosis from the above list. The items may be used once, more than once or not at all.

1. A 90-year-old woman presents in A&E with a 3-day history of vomiting and colicky central and right-sided abdominal pain. She has had no previous surgery. On examination she is dehydrated and her abdomen is distended and tympanic with obstructed bowel sounds. There is a small 2 cm tender swelling in the right groin with overlying erythema.

2. A 46-year-old woman is referred by her GP to A&E with a 48-hour history of abdominal pain, distension and vomiting. She has had several previous admissions for similar symptoms. On examination she has scars from previous operations which include a hysterectomy and a laparotomy.

3. A 6-month old baby is referred to the paediatric on-call team because of attacks of screaming associated with drawing up of the legs. The baby has vomited and is clinically dehydrated and unwell. On examination there is blood and mucus per rectum.

4. A 67-year-old man presents in A&E with a 4-day history of severe lower abdominal cramps and vomiting. He has not opened his bowels for 3 days and has not passed flatus today. On direct questioning he has had vague lower abdominal pains and some diarrhoea for some months and may have lost some weight. The abdomen is distended on examination and bowel sounds are obstructed. The rectum is empty.

5. An 80-year-old man with severe Parkinson's disease is a long-term nursing home resident. The nurses have called the GP out because he has been distressed for some days and has not been eating or drinking. The patient has a reduced level of consciousness and is dehydrated. The abdomen is very distended and a plain abdominal radiograph demonstrates a single, hugely dilated loop of colon.

8. THEME: POSTOPERATIVE PYREXIA

A   Anaesthetic drugs
B   Anastomotic dehiscence
C   Basal atelectasis
D   Deep vein thrombosis
E   Pelvic abscess
F   Phlebitis
G   Respiratory tract infection
H   Subphrenic abscess
I   Transfusion reaction
J   Urinary tract infection
K   Wound infection

The following are descriptions of patients with postoperative pyrexia with or without associated pain. Please select the most appropriate diagnosis from the above list. The items may be used once, more than once or not at all.

1. A 62-year-old woman undergoes a right hemicolectomy for caecal carcinoma. She is given an epidural for pain relief but this falls out on leaving theatre recovery. A PCA is started but only after some delay during which she has significant pain. On the first post operative day she has a temperature of 37.9°C.

2. A 92-year-old woman undergoes a laparotomy for small bowel obstruction. She has a protracted recovery and is still catheterised at day 14 post operatively because of problems with mobilisation. You are called because she develops a temperature of 38.7°C. She has no cough or GI symptoms and is eating and drinking normally.

3. A 12-year-old boy undergoes a difficult appendicectomy for gangrenous appendicitis. He makes an initial rapid recovery and goes home on the third postoperative day. Four days later, his mother brings him back to A&E with further lower abdominal pain and a swinging pyrexia of 39°C. The wound is clean but there is tenderness and guarding in the right iliac fossa.

4. A 66-year-old woman undergoes a laparotomy with oversewing of a perforated duodenal ulcer. Five days postoperatively she develops a swinging pyrexia of 38.6°C with rigors. On examination, there is some right upper quadrant tenderness. She has right basal crackles and a small right pleural effusion on chest radiograph.

5. A 76-year-old man undergoes an anterior resection for rectal cancer. On the third postoperative day he develops severe lower abdominal pain. On examination he is septic with a high temperature, reduced conscious level and abdominal distension with peritonism in the lower abdomen.

9. THEME: UROGYNAECOLOGICAL DISORDERS

A Congenital abnormality of the genito-urinary tract
B Cystocele
C Detrusor overactivity
D Enterocele
E Genuine stress incontinence (GSI))
F Interstitial cystitis
G Rectocele
H Urinary tract infection (UTI)
I Uterovaginal prolapse
J Vesicovaginal fistula

From the above list please choose the item most likely to cause the clinical picture described. The items may be used once, more than once, in combination or not at all.

1. A 38-year-old woman describes urinary frequency, urgency and stress incontinence on coughing and laughing for the last 6 months. Examination of the urogenital tract reveals no abnormality. Her symptoms improve markedly on tolteridine, an anticholinergic agent.

2. A 45-year-old woman describes urinary incontinence almost continuously. It started shortly after a 'difficult' hysterectomy for fibroids. Examination reveals a moist vagina and vulva but no demonstrable stress incontinence on coughing.

3. A 60-year-old woman describes a feeling of 'something coming down' in the vagina. She also describes frequency and difficulty passing urine, having to insert a finger into the vagina to aid voiding.

4. A 28-year-old woman describes urinary frequency, urgency and dysuria. She had a diagnostic laparoscopy 1 week previously for pelvic pain with no cause found for the pain. Examination reveals no abnormality.

5. A 58-year-old woman describes urinary frequency and stress incontinence on coughing and laughing for the last 6 months. Examination of the urogenital tract reveals moderate urogenital atrophy but no other abnormalities. Urodynamic investigation (UDS) shows no increase in detrusor pressure during witnessed episodes of stress incontinence.

10. THEME: DISEASES OF THE LARGE INTESTINE

A   Adenocarcinoma
B   Adenoma
C   Amoebiasis
D   Angiodysplasia
E   Crohn's disease
F   Diverticular disease
G   Hirschsprung's disease
H   Ischaemic colitis
I   Pseudomembranous colitis
J   Ulcerative colitis

From the above list, please select the disease that each of the following patients is most likely to have. The items may be used once, more than once or not at all.

1. A 50-year-old man presents with a recent onset of bright red rectal bleeding. Flexible sigmoidoscopy shows a pedunculated polyp in the rectum. The polyp has a lobulated red surface and is 1 cm in size.

2. A 75-year-old woman who had a total hip replacement 5 days previously develops diarrhoea on the orthopaedic ward. She had been treated with prophylactic antibiotics around the time of surgery. Stool culture grows *Clostridium difficile*.

3. A 35-year-old man presents with abdominal pain and bloody diarrhoea 1 month after returning from holiday to India. Colonoscopy shows multiple flask-shaped ulcers throughout the colon. Biopsies of the ulcerated areas shows PAS-positive trophozoites with ingested red cells in the ulcer slough.

4. A 75-year-old man presents with a 2-month history of left-sided abdominal pain and altered bowel habit. On examination he has a pyrexia of 37.8°C and is tender in the left iliac fossa. Barium enema shows narrowing of the sigmoid colon and multiple outpouchings that communicate with the lumen. No evidence of a mass lesion is seen.

5. A 23-year-old woman presents with a 4-week history of profuse bloody diarrhoea and abdominal pain. Colonoscopy reveals diffuse mucosal erythema starting in the rectum and extending in continuity to the splenic flexure. Stool cultures on three consecutive occasions are negative. Colonic biopsies show diffuse chronic inflammation in the lamina propria with crypt abscesses and crypt distortion. No granulomas are seen.

11. THEME: LARYNX

A Arytenoid cartilage
B Cricoid cartilage
C Epiglottis
D External laryngeal nerve
E Inferior thyroid artery
F Internal laryngeal nerve
G Recurrent laryngeal nerve
H Superior laryngeal nerve
I Thyrohyoid membrane
J Thyroid cartilage

For each of the following descriptions, please choose the most appropriate structure from the above list. The items may be used once, more than once or not at all.

1. Innervates the lateral cricoarytenoid muscle.

2. Gives attachment to both sides of the conus elasticus.

3. Gives anterior attachment to the vocal fold.

4. Gives posterior attachment to the quadrangular membrane.

5. Is a posterior relation of the tongue.

12. THEME: NERVE SUPPLY OF THE MUSCLES OF THE LOWER LIMB

A   Common peroneal (lateral popliteal) nerve
B   Deep peroneal (anterior tibial) nerve
C   Femoral nerve
D   Medial plantar nerve
E   Obturator nerve
F   Sciatic nerve
G   Superficial peroneal (musculocutaneous) nerve
H   Superior gluteal nerve
I   Sural nerve
J   Tibial (posterior tibial) nerve

For each of the following muscles please choose the nerve that innervates it from the above list. The items may be used once, more than once or not at all.

1. Gluteus medius.

2. Semimembranosus.

3. Tibialis anterior.

4. Peroneus longus.

5. Soleus.

Paper 5 answers

1. HEART FAILURE

1. **G – Ischaemic cardiomyopathy**

   This gentleman has signs of biventricular failure. He has peripheral oedema and dyspnoea which may be due to pulmonary oedema, a pleural effusion or indeed low output failure. His ECG confirms signs of old (i.e. non-acute) ischaemic heart disease with left axis deviation, poor anterior R wave progression and a partial left bundle branch block. He will need treatment with diuretics and if possible an ACE inhibitor and/or cardioselective β blocker.

2. **B – Aortic regurgitation**

   This young man has developed acute infective endocarditis probably caused by a staphylococcal infection. He has had an intravenous cannula, which is probably the source of the infection, and shows the importance of their aseptic insertion and removal as soon as they are no longer required. He will require intravenous flucloxacillin and probably aortic valve replacement.

3. **I – Mitral stenosis**

   This woman has signs consistent with mitral stenosis (MS) and secondary tricuspid regurgitation (TR). She has a soft mid diastolic murmur (MS) and a loud PSM (TR) with a low volume pulse in atrial fibrillation. She has now developed cardiac failure and will need treatment with diuretics, digoxin and prophylactic warfarin or aspirin. If she is agreeable she should be considered for mitral valve replacement.

4. **E – Cardiac tamponade**

   This young man has probable TB pericardial effusion leading to signs of a potential tamponade. Kussmaul's signs (the paradoxical rise in the JVP with inspiration), the poorly heard heart sounds and the low voltage complexes of his ECG are all consistent with a tamponade and he requires urgent pericardiocentesis. He will also need anti-TB treatment for at least 6 months.

5. **J – Pulmonary fibrosis**

   This man has developed cor-pulmonale, i.e. cardiac failure secondary to his chronic lung condition. He has signs of pulmonary fibrosis as evidenced by the fixed bibasal crepitations and finger clubbing with associated hypoxia and desaturation. This chronic condition has led to pulmonary hypertension and secondary right, and then left heart failure.

2. DEFINITIVE UROLOGICAL INVESTIGATIONS

1. F – PSA

This man has developed symptoms of bladder outflow tract obstruction. In a middle-aged gentleman this is most likely to be due to prostatic enlargement, which may be confirmed on PR examination. He has no associated systemic symptoms, normal FBC, U&Es, CCa^{2+} and chest radiograph. The most likely diagnosis is benign prostatic hypertrophy although carcinoma must still be excluded. The differentiating investigation is a serum prostatic specific antigen (PSA). If the PSA is within the normal range the patient should be started on an à blocker or considered for surgical resection.

2. A – Anti-dsDNA antibody

This patient has developed systemic lupus erythematosus (SLE) as evidenced by her malar rash and renal failure. The renal impairment is secondary to a glomerulonephritis which maybe membranous, focal segmental, diffuse or even minimal change disease. However it may be that even lupus patients with apparently normal renal function have some immune mediated changes within the kidney visible only on microscopy. SLE is characterised by the presence of dsDNA antibodies, particularly in the presence of active nephritis. This may be associated with low C3 and C4 levels and a raised ESR in the presence of relatively normal CRP levels.

3. B – Anti-GBM antibody

This patient has developed renal impairment and pulmonary changes consistent with haemorrhage. This combination maybe associated with Goodpasture's syndrome, more recently renamed anti-glomerular basement membrane disease (anti-GBM disease) or in a chronic setting Wegner's granulomatosis may present in a similar manner but would usually involve the upper respiratory tract as well. The common antigen in anti-GBM disease is a component of type iv collagen which forms a major structural component of the basement membrane found within the alveolus and glomerulus alike.

4. J – Ultrasound scan of the renal tract

This patient has a strong family history of renal disease and two relatives have died suddenly of intracranial haemorrhages. She now presents with renal failure, haematuria and polycythaemia. This clinical picture is highly suggestive of adult polycystic kidney disease (APCKD). The diagnosis may easily be confirmed on renal ultrasound scan. APCKD is the commonest congenital abnormality of the renal tract leading to renal failure and should be screened for in all first-degree relatives. It is an autosomal dominant disorder, unlike the childhood form which is inherited in an autosomal recessive manner.

5. E – Plasma electrophoresis

This elderly woman has presented with back pain. Subsequent routine investigations have confirmed a pancytopenia, an ESR >100, hypercalcaemia and acute renal failure, suggesting probable multiple myeloma. The diagnoisis is confirmed by the presence of a monclonal gammopathy with associated immunoparesis on plasma electrophoresis, Bence Jones proteins in the urine and plasma cells on a blood film or in the bone marrow. Renal failure occurs due to four or five processes in myeloma, collectively called 'myeloma kidney': (1) dehydration – due to being unwell; (2) glomerulonephritis; (3) increased urinary tract infections – due to the immunoparesis; (4) hypercalcaemia – leading to nephrocalcinosis and renal stones; and (5) obstruction of the tubules by the light chains.

3. DYSPHAGIA

1. **C – Motor neurone disease**
   This woman has symptoms of 'bulbar problems'. She has high level dysphagia and nasal regurgitation suggestive of an oropharyngeal neuromuscular problem. She has also developed speech problems and limb weakness. This clinical picture is highly suggestive of motor neurone disease, however the diagnosis is one of exclusion and other pathologies should be excluded using MRI of the cervical spine and brain, EEG and EMG.

2. **D – Oesophageal candidiasis**
   This patient has had multiple courses of antibiotics and steroids implying he has been seriously ill and this will lead to opportunistic infection such as candidiasis and to *Clostridium difficile* and MRSA infections. Patients often complain of hoarseness of voice if the candidiasis has affected their pharynx or dysphagia as in this case. Patients should be treated with a single dose of fluconazole 150 mg, nystatin or amphotericin.

3. **I – Presbyoesophagus**
   Presbyoesophagus or 'corkscrew' oesophagus is a further diagnosis of exclusion and is due to dysfunctional peristalsis. This may occur throughout the GI tract in older patients and leads to dysphagia in the upper GI tract and constipation in the colon. Benign and malignant lesions are common in the older patient and dysphagia should be investigated with barium swallow and/or upper GI endoscopy, constipation with colonoscopy or CT abdomen with contrast.

4. **E – Oesophageal carcinoma**
   Carcinoma of the oesophagus is commoner in Chinese people and presents with increasing dysphagia, initially to solids and then progressively to liquids. Risk factors includes underlying oesophageal disorders such as achalasia and Barret's oesophagus, cigarette smoking and spicy foods.

5. **A – Achalasia**
   Achalasia of the oesophagus is an idiopathic disorder due to an atonic segment in the lower oesophagus, similar to Hirchsprung's disease in the rectum. It produces low-level dysphagia to solids and patients often complain of vomiting up undigested food. It is improved symptomatically if the patient takes smaller mouthfuls and washes the food down with large volumes of liquid. Definitive treatment involves forceful dilatation of the lower oesophageal sphincter or in poorly responsive cases surgical division of the segmental muscle wall.

4. WEAKNESS

1. **H – Motor neurone disease**
   This patient has signs/symptoms of limb weakness and bulbar problems, i.e. speech and swallowing difficulties, consistent with motor neurone disease. Motor neurone disease is a diagnosis of exclusion and must be differentiated from other pathologies such as multi-infarct disease and late onset myasthenic syndrome.

2. **G – Hypokalaemia**
   Hypokalaemia may make patients feel very weak and lethargic and is common in patients on several diuretics. The hypokalaemia can be avoided by the addition of spironolactone, amiloride and/or an ACE inhibitor.

3. **J – Thyrotoxic proximal myopathy**
   This young woman has developed a proximal myopathy secondary to thyrotoxicosis. The major endocrine disorders associated with 'excess', i.e. acromegaly, Cushing's and diabetes (hyperglycaemia), can all produce a proximal myopathy.

4. **F – Guillain–Barré syndrome**
   This patient has developed a mixed motor-sensory neuropathy 10 days after a respiratory tract infection. This is consistent with Guillain–Barré syndrome. Patients with *Campylobacter* antibodies or evidence of HIV infection suffer a more rapidly progressive, malignant form of this disorder often requiring ventilatory support. The patient's respiratory function should be monitored using serial spirometry measurements and not PEFR.

5. **B – Amyotrophy**
   This man has developed a proximal motor neuropathy associated with his diabetes. This is known as diabetic amyotrophy. The patient should improve with insulin therapy. Non-responders need other causes of proximal myopathy excluded.

5. NEW THERAPEUTIC INTERVENTIONS

This set of questions is difficult for the undergraduate and probably most postgraduates! However we have included them because they illustrate that medicine is an ever increasing field and that keeping up with innovation and change requires the doctor of today to maintain lifelong learning or find themselves very quickly 'behind the times'. Immunomodulators and monoclonal antibody therapies will become increasingly common, particularly in autoimmune disease, chronic inflammatory conditions and malignancies.

1. **F – β Interferon**

   This patient has relapsing–remitting multiple sclerosis. Several new agents have been licensed recently which are shown to reduce the frequency of the relapses. β interferon and glatiramer are given to patients who have had at least one relapse in the past 18 months (both should only be given in specialist centres). β interferon commonly causes a 'flu-like' illness but may cause personality changes, severe depression and even suicidal ideation. Glatiramer is an 'immunomodulator' made up of synthetic peptides. Like β interferon it may cause local irritation at the injection site but its main side effects include tachycardia, palpitations and shortness of breath.

2. **H – Infliximab**

   This patient should be given the monoclonal antibody (mAb) therapy, infliximab, which is used in specialist centres for severe, relapsing Crohn's disease and in particular treatment resistant fistulae. It works against the pro-inflammatory cytokine tumour necrosis factor-α (TNF-α). It may cause worsening heart failure and reactivate tuberculosis infection. Infliximab is also used in the treatment of rheumatoid arthritis.

3. **A – Abciximab**

   This man has unstable angina following a prolonged episode of chest pain. Despite being in hospital and on maximal therapy he continues to get exertional chest pain and should be started on the glycoprotein receptor antagonist, abciximab. This monoclonal agent is directed against the GIIb/IIIa receptor on the platelet, stopping it binding to fibrinogen and thus blocking clot formation.

4. **D – α Interferon**

   This patient has active HCV infection and would be eligible for interferon α therapy but its use is contraindicated because of his history of depression and parasuicide. In approximately 40% of treated patients, α interferon causes seroconversion from HBe antigen to antibody (showing viral replication has been inhibited). This in turn may cause reversal of some of the liver damage sustained during the active infection. Paradoxically, patients with the more severe disease are more likely to respond than those with minimal changes in the liver. α Interferon may also be given for its antitumour effects in lymphoma and some solid tumours.

5. G – Granulocyte colony-stimulating factor

Granulocyte colony-stimulating factor (GCSF) is used prophylactically in patients undergoing chemotherapy to try to avoid neutropenia and its associated severe sepsis, particularly in patients who have already had one such episode.

Of the others (and there will be more in the near future)

- Aldesleukin – Recombinant IL-2, is used in metastatic renal carcinoma with limited success. It is very toxic and has several severe side effects.
- Alemtuzumab – Monoclonal therapy directed against B-cell lymphocytes. It is principally used in chemotherapeutic resistant chronic lymphatic leukaemia (CLL). Both alemtuzumab and rituximab may cause severe acute dyspnoea one to two hours after infusion, due to the sudden release of cytokines (cytokine release syndrome).
- Basiliximab – Monoclonal therapy directed against T-cell lymphocyte proliferation. It is used with ciclosporin and steroid immunosuppression to avoid acute rejection in allogenic renal transplant.
- Rituximab – Like alemtuzumab, this is a monoclonal therapy directed against B-cell lymphocytes. It is used in chemotherapy resistant follicular and large B-cell non-Hodgkin's lymphoma.
- Trastazumab – This is a monoclonal therapy directed against the human epidermal growth factor receptor 2 (HER2), which is overexpressed by some breast cancers.

6. JAUNDICE

1. **I – Pancreatic carcinoma**

   The patient has an obstructive jaundice picture with progressive symptoms suggestive of underlying pancreatic carcinoma. Cholangiocarcinoma and multiple liver metastases can present similarly but the former is much less common than pancreatic cancer (this is therefore the more likely diagnosis) and the latter is associated with a palpable liver not gallbladder. Other characteristic symptoms of pancreatic cancer include severe abdominal and back pain. Investigations include USS, CT and ERCP and cytology.

2. **F – Gallstones**

   This lady has previous characteristic symptoms of gallstones and now presents with obstructive jaundice due to impaction of gallstone in the common bile duct. The gallbladder is not palpable because, despite the obstruction, the gall-bladder will not expand due to previous inflammation and scarring. This forms the essence of Courvoisier's law which roughly states 'when the gallbladder is palpable and the patient is jaundiced, the cause is not gallstones' (as in patient 1). This in practice does have a few exceptions but is at least a useful guide, especially during your student years.

3. **J – Sclerosing cholangitis**

   Benign stricturing of the bile ducts can occur in response to localised inflam-mation (chronic pancreatitis, chronic DU, parasitic infection), trauma (usually operative) or be due to sclerosing cholangitis. This is an obscure disorder of uncertain aetiology that results in fibrous obliteration of the biliary tract. It is a relatively uncommon complication of ulcerative colitis and is more common in males with the disease.

4. **A – Acute viral hepatitis**

   The patient has an acute presentation with jaundice and systemic upset. Whilst this could also be typical of ascending cholangitis, the patients young age and tender hepatomegaly make acute viral hepatitis the most likely diagnosis. Diagnosis may be confirmed by viral serological testing.

5. **E – Cirrhosis (in this case primary biliary cirrhosis)**

   The presentation is typical for this disorder in terms of sex and age. This autoimmune disorder is confirmed by the finding of antimitochondrial anti-bodies and proven by characteristic histology from liver biopsy. Cirrhosis is one of the principal causes of jaundice and itself has many causes of which primary biliary cirrhosis is a less frequent cause than alcohol and chronic active (viral) hepatitis.

7. INTESTINAL OBSTRUCTION

1. **G – Hernia, in this case a femoral hernia**
   Hernias are the second most common causes of small intestinal obstruction in the West after adhesions. The presence of a hernia should always be sought by careful examination. Femoral hernias, whilst less common than inguinal hernias, are particular offenders for causing obstruction. Surgical treatment is indicated.

2. **A – Adhesions**
   This is the most common cause of small intestinal obstruction in the West. Why some patients develop adhesions and others do not is a cause for much speculation. Treatment should be initially conservative for about 48 hours (NBM, intravenous fluids, NG tube, correct any U&Es abnormalities) provided there are no signs of strangulation. Thereafter the decision regarding surgery is dependent on individual case findings.

3. **H – Intussusception**
   Intussusception is telescoping of a segment of intestine into an adjacent one. The condition is encountered most commonly in infancy but can occur in adults when a precipitating factor (lead point) is usually present, eg polyp. Treatment may be hydrostatic by barium enema or surgical.

4. **C – Colonic carcinoma**
   The presentation is of large bowel obstruction, the common causes of which in this age group include carcinoma, diverticular disease and volvulus. Carcinoma is suggested by the preceding history. Treatment is resuscitation then surgical resection.

5. **K – Volvulus**
   This occurs when a segment of bowel twists on its mesentery causing obstruction and later often strangulation. The common sites are the sigmoid colon and caecum but the condition can also affect the small intestine. The patient is commonly very elderly and infirm as in this case. Treatment is resuscitation and surgical resection often with end stoma formation, e.g. Hartmann's procedure (although endoscopic attempts at reduction can be made initially).

8. POSTOPERATIVE PYREXIA

The postoperative patient with pyrexia is a common source of annoyance during your surgical house post. It requires an organised approach and the diagnosis is usually evident if you are aware of the common causes listed in the question.

1. **C – Basal atelectasis**
   This is the commonest cause of early pyrexia postoperatively (the other being anaesthetic drugs). It classically occurs in a patient as described in whom inadequate analgesia leads to reduced respiratory excursion and coughing. The resultant hypoventilation of the lung bases leads to localised small airway collapse and is accompanied usually by low-grade pyrexia.

2. **J – Urinary tract infection**
   This should always be near the top of the list in any patient who is catheterised, especially the elderly convalescent.

3. **E – Pelvic abscess**
   This is the only common significant complication of appendicectomy. Wound infections are more common but less serious. The patient should be warned of these two specific complications during consent for surgery.

4. **H – Subphrenic abscess**
   This can occur following any inflammatory/infective process in the upper abdomen but also commonly as a result of secondary infection of a haematoma in the region, e.g. postsplenectomy. The swinging nature of the pyrexia again suggests a collection of pus and the chest radiograph findings are supportive – caused by transdiaphragmatic irritation of the pleura.

5. **B – Anastomotic dehiscence**
   The nature of surgery (anterior resection, i.e. left-sided anastomosis) and clinical findings suggest this diagnosis. This is a regrettable and serious complication that carries a significant mortality. Treatment is urgent resuscitation, surgery and usually postoperative ITU care.

9. UROGYNAECOLOGICAL DISORDERS

1. C – Detrusor overactivity

The two most common causes of stress incontinence are GSI and detrusor over-activity. Stress incontinence is most common in the peri- and postmenopausal period due to pelvic floor and sphincter deficiencies, exacerbated by the hypo-oestrogenic state (GSI). GSI is a little less likely in a 38-year-old but still possible. The symptoms described can occur in most of the listed conditions but the irritative symptom of urgency is more common with detrusor overactivity than GSI. The fact that symptoms improve with tolterodine (anticholinergic) makes detrusor overactivity most likely as this would be unlikely to improve UTI, interstitial cystitis or GSI.

2. J – Vesicovaginal fistula

Continuous urinary incontinence tends to suggest either bypass of the normal sphincter mechanism (V-V fistula or congenital abnormality, e.g. aberrant ureter) or very severe sphincter deficiency (GSI). The timing of the symptoms immediately after a difficult surgical procedure is again highly suggestive of a V-V fistula as unrecognised bladder trauma (more likely during a difficult operation) can lead to subsequent fistula formation in the postoperative period. An aberrant ureter usually presents in childhood or adolescence. Intrinsic sphincter deficiency severe enough for continuous leaking is rare.

3. B – Cystocele

'Something coming down' is a common pressure symptom of prolapse, depending upon whether there is the laxity of the anterior (cystocele) or posterior (rectocele) vaginal wall or direct utero-vaginal (U-V) prolapse. Enterocele is commonly seen when bowel contents prolapse into the top of the vaginal vault after hysterectomy. The fact that the symptoms are urinary tends to suggest prolapse of the anterior compartment. Voiding difficulty is rare in women and is likely to be due to significant cystocele allowing the bladder to move from its normal anatomical position and kink the urethra causing obstruction to outflow and hence frequency and voiding difficulty. Manual replacement of the cystocele corrects this and aids micturition.

4. H – Urinary tract infection (UTI)

Sudden onset of frequency, urgency and dysuria in a young, fit woman suggests UTI as the most likely cause. The fact that she had a laparoscopy the previous week means she was likely to have been catheterised thus further increasing the risk of UTI. Interstitial cystitis and detrusor overactivity are possible but the former is rare and the latter does not usually cause dysuria.

5. E – Genuine stress incontinence (GSI)

Stress incontinence is most common in the peri- and postmenopausal period due to pelvic floor and sphincter deficiencies exacerbated by the hypo-oestrogenic state (GSI). Frequency tends to become a habitual symptom to try and reduce the number of episodes of incontinence. The major use of UDS is to make a firm diagnosis when there are mixed urinary symptoms and also before any bladder neck surgery. Detrusor pressure is calculated by subtracting the intra-abdominal pressure (rectal transducer) from the intravesical pressure (bladder transducer). If the stress incontinence is due to detrusor overactivity there are unprovoked rises in detrusor pressure at the time of stress incontinence – in their absence it confirms the diagnosis of GSI.

10. DISEASES OF THE LARGE INTESTINE

1. **B – Adenoma**
   Adenomas are benign neoplasms of glandular epithelium. Adenomas of the large intestine can be classified as tubular, villous or tubulovillous. Tubular adenomas are pedunculated and have a lobulated red surface. Villous adenomas are sessile and have seaweed-like fronds. Adenomas have distinct malignant potential and are thought to be the precursor of adenocarcinomas of the colorectum. This patient's polyp is unlikely to have developed into an adenocarcinoma because it is pedunculated and small.

2. **I – Pseudomembranous colitis**
   Pseudomembranous colitis is caused by the A and B toxins produced by toxigenic strains of *Clostridium difficile*. It usually occurs several days after commencement of broad spectrum antibiotic therapy and most commonly affects elderly hospitalised patients. Diarrhoea (rarely with blood) and abdominal cramps are the common symptoms. Sigmoidoscopy may reveal an erythematous ulcerated mucosa with patchy, white membranes. In a minority of patients, however, only the proximal colon is affected and sigmoidoscopy is therefore normal.

3. **C – Amoebiasis**
   Infection with *Entamoeba histiolytica* causes amoebiasis. Several of the diseases on this list can lead to colonic ulceration, but only in ameobiasis are the ulcers typically flask-shaped. The finding of PAS-positive trophozoites with ingested red cells is diagnostic of amoebiasis.

4. **F – Diverticular disease**
   A diverticulum is a blind-ending mucosal-lined outpouching that communicates with the lumen of the organ in which it arises. The gut is the most common site of origin and, although diverticula can be found anywhere in the gut, 95% are located in the sigmoid colon. Diverticular disease is common in the elderly, the prevalence approaching 50% in adults over 60 years of age. Its pathogenesis seems to be related to the low fibre diet eaten in Western countries with consequent reduction in stool bulk and raised intraluminal pressure. Thickening of the bowel wall is associated with formation of diverticula and this can lead to development of strictures, thus simulating a carcinoma. In this patient, the diverticula have become inflamed (known as diverticulitis), as indicated by the pyrexia and abdominal tenderness.

5. **J – Ulcerative colitis**
   The main differential diagnosis of bloody diarrhoea in this age group lies between infective colitis and idiopathic inflammatory bowel disease. The fact that repeated stool cultures are negative makes infective colitis less likely. The colonoscopic appearances of diffuse erythema without skip lesions favour ulcerative colitis over Crohn's disease. The biopsy changes (severe chronic inflammation with crypt abscesses and crypt architectural distortion and lack of granulomas) are typical of ulcerative colitis.

11. LARYNX

1. G – Recurrent laryngeal nerve
This nerve provides sensory innervation to the trachea and larynx below the vocal cords and innervates all muscles of the larynx except the cricothyroid. The superior laryngeal nerve pierces the thyrohyoid membrane and divides into an external laryngeal nerve supplying the cricothyroid muscle and an internal laryngeal nerve providing sensation to the larynx above the vocal cords.

2. B – Cricoid cartilage
The conus elasticus (cricothyroid membrane) of each side meet and are strengthened in the midline anteriorly by the cricothyroid ligament. The upper free border is the vocal fold.

3. J – Thyroid cartilage
The vocal fold extends from the back of the laryngeal prominence of the thyroid cartilage to the vocal process on the arytenoid cartilage. It is covered with mucous membrane and forms the vocal cord. Action of the cricothyroid muscle alters tension in the cord and the shape of the rima glottidis between the cords is altered by gliding and rotation of the arytenoid cartilages on the cricoid.

4. A – Arytenoid cartilage
The aryepiglottic (quadrangular) membrane passes from the sides of the epiglottis to the anterior border of the arytenoid cartilage. The lower free border is the vestibular fold and a pouch (laryngeal sinus) bulges laterally between the vestibular and vocal folds.

5. C – Epiglottis
The epiglottis is attached to the thyroid cartilage above the vocal fold and extends upwards behind the tongue, with the piriform fossa of the pharynx recessed on each side. In swallowing, the larynx is raised bringing the epiglottis over the superior opening.

12. NERVE SUPPLY OF THE MUSCLES OF THE LOWER LIMB

1. **H – Superior gluteal nerve**
   The nerve also supplies the gluteus minimus and tensor fascia lata. The gluteus maximus is supplied by the inferior gluteal nerve.

2. **F – Sciatic nerve**
   The semimembranosus is the most medial of the hamstring group of muscles. The sciatic nerve supplies all of them and also the ischial part of the adductor magnus muscle.

3. **B – Deep peroneal (anterior tibial) nerve**
   This nerve is a branch of the common peroneal nerve and supplies all muscles of the anterior (dorsiflexor) group in the anterior compartment of the leg, and also the extensor digitorum brevis on the dorsum of the foot.

4. **G – Superficial peroneal (musculocutaneous) nerve**
   The nerve passes around the neck of the fibula and is vulnerable to injury at this site. It also innervates the peroneus brevis muscle.

5. **J – Tibial (posterior tibial) nerve**
   The tibial nerve innervates all the muscles of the calf.

PAPER 6

Paper 6 questions

1. THEME: ANTIHYPERTENSIVE AGENTS

A Amlodipine
B Atenolol
C Bendrofluazide
D Doxazosin
E Hydralazine
F Indapamide
G Losartan
H Methyldopa
I Moxonodine
J Ramipril

The following patients have all presented with hypertension. Please choose the most appropriate single antihypertensive agent from the above list.

1. A 58-year-old man is seen in his GP practice with BP = 220/100. He is a smoker but his total cholesterol 4.8 mmol/l, RBG 4.3 mmol/l, and he has no other cardiovascular risk factors. He also complains of prostatism but on PR there is a smoothly enlarged prostate and his PSA is 3.2 mg/l.

2. A 47-year-old obese woman is seen by her GP for hypertension = 170/90. Of note her routine investigations reveal RBG 11.3 mmol/l, total cholesterol 6.9 mmol/l and her ECG shows changes consistent with the voltage criteria of LVH.

3. A 32-year-old primigravida is seen at 24/40 in antenatal clinic complaining of increased lethargy and malaise. Her BP = 160/80 on two separate occasions, urinary analysis protein +, nil else. She is started on an antihypertensive and her BP settles.

4. A 62-year-old female smoker is seen in her GP surgery with episodic angina and chest pain which is short lived and relieved immediately by rest. A routine serum lipid profile and glucose were normal 3 months earlier. Her BP is elevated at 160/100.

5. A 64-year-old man is seen by his GP 6 weeks after discharge from hospital for an acute myocardial infarction. Since discharge he has had a persistent dry/irritating cough. He is on aspirin, metoprolol, lisinopril and GTN spray PRN. The GP stops one of the medications and exchanges it for another agent.

2. THEME: THE MULTIDISCIPLINARY TEAM

A   Chiropodist
B   Community psychiatric nurse (CPN)
C   Dementia support worker
D   Dietician
E   District nurse
F   Occupational therapist
G   Orthotist
H   Physiotherapist
I   Social worker
J   Specialist nurse

For each of the following scenarios please list the members of the multidisciplinary team who should be involved in the patient's care. You may use the members once, more than once, in combination or not at all.

1. An independent 54-year-old man is seen in outpatients department with left-sided foot drop which has led to several falls. He improves with a splint and therapy.

2. A 61-year-old woman with longstanding type II diabetes mellitus is discharged from hospital on insulin. She has severe visual impairment secondary to her retinopathy, and peripheral sensory neuropathy. She needs assistance with most ADLs but is mobile with guidance about the ward.

3. A 79-year-old man with moderate cognitive impairment is seen with his wife. She feels she can no longer cope with him at home but she is reluctant to have him 'put in a home'. He has no other medical history of note and is only on donepezil. He consistently says he 'wants to stay with my Bessie' (his wife). They have no services at present.

4. A 21-year-old man is admitted to A&E with diabetic ketoacidosis, his first presentation of diabetes mellitus. He recovers slowly over 72 hours and is seen by the various members of the multidisciplinary team before discharge home.

5. A 41-year-old schizophrenic man is admitted to A&E with a respiratory tract infection. His neighbours say he has been acting strangely for 3 months and is not really looking after himself. He improves and the consultant feels he is ready for discharge but the patient cannot get his shoes on secondary to onychogryphosis.

3. THEME: JAUNDICE

A   Autoimmune hepatitis
B   Carcinoma of the head of the pancreas
C   Epstein–Barr virus (EBV)
D   Gallstones
E   Haemochromatosis
F   Hepatitis A virus (HAV)
G   Hepatitis B virus (HBV)
H   Primary biliary cirrhosis
I   Sclerosing cholangitis
J   Wilson's disease

The following patients have all presented with jaundice. Please choose the most appropriate cause from the above list. The items may be used once, more than once, in combination or not at all.

1. A 43-year-old man presents to his GP with increasing polydypsia. On examination he appears to be slightly 'suntanned' despite not having been in the sun for 6 months. He has spider naevi and gynaecomastia and 3 cm hepatomegaly below the right costal margin. His BM stix is 17.9 mmol/l. Routine investigations reveal FBC: Hb 8.7 g/dl, MCV 101 fl, WCC 3.9×10^9/l, Plt 88 $\times 10^9$/l; RBG 23.2 mmol/l; LFTs: Tbil 27 μmol/l, AST 65 iu/l, ALT 51 iu/l, Alk phos 555 iu/l, Alb 31 g/l; ferritin 12,770 μg/l.

2. A 38-year-old woman is seen in medical outpatients with a 2-month history of weight loss associated with recent onset of jaundice. On examination she has spider naevi, Dupytren's contracture and 4 cm hepatomegaly below the right costal margin. The diagnosis is confirmed by the presence of anti-smooth muscle and anti-LKM-1 antibodies. She improves quite rapidly with corticosteroids.

3. A 27–year-old woman with poorly controlled sickle cell disease is admitted to hospital with severe abdominal pain, pyrexia and vomiting. On examination she is jaundiced, has generalised abdominal pain with some, more localised tenderness in the right upper quadrant. Initial investigations reveal FBC: Hb 5.5 g/dl, MCV 87 fl, WCC 23.9×10^9/l, Plt 411 $\times 10^9$/l; U&Es: Na$^+$ 141 mmol/l, K$^+$ 4.7 mmol/l, urea 12.9 mmol/l, Cr 112 μmol/l. LFTs Tbil 47 μmol/l, AST 72 iu/l, ALT 66 iu/l, Alk phos 871 iu/l, Alb 34 g/l.

4. A previously fit and well 35-year-old man returns from India with a week's history of worsening abdominal pains, diarrhoea, vomiting and a fever. Over the last 72 hours he has also become jaundiced. His investigations reveal LFTs Tbil 38 μmol/l, AST 332 iu/l, ALT 219 iu/l, Alk phos 238 iu/l, Alb 32 g/l and an acute phase IgM response confirming the presence of an RNA virus.

5. A 27-year-old man with known ulcerative colitis is seen in the gastroenterology clinic for his 6-month check up. He reports he has been well with no recent acute exacerbations of his colitis. However in the last few months he has had occasional upper abdominal pains associated with pruritis and more recently an episode of jaundice. Routine investigations reveal LFTs: Tbil 18 μmol/l, AST 22 iu/l, ALT 19 iu/l, Alk phos 438 iu/l, Alb 39 g/l. The diagnosis is confirmed on ERCP which shows 'occasional beading of the biliary tree'.

4. THEME: DEMENTIA

A   Alzheimer's disease
B   Creutzfeld–Jakob disease
C   Huntington's chorea
D   Hypothyroidism
E   Lewy body disease
F   Neurosyphilis
G   Normal pressure hydrocephalus
H   Pick's disease
I   Pseudodementia
J   Vascular dementia

The following patients have all presented with dementia. Please choose the most appropriate cause from the above list. The items may be used once, more than once or not at all.

1. A 48-year-old man presents to his GP with increasing confusion and memory problems and abnormal movements of his limbs. His wife is very concerned about him as she remembers that his father had a similar problem in his late 40s and died very soon after they were married.

2. A previously fit and well 69-year-old woman presents to her GP with a 6-month history of insidious worsening of her memory. She has until recently been very independent but can now no longer find her way to the local shops. Her MMSE is 24/30 but examination and routine investigations including FBC, U&Es, RBG, LFTs, CCa^{2+}, TFTs, ESR and radiograph are all within normal limits. Her CT head scan shows cerebral atrophy but nil else of note. She makes some improvement with donepezil.

3. A 71-year-old woman presents to Medicine for the Elderly Outpatients with a 3–4-month history of confusion, falls and urinary incontinence. Her AMTS is 6/10 and she is noted to have a dyspraxic gait. Her blood tests including FBC, U&Es, RBG, LFTs, CCa^{2+}, TFTs, VDRL and ESR are all within normal limits as is her chest radiograph and ECG. Her CT head scan shows ventricular dilatation disproportionate to her degree of cerebral atrophy.

4. An 84-year-old man is admitted to hospital with acute on chronic confusion. His wife who has been caring for him at home with no social services feels she can no longer cope. He is treated for a urinary tract infection and improves but his AMTS remains 4–5/10. His CT head scan shows mild to moderate cerebral atrophy but subsequent investigations confirm serum and CSF TPHA and FTA are positive.

5. A 62-year-old woman presents to Medicine for the Elderly Outpatients with a 6–8–month history of increasing speech problems. During the clerking the SHO notes her to be confusing and muddling words and phrases. Her MMSE is 28/30. Subsequent CT head scan shows marked atrophy of the temporal regions.

5. THEME: ANTIBIOTICS

A   Benzylpenicillin
B   Cefotaxime
C   Cefuroxime
D   Ciprofloxacin
E   Clarithromycin
F   Doxycycline
G   Flucloxacillin
H   Metronidazole
I   Trimethoprim
J   Vancomycin

The following patients have all presented with sepsis. Please choose the most appropriate antibiotic therapy from the above list. You may use the antibiotics once, more than once, in combination or not at all. (The patients have no known drug allergies.)

1. A 29-year-old man with poorly controlled type 1 diabetes mellitus is admitted to A&E with a hot painful red left calf with pyrexia. On examination he is well but has a temperature of 39.5°C and is tachycardic 120 bpm. He has a marked right lower limb cellulitis spreading over the anterolateral aspect of his shin.

2. A 59-year-old man and his wife return from St Petersburg after celebrating their 30th wedding anniversary with diarrhoea and vomiting. The man has noted 'sulphur' on his breath and both admit to offensive watery stools with urgency and frequency.

3. A 19-year-old man presents to the GUM clinic with a urethral discharge and dysuria. Gonococcal cultures and microscopy are negative but the diagnosis is confirmed as *Chlamydia trachomatis* after antibody tests are positive.

4. A 78-year-old woman is re-admitted to hospital a week after discharge with profuse, offensive watery diarrhoea. She was previously admitted with pneumonia which required several courses of antibiotics before she was discharged.

5. A 17-year-old woman is admitted to hospital with a severe headache worsening over two days. She has marked photophobia, neck stiffness and temperature of 39.2°C but no associated rash. Lumbar puncture confirms Gram-positive intracellular diplococci in the CSF.

6. THEME: CONSTIPATION

A   Colonic carcinoma
B   Constipation-predominant IBS
C   Diabetes mellitus
D   Diverticular disease
E   Hypercalcaemia
F   Hypothyroidism
G   Iatrogenic: drug threrapy
H   Idiopathic megacolon
I   Pelvic nerve/spinal cord injury
J   Simple constipation

The following patients have all presented with constipation. Please select the most appropriate diagnosis from the above list. The items may be used once, more than once or not at all.

1. A 66-year-old woman is seen in surgical outpatients with a long history of alternating constipation and loose stool associated with left iliac fossa pain. She now complains of 3 months constipation. She tells you that she had a barium enema 1 year ago and although she cannot recall the diagnosis was told to eat a high fibre diet.

2. A 40-year-old woman with chronic back pain presents in A&E with a 5-day history of lower abdominal pain and urinary incontinence. She has not opened her bowels for a similar period. On examination, she has a palpable bladder and catheterisation drains 1100 ml urine. There is poor sphincter tone and absent perianal sensation.

3. A 62-year-old man is referred to surgical clinic with a 6-week history of constipation. His bowels are open once per 2 days passing small hard stools after a lot of straining. Previously he opened his bowels every morning with soft stool. He has also noticed some vague cramping lower abdominal pain. Examination including proctosigmoidoscopy is normal. Investigations reveal: Hb 9.8 g/dl, MCV 73.3 fl.

4. A 14-year-old boy presents in A&E with lower abdominal pain. His mother informs you that he has had severe constipation since infancy and encopresis for which he was regularly admitted for manual evacuation at the children's hospital. On examination, there is a large indentable mass arising from the pelvis.

5. A 66-year-old woman with chronic back pain presents in A&E with colicky lower abdominal pain. She has not opened her bowels for 4 days. Her problems started after an upper GI endoscopy for dyspepsia when she was diagnosed with gastric erosions. She was discharged on a variety of new medications which she has not brought with her today.

7. THEME: DISORDERS OF THE FEMALE BREAST

A   Breast abscess
B   Carcinoma of the breast
C   Cystosarcoma phylloides
D   Duct papilloma
E   Fat necrosis
F   Fibroadenoma
G   Fibroadenosis
H   Galactocele
I   Mammary duct ectasia
J   Mammary fistula

The following female patients all have conditions of the breast. Please select the most appropriate diagnosis from the above list. The items may be used once, more than once or not at all.

1. A 35-year-old presents with several years of cyclical pain in both breasts and the recent feeling of a lump in the right breast. On examination there is diffuse nodularity in both axillary tails which are slightly tender on palpation. Fine needle aspiration of a prominent nodule on the right results in aspiration of 5 ml of clear, brownish fluid with resolution of the lump. Cytology shows cellular debris with no malignant cells.

2. A 52-year-old presents with a painless lump in the left breast that she noticed 5 weeks ago. On examination a hard, irregular 3 cm lump is palpable in the upper outer quadrant. There are no obvious skin changes but the breast appears slightly asymmetric with respect to the right side when the arms are raised above the patient's head.

3. A 28-year-old presents 3 weeks after the birth of her first child with pain in the right breast. On examination she has a large 6 cm very tender swelling adjacent and medial to the nipple.

4. A 43-year-old presents with a 3-week history of blood-stained nipple discharge. Examination is unremarkable with no lumps palpable in either breast.

5. An 18-year-old presents having noticed a painless lump in her left breast 2 weeks ago. On examination a discrete hard, highly mobile 1 cm lump is palpable in the medial breast. There are no skin changes or nipple discharge. Fine needle aspiration cytology shows benign cells.

8. THEME: MUSCULOSKELETAL CAUSES OF BACK PAIN

A   Ankylosing spondylitis
B   Metastatic carcinoma
C   Osteoporosis
D   Prolapsed intervertebral disc
E   Pyogenic spondylitis
F   Scheuermann's disease
G   Spinal stenosis
H   Spinal tuberculosis
I   Spondylolisthesis
J   Spondylosis

The following patients all present with back pain of musculoskeletal origin. For each, please select the most appropriate diagnosis from the above list. The items may be used once, more than once or not at all.

1. A 45-year-old care worker presents with acute back pain and right-sided buttock pain and sciatica following lifting a patient into bed. On examination he has reduced right-sided straight leg raising. Neurological examination is normal.

2. A 70-year-old man presents in A&E with severe lower thoracic back pain of 3-weeks duration. He has attended his GP several times and is now on maximal doses of coproxamol and voltarol. The pain, initially on movement, is now constant day and night and he is unable to sleep. Neurological examination is normal.

3. A 13-year-old girl complains of thoracolumbar backache. Her mother has also noted that she has become increasingly round-shouldered. On examination the patient has a fixed smooth thoracic kyphosis. Neurological examination is normal.

4. A 60-year-old man complains of a 5-year history of backache. The pain, which started following an acute injury initially, now occurs almost daily, especially after lifting or standing/sitting for prolonged periods. It is felt in the lumbar region and buttock. On examination there is mild tenderness over the lumbar spine and reduced movement. Neurological examination is normal.

5. A 60-year-old man complains of a 6-month history of back pain and an aching pain and weakness in both calves when walking. The pain starts with ambulation and resolves only after resting for some time following exercise especially if leaning forward. All foot pulses are present. Neurological examination is normal.

9. THEME: BLEEDING PER VAGINA IN PREGNANCY

A   Abruptio placentae
B   Atonic uterus
C   Disseminated intravascular coagulation (DIC)
D   Local cervical pathology, e.g. cervical ectropion
E   Marginal bleed
F   Obstetric tear
G   Placenta praevia
H   Retained products of conception (RPOC)
I   Uterine rupture
J   Vasa praevia

From the above list please choose the item most likely to cause the clinical picture described. The items may be used once, more than once, in combination or not at all.

1. A 30-year-old primiparous woman has just had a spontaneous vaginal delivery. The antenatal period was complicated by idiopathic polyhydramnios. She starts bleeding heavily PV immediately after delivery. The third stage of labour appears to be complete.

2. A 30-year-old multiparous woman is in labour. She has had one previous child by emergency LSCS. Her labour is initially uneventful but becomes prolonged, and cervical dilatation arrests at 8 cm. She suddenly experiences brisk vaginal bleeding accompanied by a fetal bradycardia. On vaginal examination the presenting part is no longer palpable in the pelvis.

3. A 30-year-old primiparous woman has recently had a spontaneous vaginal delivery. She had been induced for moderately severe pre-eclampsia. All stages of labour appeared to be complete. Despite all appropriate measures she has a major PPH. Examination under anaesthesia reveals an empty uterus. Her bleeding per vagina continues and it is noted that she is now also bleeding from her cannulation sites.

4. A 30-year-old primiparous woman is at 32/40 gestation. Her antenatal period has been uneventful until she awakes one night with moderate PV bleeding associated with abdominal pain and uterine contractions. On arrival at hospital her pulse and blood pressure are normal as is the fetal heart, but there is uterine tenderness with palpable contractions. Speculum examination is unremarkable except for a small amount of fresh blood in the vagina.

5. A 30-year-old primiparous woman is induced at 42 weeks for post-maturity. Following prostaglandin treatment an artificial rupture of membranes (ARM) is performed at 3 cm cervical dilatation. Her antenatal period has been uneventful up to this point. On examination there is a longitudinal lie with a cephalic presentation with 2/5ths of the head palpable per abdomen. Immediately after the ARM, there is brisk vaginal bleeding which continues until emergency LSCS is required.

10. THEME: DISEASES OF THE LUNG AND PLEURA

A   Adenocarcinoma of the bronchus
B   Emphysema
C   Lobar pneumonia
D   Malignant mesothelioma
E   *Pneumocystis* pneumonia
F   Pulmonary hypertension
G   Sarcoidosis
H   Small cell carcinoma of the bronchus
I   Squamous cell carcinoma of the bronchus
J   Tuberculosis

From the above list, please select the disease that each of the following patients is most likely to have. The items may be used once, more than once or not at all.

1. A 70-year-old vagrant man presents with a 2-week history of productive cough, fever and worsening dyspnoea. On examination he is extremely unwell with cyanosis, tachycardia and hypotension. His chest radiograph shows complete consolidation of the left lower lobe.

2. A 35-year-old black woman presents with a six-month history of shortness of breath, night sweats and weight loss. Her chest radiograph shows bilateral hilar lymphadenopathy. Transbronchial biopsy shows non-necrotising epithelioid granulomas within the interstitium. A special stain for acid-fast bacilli is negative.

3. A 62-year-old male smoker presents with haemoptysis for 2 weeks. In addition he has severe pain in the left shoulder and left arm. His chest radiograph shows a large mass at the apex of the left lung. Sputum cytology reveals malignant keratinised cells.

4. A 35-year-old HIV-positive man develops shortness of breath accompanied by a dry cough. His chest radiograph shows bilateral reticulonodular shadowing. Sputum culture is negative. Transbronchial biopsy shows alveoli filled with a foamy eosinophilic material and numerous boat-shaped organisms staining positively with a silver stain.

5. A 65-year-old man, a life-long heavy smoker, presents with recent onset of haemoptysis and dyspnoea. On examination he has a moon face and truncal obesity. Biochemical investigations show hypokalaemia. His chest radiograph shows a large mass at the hilum of the right lung.

11. THEME: ANATOMY OF THE ALIMENTARY TRACT

A   Appendix
B   Duodenojejunal flexure
C   First part of duodenum
D   Hepatic flexure of the colon
E   Ileocaecal valve
F   Jejunum
G   Mesentery of the sigmoid colon
H   Pylorus
I   Second part of the duodenum
J   Splenic flexure of the colon

For each of the following descriptions, please choose the most appropriate structure from the above list. The items may be used once, more than once or not at all.

1. Lies to the left of the 2nd lumbar vertebra.

2. Is in contact with the fundus of the gallbladder.

3. Has mucosa characterised by prominent villi.

4. Lies on the lower pole of the right kidney.

5. Overlies the bifurcation of the left common iliac artery.

12. THEME: OPENINGS IN THE BASE OF SKULL

A   Anterior condylar canal
B   Carotid canal
C   Foramen lacerum
D   Foramen ovale
E   Foramen spinosum
F   Inferior orbital fissure
G   Jugular foramen
H   Optic canal
I   Posterior condylar canal
J   Superior orbital fissure

For each of the following descriptions, please choose the most appropriate skull-base opening from the above list. The items may be used once, more than once or not at all.

1.   Transmits the nerve supplying the stylopharyngeus muscle.   ☐

2.   Transmits the nerve supplying the intrinsic muscles of the tongue.   ☐

3.   Transmits the nerve supplying the upper incisor teeth.   ☐

4.   Transmits the nerve supplying the superior oblique muscle.   ☐

5.   Transmits the nerve supplying the medial pterygoid muscle.   ☐

Paper 6 answers

1. ANTIHYPERTENSIVE AGENTS

1. **D – Doxazosin**

   This man has essential hypertension and is a smoker but has no other apparent cardiovascular risk factors. He should be encouraged to stop smoking. In view of his prostatic symptoms he required a per rectal examination and a serum PSA to exclude malignant disease. Since they are within normal limits he should be started on doxazosin.

2. **J – Ramipril**

   This obese woman has diabetes mellitus, hypercholesterolaemia and should be started on an ACE inhibitor. She will also need a statin and dietetic advice on a diabetic diet and weight loss.

3. **H – Methyldopa**

   Pregnancy-induced hypertension is an interesting therapeutic dilemma. Most antihypertensive agents are not licensed for use in pregnancy mainly because of the theoretical risk to the fetus and ethical issues about the introduction of untested agents in this group of patients. Methyldopa, which is an extremely effective agent, has a long history of use in pregnancy, thus is still used. It famously causes autoimmune haemolytic anaemia and this needs to be screened for with regular monitoring of the full blood count.

4. **B – Atenolol**

   This woman has developed unstable angina associated with hypertension, a common combination. To treat both disorders a β blocker or calcium channel blocker could be used. However a β blocker has positive prognostic effects and if tolerated is the treatment of choice. She should also have other risk factors addressed and in particular needs to be encouraged to stop smoking.

5. **G – Losartan**

   This man has been on an ACE inhibitor which has caused his dry cough. Although at the present time there is little research data on the effects of angiotensin II inhibitors in ischaemic heart disease they have been proposed as replacement agents when an ACE inhibitor is not tolerated.

   In recent years target BPs have changed quite considerably particularly in the presence of other cardiovascular risk factors, eg ischaemic heart disease, stroke disease, diabetes and smoking. Blood pressure in this situation should be reduced to ≤ 140/80. As with the scenarios above the agents used should be tailored to the patients' needs and co-morbidity but most importantly need to be effective at reducing the blood pressure to acceptable targets.

2. MULTIDISCIPLINARY TEAM

1. G & H – Orthotist and physiotherapist

This man has a mononeuropathy (due to a common peroneal palsy) causing left-sided foot drop. This may be idiopathic or due to a systemic disorder such as diabetes mellitus or a systemic vasculitis, eg Wegener's granulomatosis. It may also herald a lumbar spine problem. The treatment includes a foot splint to maintain the ankle in 'neutral' and thus stop the foot 'catching' on the floor leading to falls. He should also benefit from some physiotherapy.

2. A, D, E, F, I & J – Dietician, district nurse, chiropodist, occupational therapist, social worker and specialist nurse

This patient is chronologically quite young (61 years) but due to her poorly controlled type II diabetes mellitus has multiple disabilities and is biologically quite old. She needs a lot of help to maintain her independence at home and pre-discharge planning is vital in such a case. Almost all members of the multi-disciplinary team have a role to play in her care and this case shows the importance of good multidisciplinary team work.

3. A, D, F, H & I – Dietician, chiropodist, occupational therapist, physiotherapist and social worker

This situation is not uncommon in medicine for the older patient. Carers often reach a point of 'despair' where they feel isolated and undersupported as well as guilty for thinking about placing their loved one in care. With good community support and services both partners can enjoy a far better quality of life.

4. E & J – District nurse and specialist nurse

This patient needs empathetic education and support to help him come to terms with his new diagnosis. The diabetic specialist nurse is the patient's main contact during his hospital stay and often bears the brunt of feelings of denial or anger. With good education and a strong multidisciplinary team patients can be helped through this difficult period.

5. B & I – Community psychiatric nurse and social worker

This man will also need strong multidisciplinary team support pre- and post-discharge if he is to continue living independently.

3. JAUNDICE

1. E – Haemochromatosis
This man has developed chronic liver disease secondary to haemochromatosis. This may be a primary, idiopathic disorder that is inherited in an autosomal recessive manner. Although it more commonly occurs in association with alcohol excess, alcohol is a contributory rather than causative agent. Secondary haemochromatosis occurs in patients who ingest excessive amounts of iron or more commonly receive multiple blood transfusions. Haemochromatosis leads to excess iron within the body which is deposited in various organs, most commonly the liver (cirrhosis and hepatocellular carcinoma), pituitary (hypogonadism), myocardium (cardiomyopathy) and pancreas (diabetes mellitus). The suntanned appearance is due to melanin (not iron) deposition in the skin.

2. A – Autoimmune hepatitis
This woman has developed autoimmune hepatitis defined by the presence of the anti-smooth muscle and anti-LKM-1 antibodies (liver/kidney microsomal antibodies). This is an autoimmune disorder which has two peaks of incidence. A childhood illness which is characterised by the presence of the anti-LKM antibodies and is closely associated with other autoimmune disorders such as vitiligo, thyroid disease and diabetes mellitus. It is characterised clinically by a rapidly progressive liver condition with cirrhosis. The second peak occurs in young adults and may be more insidious in its progress. It is associated with the presence of anti-smooth muscle antibodies and, to a lesser extent, anti-mitochondrial and anti-LKM-1 antibodies. It responds well to corticosteroids but may rapidly relapse on their withdrawal.

3. D – Gallstones
Sickle cell disease predisposes patients to the development of gallstones because of the constant episodes of haemolysis. The cholecystitis has precipitated a sickle crisis for which she needs intravenous antibiotics (cefuroxime and metronidazole), fluids, blood transfusion and analgesia.

4. F – Hepatitis A virus
This man has developed an acute hepatitis secondary to a hepatitis A viral (HAV) infection. This RNA virus is endemic in areas of poverty and poor public health and is spread by the faecal–oral route. HAV and HEV cause an acute viral illness associated with diarrhoea, fever and jaundice. They do NOT have a chronic phase and are usually self-limiting but may rarely progress to fulminant liver failure.

5. I – Sclerosing cholangitis
This gentleman has developed sclerosing cholangitis, which is an idiopathic condition leading to acute/chronic inflammation within the biliary tree and subsequent fibrosis and strictures. It may be a primary idiopathic condition but is commonly associated with inflammatory bowel disease (ulcerative colitis more commonly than Crohn's) and HIV infection. Half of the cases run a slow, benign course whilst the rest may require liver transplant.

4. DEMENTIA

1. C – Huntington's chorea

Huntington's chorea is an autosomal dominant disorder characterised by early onset of progressive cognitive impairment and chorea. The gene defect has recently been localised to chromosome 4. The disorder leads to progressive destruction within the caudate nucleus and putamen and leads to loss of GABA and acetylcholine synthesis in these important extrapyramidal areas. The disorder is incurable and symptomatic treatment, education, genetic screening and support for patient and family remain the mainstay of therapy.

2. A – Alzheimer's disease

Alzheimer's disease is the commonest of all the dementia syndromes, although more recently with the advent of newer imaging techniques such as PET scanning sub-syndromes of the condition are now being defined. Alzheimer's is characterised by insidious worsening of global cognitive impairment with early memory impairment, problems with language skills and visuospatial problems leading to the patient getting lost in well known surroundings. Depression and other psychiatric symptoms may be early features, although delusions and hallucination occur in only 10–15% of cases. The acetylcholinesterase inhibitors are a relatively new group of medications which are used particularly early in this condition, although research has suggested they may have a role in the more severely cognitively impaired, as well as in Lewy body dementia.

3. G – Normal pressure hydrocephalus

This patient has presented with the classical triad of normal pressure hydrocephalus, namely cognitive impairment, gait dyspraxia and urinary incontinence. The label 'normal pressure' is a misnomer as the CSF pressure varies in peaks and troughs, which may be demonstrated on the insertion of an intraventricular manometer. The treatment of this condition is the neurosurgical insertion of a ventriculoperitoneal shunt.

4. F – Neurosyphilis

Neurosyphilis is a relatively uncommon cause of dementia in the UK but syphilis serology tests are still often included in dementia screens. VDRL may be a false positive in the elderly due to old age, co-existing chronic inflammatory conditions or in the Afro-Caribbean population due to previous yaws or pinta infection. If VDRL is positive, the more specific TPHA and FTA should be sent to exclude or refute the diagnosis of syphilis. If they are subsequently positive a lumbar puncture should be performed to confirm the presence of CSF VDRL which if significantly positive confirms active neurosyphilis. Patients with confirmed neurosyphilis should be treated with an appropriate course of penicillin. In late presentations of the condition (which is the most common in the older population) the treatment will produce little reversibility but will stop the progression of the condition.

5. **H – Pick's disease**

This woman presents with typical features of Pick's disease or lobar dementia. This form of dementia typically presents with relatively well preserved cognition in the early stages of the disease but either focal frontal or temporal signs, due to focal atrophy of these lobes. Patients with frontal pathology present with personality changes, disinhibition, inertia, lack of planning and self-regard. Temporal features principally focus around speech and language difficulties including word finding and reduced vocabulary problems. As the disease progresses pateints develop a progressive aphasia and may develop an 'associative agnosia', an inability to recognise and name everyday objects, items and animals.

5. ANTIBIOTICS

1. **A & G – Benzylpenicillin and flucloxacillin**

   This patient has developed an acute cellulitis of the anterior shin. The most likely causative organisms are streptococcal or staphylococcal species and the most appropriate first line therapy includes benzylpenicillin and flucloxacillin. Patients with penicillin allergy could have cephalosporin or macrolide.

2. **H – Metronidazole**

   This couple have developed giardiasis which is treated with high-dose metronidazole (2 g/day for 3 days).

3. **E & F – Clarithromycin and doxycycline**

   This young man has developed a *Chlamydia* urethritis which should be treated with tetracycline and then a macrolide if symptoms recur. As with all sexually transmissable disease he should be counselled with regard to the use of condoms and recent sexual contacts need to be traced.

4. **H or J – Metronidazole or vancomycin**

   This older woman has develped *Clostridium difficile* diarrhoea caused by the multiple courses of antibiotics during her original admission with a chest infection. Patients require oral metronidazole or vancomycin as studies have shown the intraluminal concentration of the drug is the important part of the treatment and administering the drugs by intravenous or rectal routes are not as effective. Both metronidazole and vancomycin are poorly absorbed in the GI tract and are therefore the drugs of choice.

5. **A or B – Benzylpenicillin or cefotaxime**

   This young woman has developed meningitis (bacterial) which according to the Gram stain is due to a streptococcal infection. The most appropriate empirical antibiotic in this case would be cefotaxime as it has better CSF penetration than cefuroxime but benzylpenicillin could be used once the Gram stain result is known.

6. CONSTIPATION

1. D – Diverticular disease
The history could indicate either this diagnosis or one of constipation-predominant IBS. The fact that she has had no intervention following barium enema excludes a carcinoma and, indeed, a high fibre diet is generally recommended for diverticular disease.

2. I – Pelvic nerve/spinal cord injury
This patient has signs of cauda-equina compression. This is a neurosurgical emergency caused usually be a central disc protrusion compressing the lumbosacral nerve roots below the level of the cona medullaris at L1. Clinical signs are of lower motor neurone lesions of the affected levels and may include bilateral limb signs if higher or only bowel and bladder dysfunction if lower segments. Such debilitating disturbances may be permanent without prompt intervention.

3. A – Colonic carcinoma
A change in bowel habit such as that presented should always prompt the search for a carcinoma. In this case there is a microcytic anaemia which strongly suggests the diagnosis. In reality, a change in bowel habit to diarrhoea with rectal bleeding is more strongly suggestive than a change to constipation. The patient should undergo urgent colonoscopy or barium enema if this is not available.

4. H – Idiopathic megacolon
This is a characteristic history of this ill-understood and fairly uncommon disorder in which there is a grossly distended rectum/colon with associated severe constipation and overflow (especially evident as encopresis: incontinence at night). The diagnosis can be made on barium enema. Treatment is behavioural, psychological, medical (laxatives) and surgical: regular disimpaction, sometimes bowel resection. Megacolon can also occur in children as a result of Hirschsprung's disease and a variety of other rare syndromes. It can arise in adulthood from a variety of causes or idiopathically (cause unknown).

5. G – Iatrogenic: drug therapy
A variety of drugs can cause constipation and should always be considered in the elderly on polypharmacy. In this case, the likely offender is an opioid containing analgesic which has been added in place of NSAIDs after a diagnosis of gastric erosions.

7. DISORDERS OF THE FEMALE BREAST

1. **G – Fibroadenosis (fibrocystic disease)**
   This is a diffuse and painful benign condition of the breast in women aged 25–45 years. The condition is characterised by exacerbations and remissions that are usually cyclical with the menses. Aetiologically the disorder is probably one of abnormal expression of physiological proliferative and involutionary changes. There are four main pathological processes: adenosis, epitheliosis, fibrosis and cyst formation. The diagnosis is made by the history and examination (as above) and mammography/ultrasound, with or without cyst aspiration and cytology.

2. **B – Carcinoma of the breast**
   The age of the patient, history and findings on examination should strongly point to this diagnosis. Further symptoms include nipple bleeding. Further signs include deep or superficial tethering of the lump, skin changes such as peau d'orange or ulceration, and the finding of enlarged axillary nodes or evidence of systemic spread to bone or liver. The diagnosis can usually be confirmed by mammographic changes.

3. **A – Breast abscess**
   This is a disorder of the puerperium in which a cracked nipple leads to ascending infection with the pyogenic organism *Staphylococcus aureus*. The patient should stop feeding with the affected breast and antibiotics should be given (flucloxacillin). Drainage or aspiration is usually required. If the lump had no features of inflammation, a galactocele would be the most likely diagnosis.

4. **D – Duct papilloma**
   The most likely diagnosis is duct papilloma. This should be suspected from the age of the patient (younger than carcinoma) and the solitary symptom of recurrent blood-stained nipple discharge without the finding of a discrete lump. A true papilloma is usually single and occurs in a major duct in the subareolar area. The tumour consists of hyperplastic columnar epithelium with a rich blood supply (hence the presentation). They are entirely benign.

5. **F – Fibroadenoma**
   This is evidenced by the very young age of the patient and the characteristic features on examination i.e. hard, discrete, highly mobile (they are sometimes referred to as a 'breast mouse' on account of the mobility). Although such tumours are completely benign, most women are anxious to have them surgically excised.

8. MUSCULOSKELETAL CAUSES OF BACK PAIN

1. **D – Prolapsed intervertebral disc**
   This is a fairly characteristic description of an acute disc injury although it can also occur with trivial injuries, even coughing/sneezing. Neurological signs are present in some cases when the nerve root is compressed by the herniating disc but often there is only nerve root irritation with pain in the affected dermatome (as in this case). This is usually sciatic because L4/5 & L5/S1 are the most common levels of injury. Most herniations are posterolateral and therefore lead to unilateral symptoms. A posterior (central) disc herniation may however lead to the surgical emergency of cauda equina compression.

2. **B – Metastatic carcinoma**
   The history of relentlessly progressive severe and nocturnal pain especially in this age group should prompt a search for cancer as a cause. Common primary sites are breast, lung, prostate, kidney, thyroid and lymphoma. Primary tumours of bone especially myeloma should also be considered.

3. **F – Scheuermann's disease**
   This condition, also known as adolescent kyphosis, is twice as common in girls as boys and presents as described. The condition is thought to arise from damage to the vertebral growth plates in children who outgrow their bone strength during the pubertal growth spurt. The condition can usually be confirmed radiographically and is usually treated conservatively (physiotherapy).

4. **J – Spondylosis**
   This is the most common cause of back pain and probably the most common cause of lost hours at work in the Western world. The site is usually lumbar and the condition can probably be considered to be synonymous with osteoarthritis of the spine. The accepted pathogenetic sequence is initial degenerative disc disease leading to loss of disc height with subsequent lumbar instability and secondary osteoarthritis in the posterior facet joints. Treatment of this chronic condition is largely supportive.

5. **G – Spinal stenosis**
   The description given is characteristic of this syndrome which is caused by narrowing of the spinal canal and subsequent compression of canal contents. Disc degeneration, spondylosis and spondylolisthesis are the main aetiological factors. The syndrome must be distinguished from other causes of limb pain on exercise especially vascular claudication and osteoarthritis of the hip/knees.

9. BLEEDING PER VAGINA IN PREGNANCY

1. **B – Atonic uterus**
   The only common causes of primary PPH (blood loss > 500 ml in first 24 hours) are atonic uterus, RPOC and obstetric tears. By far the commonest of these is atonic uterus in the absence of any risk factors. Since she has had idiopathic poly-hydramnios atonic uterus is even more likely, as overdistension of the uterine wall leads to ineffective myometrial contraction after delivery of the placenta.

2. **I – Uterine rupture**
   Intrapartum bleeding is only likely to be due to placental abruption, uterine rupture and undiagnosed placenta praevia. Her major risk factor is previous LSCS and with prolonged obstructed labour she is at risk of uterine rupture. Uterine rupture only tends to occur with previous LSCS or uterine trauma, e.g. perforation or with the use of oxytocin. Uterine rupture, abruption and praevia may be associated with vaginal bleeding and fetal bradycardia if serious enough but uterine rupture is the only one where the presenting part may move out of the pelvis as it disappears through the scar rupture into the peritoneal cavity.

3. **C – Disseminated intravascular coagulation**
   The common causes of primary PPH (blood loss > 500 ml in first 24 hours) are atonic uterus, RPOC and obstetric tears. The 'complete' third stage does not exclude RPOC but the empty uterus at EUA does. Her major risk factor is moderately severe PET, which is associated with DIC in itself. The original bleeding is most likely associated with atonic uterus but the prolonged, major PPH leads to consumption of clotting factors and platelets. Spontaneous bleeding from puncture sites is a classic feature of coagulopathy.

4. **A – Abruptio placentae**
   APH may be due to placenta praevia, abruptio placentae, marginal bleed or local cervical pathology (e.g. cervical polyp/erosion/carcinoma). Local cervical pathology is classically postcoital and usually easily visible on speculum examination, which was not seen here. Abdominal pain and uterine contractions are most likely due to myometrial irritation from retroplacental bleeding in association with abruptio placentae, sometimes sufficient to trigger premature labour. Most abruptions are not major and do not lead to maternal or fetal compromise but can both extend and recur. APH with placenta praevia and marginal bleeds are usually painless.

5. **J – Vasa praevia**
   APH immediately after ARM is highly suggestive of either placenta or vasa praevia. It could be due to a coincidental abruption but this is unlikely with the timing and is more common with the sudden decompression of polyhydramnios. Given the engaged presenting part (only 2/5th palpable), a major placenta praevia is highly unlikely, as it would obstruct the pelvis. Though a minor degree of placenta praevia is possible, this is a classic story for rupture of an aberrant placental vessel that happens to traverse the cervical os (vasa praevia).

10. DISEASES OF THE LUNG AND PLEURA

1. C – Lobar pneumonia
Pneumonia is defined as inflammation of the lung parenchyma and is usually caused by bacterial infection. It presents as an acute illness characterised by cough, purulent sputum, pleuritic chest pain and fever. Bacterial pneumonia can present as one of two anatomic and radiographic patterns known as bronchopneumonia and lobar pneumonia. In bronchopneumonia there is patchy distribution of the inflammation, typically with involvement of more than one lobe. In contrast, lobar pneumonia involves an entire lobe, and there are physical signs and radiological changes indicating consolidation of that lobe. More than 90% of lobar pneumonias are caused by *Streptococcus pneumoniae*. Patients at increased risk of developing lobar pneumonia include the elderly and those with immunosuppression, debilitation, malnutrition or chronic disease.

2. G – Sarcoidosis
Sarcoidosis is a multisystem disease of unknown aetiology characterised by non-necrotising granulomas in many organs. It usually affects young adults and is more common in blacks than in whites. The most common presentation is with respiratory symptoms such as dyspnoea or with abnormalities on chest radiograph. Bilateral hilar lymphadenopathy is a characteristic feature found in 75–90% of patients. Other organs commonly affected include the eye and skin. Transbronchial biopsy is the most useful investigation, showing granulomas in 90% of patients with pulmonary sarcoidosis, even if there is no radiological evidence of lung involvement. The main differential diagnosis from the other diseases listed is tuberculosis. However, the lack of caseation within the granulomas, together with the absence of stainable acid-fast bacilli, mean that sarcoidosis is much more likely.

3. I – Squamous cell carcinoma of the bronchus
A heavy smoker who presents with haemoptysis and dyspnoea is likely to have carcinoma of the bronchus unless proven otherwise. This patient also has symptoms that indicate involvement of the lower part of the brachial plexus, namely pain in the shoulder that radiates down the arm. This occurs with a tumour at the apex of the lung that erodes the ribs and the first thoracic nerve root; it is known as a Pancoast tumour. Highly keratinised cells in sputum are indicative of atypical squamous cells (it is squamous cells that normally produce keratin), so the most likely diagnosis in this case is squamous cell carcinoma of the bronchus.

4. E – *Pneumocystis* pneumonia
Pneumocystis carinii is a ubiquitous organism that does not cause disease in normal individuals but causes a severe pneumonia in immunosuppressed patients, including those with HIV. The organism cannot be grown in culture, so diagnosis requires cytological or histological identification. Useful cytological preparations include bronchial washings or lavage. Transbronchial biopsy shows foamy eosinophilic material in the alveolar spaces. On both cytology and histology, the organism is seen as a boat-shaped or cup-shaped structure on silver stain. *Pneumocystis* pneumonia is one of the AIDS-defining diagnoses.

5. **H – Small cell carcinoma of the bronchus**

   As mentioned above, haemoptysis in a smoker is a sinister symptom and should be considered as indicative of bronchial carcinoma unless proved otherwise. The fact that this patient has a moon face, truncal obesity and hypokalaemia is strongly suggestive of Cushing's syndrome. Patients with carcinoma of the bronchus quite often present with paraneoplastic endocrinopathies. Cushing's syndrome, in which there is ectopic production of ACTH by the tumour cells, is one example. The type of bronchial carcinoma most likely to cause paraneoplastic Cushing's syndrome is small cell carcinoma as this is derived from neuroendocrine cells.

11. ANATOMY OF THE ALIMENTARY TRACT

1. **B – Duodenojejunal flexure**
   The root of the small gut mesentery passes from the flexure obliquely downwards to the right sacroiliac joint, crossing the left psoas muscle, the aorta, the inferior vena cava, right gonadal vessels, right psoas and the right ureter, to reach the ileocaecal junction.

2. **C – The first part of the duodenum**
   The pylorus lies to the right of the 1st lumbar vertebra. The first part of the duodenum is short and passes upwards and to the right before descending, the second part lying anterior to the hilum of the right kidney.

3. **F – Jejunum**
   The jejunum has prominent villi for absorption in contrast to the duodenum and colon where they are absent. The duodenum is characterised by Brunner's glands; these are mucous glands whose coiled pits extend into the submucosa.

4. **D – Hepatic flexure of the colon**
   The ascending colon is largely retroperitoneal, the flexure turns medially to become the transverse colon; the colon, its mesentery and the greater omentum overlying the small gut.

5. **G – Mesentery of the sigmoid colon**
   The sigmoid colon is attached by an inverted V-shaped mesentery to the pelvic wall. The apex of the V overlies the left ureter anterior to the bifurcation of the left common iliac artery and the left sacroiliac joint.

12. OPENINGS IN THE BASE OF SKULL

1. **G – Jugular foramen**
    The stylopharyngeus is the only muscle supplied by the glossopharyngeal nerve. This nerve, and the vagus and accessory nerves, together with the internal jugular vein and inferior petrosal sinus, pass through the jugular foramen.

2. **A – Anterior condylar canal**
    All the intrinsic and extrinsic muscles of the tongue except the palatoglossus are supplied by the 12th cranial nerve. This nerve also carries fibres from the ventral ramus of the 1st cervical nerve that supply geniohyoid and thyrohyoid muscles. The 12th nerve passes through the anterior condylar canal; the posterior condylar canal transmits an emissary vein.

3. **F – Inferior orbital fissure**
    The fissure transmits the infraorbital nerve, this being the continuation of the maxillary nerve out of the orbit. It supplies the lower eyelid and conjunctiva, the side of the nose and the upper lip, and through its anterior superior alveolar branch, the canine and incisor teeth, the lower lateral wall of the nose and the maxillary air sinus.

4. **J – Superior orbital fissure**
    The superior oblique muscle is supplied by the abducent nerve. The fissure is divided by the common tendinous attachment of the extraocular muscles into a narrow lateral part, transmitting the lacrimal, frontal and trochlear nerves, and a larger medial part transmitting the superior division of the oculomotor, the nasociliary, the inferior division of the oculomotor and the abducent nerves, from lateral to medial. The optic nerve and ophthalmic artery pass into the orbit through the optic canal.

5. **D – Foramen ovale**
    The medial pterygoid muscle is supplied by the mandibular division of the trigeminal nerve; this supplies the muscles of mastication, and also the tensor tympani and tensor veli palatini. The foramen spinosum, situated just posterior and lateral to the foramen ovale, transmits the middle meningeal vessels.

PAPER 7

Paper 7 questions

1. THEME: SECONDARY HYPERTENSION

A Acromegaly
B Chronic reflux nephropathy
C Coarctation of the aorta
D Conn's syndrome
E Cushing's syndrome
F Diabetic nephropathy
G Phaeochromocytoma
H Polycystic kidney disease
I Raised intracranial pressure
J Renal artery stenosis

The following patients have all presented with secondary causes of hypertension. Please choose the most appropriate cause from the above list. The items may be used once, more than once or not at all.

1. A 29-year-old woman attends her GP with headaches and dizziness. Her BP is measured at 230/110 on three separate occasions despite treatment and she is referred to the hospital. Routine investigations reveal U&Es: Na$^+$ 131 mmol/l, K$^+$ 2.4 mmol/l, urea 3.9 mmol/l, Cr 87 μmol/l. Further investigations reveal reduced plasma renin with a markedly raised aldosterone, despite correction of the hypokalaemia with spironolactone. ☐

2. A 34-year-old man is seen in medical outpatient department with visual 'blurring' and BP = 170/100. He is noted to have frontal bossing and bitemporal hemianopia and his BM Stix reading = 13.7 mmol/l. ☐

3. A 24-year-old woman is seen by her GP with vague abdominal pains and headaches. On examination she is plethoric, BP = 185/110 and abdominal examination reveals hepatosplenomegaly. Blood tests reveal FBC: Hb 17.9 g/dl, HCt 56.3, WCC 11.1 × 10^9/l, Plt 499 × 10^9/l; U&Es: Na$^+$ 131 mmol/l, K$^+$ 5.8 mmol/l, urea 21.9 mol/l, Cr 419 μmol/l. ☐

4. A 61-year-old man with known ischaemic heart disease and peripheral vascular disease is started on an ACE inhibitor by his GP for hypertension. Three weeks later he is admitted with increasing confusion and vomiting. Investigations reveal FBC: Hb 14.9 g/dl, MCV 88 fl, WCC 13.6 × 10^9/l, Plt 317 × 10^9/l; U&Es: Na$^+$ 131 mmol/l, K$^+$ 7.3 mol/l, urea 37.8 mmol/l, Cr 858 μmol/l. ☐

5. A 37-year-old woman is admitted to hospital with an episode of sweats, palpitations and headache associated with a BP = 240/130. Her initial blood tests including FBC, U&Es, and cardiac enzymes are all normal, but her BP is poorly controlled despite the addition of several agents. The diagnosis is later confirmed by raised urinary VMA (vanillyl mandelic acid) levels and adrenal venous sampling showing raised serum catecholamines from left and right adrenal vein.

2. THEME: AUTOSOMAL DOMINANT DISORDERS

A Achondroplasia
B Dystrophia myotonica
C Familial hypercholesterolaemia
D Gilbert's syndrome
E Hereditary spherocytosis
F Huntington's chorea
G Marfan's syndrome
H Neurofibromatosis
I Osteogenesis imperfecta
J Romano–Ward syndrome

The following patients have all presented with autosomal dominant disorders. Please choose the most appropriate cause from the above list. The items may be used once, more than once or not at all.

1. A 31-year-old man is seen in the neurology outpatient department with increasing weakness in all four limbs. On examination he has bilateral ptosis with weakness and wasting of the facial muscles and a 'prolonged' handshake.

2. A 24-year-old woman is admitted to A&E with a 6-hour history of severe central chest pain. ECG confirms an anterolateral myocardial infarct. Of note her father and brothers have ischaemic heart disease since their early 20s.

3. A 39-year-old woman is seen in the medical outpatient department with increasing skin eruptions. On examination she has several café au lait spots and multiple skin lesions. Of note her grandfather had a similar condition and became wheelchair-bound due to a spinal tumour.

4. A 41-year-old man is admitted to A&E with collapse secondary to Torsades des Pointes which spontaneously reverts. His repeat ECG shows a prolonged QTc interval. He is on no medications and subsequent serum Ca^+, Mg^+ and K^+ are normal.

5. A 28-year-old woman is admitted to hospital with a left lower lobe pneumonia with Gram-positive diplococci in the sputum. Routine investigation show FBC: Hb 13.7 g/dl, MCV 87.3 fl, WCC 19.9×10^9/l with a neutrophilia, Plt 344×10^9/l; U&Es: Na^+ 137 mmol/l, K^+ 4.9 mmol/l, urea 4.3 mmol/l, Cr 97 µmol/l; LFTs; Tbil 42 µmol/l, AST 21 iu/l, Alk phos 112 iu/l, Alb 34 g/l.

3. THEME: INFECTIVE DIARRHOEA

A Amoebiasis
B *Bacillus cereus*
C *Campylobacter jejuni*
D *Clostridium difficile*
E *Cryptosporidium*
F *Escherichia coli*
G *Gardia lamblia*
H *Salmonella enteriditis*
I *Shigella flexneri*
J *Vibrio cholerae*

The following patients have all presented with infective diarrhoea. Please choose the most appropriate cause from the above list. The items may be used once, more than once or not at all.

1. A 9-year-old girl is seen in A&E having recently returned home from a holiday in the Punjab. She has diarrhoea associated with blood and mucus and is opening her bowels three to four times per hour.

2. A 17-year-old boy is seen at home by his GP with a 24-hour history of severe cramping abdominal pains associated with diarrhoea and fever after eating some poorly cooked chicken at a barbeque. He is admitted to hsopital where the diagnosis is confirmed on stool microscopy showing motile, curved Gram-negative rods.

3. A 35-year-old woman is seen by her GP with a 12-hour history of profuse diarrhoea and vomiting after eating lukewarm rice and vegetables from a Chinese take-away. She improves after 24 hours. Subsequent stool cultures reveal a Gram-positive but aerobic bacterium in 'curled hair' colonies.

4. An 84-year-old man is readmitted to hospital 2 weeks after a prolonged admittance with recurrent chest infections. He has 'offensive, profuse diarrhoea' with abdominal pain. He is treated empirically with oral vancomycin and improves. The diagnosis is later confirmed by positive toxin test in the stool.

5. A 78-year-old woman is admitted to hospital with severe vomiting and diarrhoea. Routine investigations confirm DIC and acute renal failure. She sadly dies 2–3 days later despite intravenous antibiotics. Several other people from her nursing home are admitted with a similar clinical picture. The outbreak is traced to some contaminated beef. The organism is seen to produce Shiga-like toxin 1.

4. THEME: PERIPHERAL SENSORY NEUROPATHY

A   Alcohol excess
B   Amiodarone
C   Amyloidosis
D   Demyelination
E   Diabetes mellitus
F   Hypothyroidism
G   Isoniazid
H   Paraneoplastic
I   Uraemia
J   Vitamin B12 deficiency

The following patients have all presented with symptoms of a peripheral sensory neuropathy. Please choose the most appropriate cause from the above list. The items may be used once, more than once or not at all.

1. A 62-year-old man with known mitral valve disease is admitted to hospital with severe sunburn. On examination he is noted to have 'little lesions across his cornea' but is otherwise well. He tells the SHO on the ward he has been experiencing pins and needles in his hands and feet for some time and closer examination confirms a loss of joint position sense, vibration and light touch in his hands and feet.

2. A 24-year-old man is seen in medical outpatients with parasthesiae and numbness in his feet. He has been unable to drive in the last few weeks as he can not feel the pedals in the car and he has been having episodes of blurred vision. The diagnosis is confirmed by a MRI scan of his cervical cord and brain and delayed visual evoked responses.

3. A 79-year-old woman presents to her GP with worsening numbness in her hands and feet associated with swelling of her ankles. Subsequent investigations confirm a nephrotic syndrome and the underlying diagnosis is confirmed when the renal biopsy appears apple green under polarised light when stained with Congo red.

4. A 37-year-old woman with vitiligo presents to her GP with weight gain, increasing lethargy and malaise associated with tingling in her hands. Routine investigations reveal FBC: Hb 11.2 g/dl, MCV 99 fl, WCC 7.8 × 10^9/l, Plt 303 × 10^9/l; U&Es: Na$^+$ 127 mmol/l, K$^+$ 4.4 mmol/l, urea 4.7 mmol/l, Cr 87 μmol/l.

5. A 35-year-old vegan woman presents to her GP with increasing lethargy, malaise and numbness in her feet. Routine investigations show FBC: Hb 4.1 g/dl, MCV 122 fl, WCC 2.1 × 10^9/l, Plt 59 × 10^9/l; U&Es: Na$^+$ 135 mmol/l, K$^+$ 4.8 mmol/l, urea 3.9 mmol/l, Cr 79 μmol/l.

5. THEME: PYREXIA OF UNKNOWN ORIGIN (PUO)

A   Brucellosis
B   Cytomegalovirus
C   Epstein–Barr virus
D   Histoplasmosis
E   Hodgkin's lymphoma
F   Infective endocarditis
G   Lyme disease
H   Renal cell carcinoma
I   Sarcoidosis
J   Tuberculosis

The following patients have all presented with pyrexia of unknown origin. Please choose the most appropriate cause from the above list. The items may be used once, more than once or not at all.

1. A 64-year-old man is admitted to hospital with weight loss and abdominal pains, swinging temperature and night sweats. Routine investigation show FBC: Hb 9.7 g/dl, MCV 72.3, WCC 11.9 × 10⁹/l, Plt 375 × 10⁹/l; U&Es: Na⁺ 132 mmol/l, K⁺ 3.9 mmol/l, urea 7.9 mmol/l, Cr 127 μmol/l, RBG 6.1 mmol/l, blood cultures negative. His chest radiograph shows multiple large round lesions in both lung fields.

2. A 14-year-old schoolgirl is seen by her GP with tender lymph nodes. She is pyrexial. She is admitted to hospital where initial investigations are unremarkable including blood cultures. Her blood film confirms 'atypical lymphocytes and monocytes'.

3. A 31-year-old school teacher returns from a week's holiday caving in France. He is non-specific unwell with myalgia and low grade temperature. He also has a dry cough. Initial investigations including FBC, U&Es, LFTs and blood film are unremarkable.

4. A 24-year-old Afro-Caribbean woman is seen in medical outpatient department with fevers and a dry cough. Her chest radiograph reveals bilateral hilar lymphadenopathy and the diagnosis is confirmed with bronchoscopy and bronchoalveolar lavage.

5. A 51-year-old rambler is admitted to A&E 2–3 weeks after a walking holiday in the New Forest. He complains of arthritis, myalgia and headache. On examination he has a low grade fever and a spreading red rash but no other focal signs.

6. THEME: COMMON CAUSES OF RIGHT ILIAC FOSSA PAIN

A   Acute appendicitis
B   Crohn's disease
C   Irritable bowel syndrome
D   Mesenteric adenitis
E   Non-specific abdominal pain
F   Pelvic inflammatory disease
G   Perforated caecal carcinoma
H   Torsion ovarian cyst
I   Ureteric colic
J   Urinary tract infection

The following are descriptions of patients with common causes of right iliac fossa pain. Please select the most appropriate diagnosis from the above list. The items may be used once, more than once or not at all.

1. A 42-year-old woman is referred to outpatients with a 3-year history of right iliac fossa pain. The pain is often post-prandial and associated with bloating and a variable bowel habit both in terms of consistency and frequency of stool. She has no weight loss or rectal bleeding. Barium enema examination performed 1 year ago was normal, as were all recent blood tests and abdominal radiograph performed by her GP.

2. A 19-year-old woman is seen in A&E with a 2-day history of right iliac fossa pain. She has no gastrointestinal, urinary or gynaecological symptoms. On examination, she is afebrile and there is slight tenderness but no guarding or rebound in the right iliac fossa. Initial blood tests, abdominal radiograph and pelvic ultrasound are normal. She is admitted for observation but is discharged 2 days later after the pain resolves.

3. A 9-year-old girl is seen in A&E with a 24-hour history of right iliac fossa pain. She admits to general malaise and fever associated with a sore throat and 'cold' for 2 days prior to onset of the pain. On examination she is pyrexial, temperature 39°C, has pharyngitis and palpable tender soft jugulodigastric lymph nodes. Examination of the abdomen reveals tenderness in the right iliac fossa. Her WCC is 6.2×10^9/l.

4. A 19-year-old woman is referred to the on-call surgical team with a 3-day history of worsening right iliac fossa pain, fever and nausea. Her GP suspects appendicitis. On questioning she has a pale yellow vaginal discharge of 1 week duration and dyspareunia. On examination her temperature is 37.9°C and there is tenderness and guarding in the right iliac fossa. On pelvic examination, in addition to evident vaginal discharge, she has cervical excitation and some right adnexal tenderness. Her WCC is 13.2×10^9/l.

5. A 23-year-old woman presents in A&E with a 4-hour history of sudden onset severe right iliac fossa pain. She has tenderness and guarding localised to the right iliac fossa and suprapubic region.

7. THEME: THE PAINFUL KNEE

A   Anterior cruciate injury
B   Chondromalacia patellae
C   Infrapatellar bursitis
D   Meniscal tear
E   Osgood–Schlatter's disease
F   Osteoarthrosis
G   Osteochondritis dessicans
H   Prepatellar bursitis
I   Recurrent dislocation of the patella
J   Rheumatoid arthritis

The following are descriptions of patients with a painful knee(s). Please select the most appropriate diagnosis from the above list. The items may be used once, more than once, in combination or not at all.

1. A 16-year-old teenage girl complains of pain, principally in front of the knee, especially on ascending and descending stairs.

2. A 63-year-old patient complains of chronic pain and swelling of the knee. On examination, there is marked deformity with valgus especially apparent on standing.

3. A 23-year-old rugby player has a twisting injury of the knee after which the knee is 'locked' in partial flexion. On examination there is a small effusion and extension is limited. McMurray's test is positive.

4. A 40-year-old carpet layer presents with anterior knee pain and a painful swelling.

5. A 13-year-old young adolescent presents after school athletics with anterior knee pain and a lump over the tibial tuberosity.

8. THEME: UPPER AIRWAYS OBSTRUCTION

A   Acute epiglottitis
B   Anaphylactic reaction
C   Angioneurotic oedema
D   Bilateral recurrent laryngeal nerve paralysis
E   Carcinoma of the larynx
F   Diphtheria
G   Fracture of the larynx
H   Fracture of the mandible/midfacial fracture
I   Inhaled foreign body
J   Inhalation or ingestion of irritants
K   Ludwig's angina
L   Papilloma of the larynx
M   Reduced conscious level
N   Thyroid carcinoma

The following patients have all presented with stridor or with breathlessness. Please select the most appropriate diagnosis from the above list. The items may be used once, more than once or not at all.

1. A 16-year-old girl presents with facial oedema, dyspnoea and stridor. She is apyrexial and has no past medical history.

2. A 25-year-old man presents with a history of anterior neck injury whilst participating in karate. He is developing increasing hoarseness. On examination he has surgical emphysema of the neck.

3. A 75-year-old woman presents with a history of dyspnoea and stridor. She has noticed a swelling in the neck for the previous 2 months. On examination she has a right-sided hard, anterior neck mass that is fixed to the larynx. A lateral soft tissue radiograph of the neck shows compression of the trachea and severe narrowing of the airway.

4. A 4-year-old boy is admitted with a 6-hour history of fever, sore throat and stridor. His temperature is 39.5°C. The child's condition deteriorates and he has to be intubated.

5. A 45-year-old builder is rescued by the fire service following a gas explosion in a building. He is alert and orientated but has stridor, hoarseness and a cough productive of black sputum. He has burns to the face and upper torso and a fractured right femur.

9. THEME: GYNAECOLOGICAL PROCEDURES

A   Anterior vaginal repair
B   Colposcopy
C   Colposuspension
D   Endometrial ablation
E   Hysteroscopy
F   Laparoscopy
G   Large loop excision of the transformation zone (LLETZ)
H   Posterior vaginal repair
I   Total abdominal hysterectomy
J   Vaginal hysterectomy

From the above list please choose the procedure most appropriate for the clinical picture described. The items may be used once, more than once, in combination or not at all.

1. A 28-year-old nulliparous woman has no clinical symptoms but receives an interval cervical smear result suggestive of moderate dyskaryosis.

2. A 60-year-old multiparous woman describes frequency and urinary incontinence on coughing and laughing. Examination reveals 1st degree uterovaginal prolapse only. Her MSU is unremarkable and conservative measures fail to improve her symptoms. Urodynamic (UDS) investigation gives a diagnosis of genuine stress incontinence (GSI).

3. A 47-year-old woman has a 6-month history of heavy, irregular periods. There has been no intermenstrual or postcoital bleeding. Her examination is completely normal and she has had a normal cervical smear in the last 2 years. TVS reveals a 2 $\times$ 3 cm serosal fibroid, endometrial thickness of 14 mm and normal ovaries. She has failed to respond to medical therapy (cyclical progestagens).

4. A 30-year-old woman has increasing dysmenorrhoea and deep dyspareunia over 12 months. On examination there is marked tenderness in the posterior fornix and the uterus feels fixed and retroverted. She has already tried 3 months' empirical treatment on high-dose progestagens for presumed endometriosis, but has not improved. Her transvaginal ultrasound scan is unremarkable.

5. A 58-year-old multiparous woman has a feeling of 'something coming down' into the vagina that has been getting worse over the last 2 years. She describes mild frequency but no urgency or urinary incontinence. There are no bowel symptoms and she is not currently sexually active. Examination reveals moderate cystocele but no obvious uterovaginal prolapse, rectocele or enterocele.

10. THEME: DISORDERS LEADING TO ABNORMAL COAGULATION

A Autoimmune thrombocytopenic purpura
B Disseminated intravascular coagulation
C Essential thrombocythaemia
D Haemophilia A
E Haemophilia B
F Sickle cell disease
G Systemic lupus erythematosus
H Thrombotic thrombocytopenic purpura
I Vitamin K deficiency
J von Willebrand's disease

From the above list, please select the disorder that each of the following patients is most likely to have. The items may be used once, more than once or not at all.

Patient	Bleeding time	Prothrombin (PT) ratio	Activated partial thromboplastin time (APTT)	Factor VIII:C levels	Factor IX levels	Platelet count
1	Normal	Normal	Increased	Very low	Normal	Normal
2	Normal	Increased	Increased	Normal	Normal	Normal
3	Increased	Normal	Increased	Low	Normal	Normal
4	Increased	Increased	Increased	Low	Low	Very low
5	Normal	Normal	Increased	Normal	Low	Normal

11. THEME: ANATOMY OF THE FEMORAL REGION

A   Femoral artery
B   Femoral canal
C   Femoral nerve
D   Femoral vein
E   Iliopsoas muscle
F   Inguinal ligament
G   Pectineal ligament
H   Pubic tubercle
I   Reflected pectineal part of the inguinal ligament
J   Saphenous opening

For each of the following descriptions, please choose the most appropriate structure from the above list. The items may be used once, more than once or not at all.

1. Lateral relationship of the femoral artery.

2. Medial relationship of the neck of the femoral canal.

3. Posterior relationship of the femoral canal.

4. Site where a femoral hernia becomes subcutaneous.

5. Structure above and medial to the opening of the femoral canal.

12. THEME: MUSCLE ATTACHMENTS OF THE LOWER LIMB

A   Adductor longus
B   Adductor magnus
C   Biceps femoris (long head)
D   Gastrocnemius
E   Iliopsoas
F   Peroneus longus
G   Semitendinosus
H   Soleus
I   Tibialis posterior
J   Vastus lateralis

For each of the following attachments please choose the most appropriate muscle from the above list. The items may be used once, more than once, in combination or not at all.

1.   Lesser trochanter of the femur.   ☐

2.   Linea aspera of the femur.   ☐

3.   Above and posterior to the lateral femoral condyle.   ☐

4.   The upper two-thirds of the lateral surface of the fibula.   ☐

5.   Tuberosity of the navicular.   ☐

Paper 7 answers

1. SECONDARY HYPERTENSION

1. **D – Conn's syndrome**
    This young woman has hypertension associated with hypokalaemia. This may be due to Conn's syndrome (primary hyperaldosteronism) or Cushing's syndrome. The subsequent investigations after correction of her hypokalaemia reveal hyperaldosteronism and reduced plasma renin activity indicating Conn's syndrome. Causes include adrenal adenomas and bilateral adrenal hyperplasia which are treated by surgical excision or with spironolactone and antihypertensive agents respectively.

2. **A – Acromegaly**
    This man has several features of acromegaly including frontal bossing and bitemporal haemianopia. He also has hypertension and proximal myopathy. The diagnosis should be confirmed by dynamic pituitary testing showing poorly suppressable, elevated growth hormone levels and MRI imaging of the pituitary fossa. The treatment is usually neurosurgical excision of the tumour either transnasally or transfrontally with post-operative radiotherapy.

3. **H – Polycystic kidney disease**
    This woman has signs of polycythaemia (plethoric) hypertension and large upper abdominal masses. Blood tests confirm the polycythaemia and reveal renal impairment. This is the clinical picture of polycystic kidney disease. Adult polycystic kidney disease is an autosomal dominant disorder which may present in early adulthood with local symptoms such as urinary infections (recurrent), haematuria, abdominal pain, renal failure or renal stones, and systemic symptoms including polycythaemia, anaemia, hypertension and subarachnoid haemorrhage due to the association with Berry aneurysms.

4. **J – Renal artery stenosis**
    This patient has known ischaemic heart disease and pulmonary vascular disease which imply he has generalised atherosclerosis. Significant pulmonary vascular disease is associated with a 25–30% risk of significant renal artery stenosis and is a contraindication to starting an ACE inhibitor unless the kidneys and renal arteries are imaged. Renal artery stenosis and aortic stenosis are both contraindications to starting on ACE inhibitors as this causes a rapid deterioration in both of these conditions.

5.   G – Phaeochromocytoma

This patient has poorly controlled blood pressure despite the addition of several antihypertensive agents. Subsequent investigations show a raised 24-hour urinary VMA (vanillyl mandelic acid) and serum catecholamines on adrenal venous sampling. VMA is a metabolite of adrenaline and noradrenaline excreted in the urine. Other investigations include (i) a radio labelled I^{131}-MIBG (metaiodobenzylguanidine) scan which is preferentially taken up at sites of sympathetic overactivity and (ii) a CT scan of the abdomen to visualise the tumour. The treatment includes an α and β blocker, always starting with α blockade and then β blockade (if required). If started in the alternate way, unopposed α activity is potentially life threatening. Definitive surgical excision of the tumour is usually curative, however expert endocrine opinion, surgery and anaethesia are required.

2. AUTOSOMAL DOMINANT (AD) DISORDERS

1. **B – Dystrophia myotonica**
   This man has bilateral ptosis and facial weakness associated with a 'prolonged handshake', all features of dystrophia myotonica. Myotonica means 'continued muscle contraction after cessation of voluntary effort' and is characteristically seen when asking the patient to perform a given task and then asking them to stop, e.g. 'Squeeze my fingers – and now stop'. The patient is not able to let go. The syndrome is characterised by mild intellectual impairment, frontal balding, cataracts, cardiomyopathy and conduction system defects. The disorder becomes apparent between 20 and 40 years old and is insidiously progressive.

2. **C – Familial hypercholesterolaemia**
   This patient has the commonest autosomal dominant disorder in the Western world, familial hypercholesterolaemia (FH). This condition causes premature macrovascular atherosclerosis and subsequent ischaemic heart disease, stroke and peripheral vascular disease. Treatment is with high-dose statins and family screening. All secondary risk factors such as hypertension, diabetes mellitus and smoking should also be addressed.

3. **H – Neurofibromatosis**
   This patient has developed several stigmata of neurofibromatosis including the skin tumours and café, au lait spots (more than five is considered pathological). The disorder has been divided into a peripheral, type I (chromosome 17) and central, type II (chromosome 22) syndrome.

4. **J – Romano–Ward syndrome**
   This patient has developed Torsades des Pointes secondary to a prolonged QTc interval caused by his Romano–Ward syndrome. Other causes include Jevell–Lange–Nielson (AR), hypocalcaemia, hypomagnesaemia and hypokalaemia, severe bradycardia (tachy-brady syndrome), ischaemic heart disease and drugs including antipsychotics, antihistamines and antiarrhythmics, e.g. amiodarone.

5. **D – Gilbert's syndrome**
   This patient has a severe streptococcal pneumonia and an associated hyper-bilirubinaemia with otherwise normal liver function tests. This is caused by Gilbert's syndrome which is a benign condition leading to hyperbilirubinaemia in times of stress. The underlying cause needs treating and the patient should be told of the condition to stop 'overzealous' doctors subjecting them to further liver function tests and imaging! Their family should also be screened.

3. INFECTIVE DIARRHOEA

1. **I – *Shigella Flexneri***

    This girl has developed shigellosis or bacillary dysentery which worldwide is one of the commonest causes of infant and childhood mortality. The four species of *Shigella* cause a spectrum of disease from a mild, even asymptomatic infection, up to a life threatening dysentery with bloody diarrhoea associated with mucus and pus. They are spread by the faecal–oral route. *Shigella dysenteriae* is found in tropical areas and causes severe enteritis with systemic complications due to the production of an enterotoxin, cytotoxin and neurotoxin. It requires antibiotic treatment. In the UK *Shigella sonnei* and *flexneri* are more common and causally cause a more benign, self-limiting condition.

2. **C – *Campylobacter jejuni***

    This young man has developed *Campylobacter* food-poisoning, one of the commonest causes of food poisoning in the UK. It is associated with meat, chicken and dairy products. It is usually a self-limiting condition but may occasionally cause severe systemic upset and require antibiotic treatment with ciprofloxacin or clarithromycin.

3. **B – *Bacillus cereus***

    This woman has developed an acute gastroenteritis secondary to a *Bacillus cereus* infection. This Gram-positive bacillus causes a rapid onset of vomiting and diarrhoea within 2 to 6 hours of the ingestion of affected foods. It is characteristically associated with poorly heated/reheated rice causing germination and multiplication of the bacilli and toxin production. The disorder is self-limiting and symptoms last only 24–48 hours.

4. **D – *Clostridium difficile***

    This man has developed *Clostridium difficile* diarrhoea due to his prolonged admission and antibiotic treatment for his recurrent infection. Several studies have shown experienced nurses to be 90% sensitive in their diagnosis of *Clostridium difficile* so if Sister says 'C. Diff diarrhoea' …it invariably is! Treatment includes *oral* metronidazole or vancomycin as it is the intraluminal concentration of the antibiotic which is important. Other treatment includes supportive treatment with intravenous or oral fluids.

5. **F – *Escherichia coli***

    This group of patients have developed an *E. coli* infection. The various strains of this organism produce several different toxins including an *enterotoxin* which is secreted by the non-invasive ETEC group. This usually produces a self-limiting condition lasting for a few days but may produce a more severe illness with cholera like symptoms and signs. The more severe *cytototoxin* producing group includes the strain *E. coli* O157 which produces the Shiga-like toxin which may lead to a severe diarrhoeal illness associated with acute renal failure and DIC – the haemolytic uraemic syndrome. This is particularly common in children and the elderly and is often fatal without early treatment.

4. PERIPHERAL SENSORY NEUROPATHY

1. **B – Amiodarone**
   This man has been placed on amiodarone which has led to several side effects including a peripheral sensory neuropathy. Amiodarone is principally used in older patients with poorly controlled paroxysmal atrial fibrillation, sustained atrial fibrillation and paroxysmal ventricular tachyarrhythmia, although more recently implantable defibrillator devices have superseded the latter role. It has numerous side effects including: (1) skin – photosensitivity (patients can claim free suntan lotion!), a slate grey pigmentation and erythema multiforme; (2) pulmonary fibrosis (very uncommon at doses below 400 mg per day); (3) dysthyroid disease – amiodarone affects the thyroid's physiology at multiple levels and may cause hypo- or hyperthyroid disease, which may or may not be clinically manifest; (4) hepatitis – again this may or may not be clinically manifest; and (5) microcorneal deposits of the eye. Most of the side effects are totally reversible on withdrawal of the drug but patients (as with all drug therapy) must be warned of the important side effects on starting the drug.

2. **D – Demyelination**
   This young man has developed episodic visual blurring and symptoms of a peripheral sensory neuropathy. His investigations will show 'plaques' of demyelination within the cervical cord, brain stem, periventricular white matter and cerebellum. The delayed visual evoked responses also help to confirm the diagnosis of multiple sclerosis. The treatment of this condition will depend on the patient's wishes and the pattern of the subsequent disease.

3. **C – Amyloidosis**
   This patient has developed amyloidosis leading to a nephrotic syndrome and a peripheral sensory neuropathy (although it is a relatively uncommon cause of neuropathy). The diagnosis is confirmed by the appearance of amyloid proteins in biopsy tissue, usually taken from the gums or rectum. The classical appearance is of an apple green appearance under polarised light having been stained with Congo red.

4. **F – Hypothyroidism**
   This woman with vitiligo has clinical and investigative evidence of hypothyroidism. She has weight gain, lethargy and symptoms of a sensory neuropathy, a macrocytosis and hyponatraemia. The diagnosis should be confirmed with thyroid function tests and the patient started on thyroxine replacement therapy, titrated slowly against clinical and biochemical response.

5.   **J – Vitamin B12 deficiency**
     This woman has developed B12 deficiency as evidenced by the symptoms of anaemia, the peripheral sensory neuropathy and the confirmatory investigations including a gross macrocytosis in association with a pancytopenia. Although her vegan diet is the most likely cause she needs an autoantibody screen to exclude pernicious anaemia and related autoimmune diseases such as thyroid disease. She will also require B12 and folate levels, as well as glucose, thyroid function tests, liver function tests and a history taken to exclude alcohol excess and drug side effects. Treatment consists of a loading course of hydroxycobalamine (three 1 mg doses over 1 week) and then single repeat doses every 3 months.

5. PYREXIA OF UNKNOWN ORIGIN (PUO)

1. H – Renal cell carcinoma

This man has a microcytic anaemia, mild renal impairment and his chest radiograph shows multiple, large lesions or cannonball metastases. This presentation is consistent with renal cell carcinoma. The diagnosis may be confirmed on renal ultrasound scan, urine cytology and CT scan of the abdomen.

2. C – Epstein–Barr virus

This schoolgirl has developed a severe EBV infection. Sepsis and in particular viral infection produce tender lymphadenopathy as opposed to haematological malignancy which produces characteristically non-tender lymphadenopathy. EBV infection is confirmed by the 'monospot' test and Paul–Bunnell test. The monospot confirms the presence of the associated atypical mononuclear cells on blood film. The Paul–Bunnell test confirms the presence of heterophile IgM antibodies. These lead to agglutination of sheep red blood cells in vitro. Rising EBV IgM titres are also commonly used in hospitalised patients.

3. D – Histoplasmosis

This man has developed a primary histoplasmosis infection. The infection is caused by a fungus whose spores may survive in moist soil or bat and/or bird droppings for several years. It is a 'classic' infection of cavers who explore caves in endemic areas. The primary infection is often asymptomatic but may present with a PUO, flu-like illness and a dry cough. Secondary complications in the lung include secondary bacterial infection, pleural effusions and pleurisy. A chronic pulmonary infection may develop which is almost identical to pulmonary TB.

4. I – Sarcoidosis

This Afro-Caribbean woman has developed pulmonary sarcoidosis as evidenced by the bilateral hilar lymphadenopathy on chest radiograph, the clinical presentation. The diagnosis is confirmed on bronchoscopy and biopsy and bronchoalveolar lavage (BAL) which will show non-caeseating granulomatous infiltration with inflammatory cells and T-helper cells.

5. G – Lyme disease

This patient has developed Lyme disease, a spirochaete infection spread by ticks (which live on the deer of the New Forest). There are three distinct phases of the disease.

(1) Non-specific flu-like illness associated with myalgia, arthralgia, fever, lymphadenopathy but characterised by a spreading red rash – erythema chronicum migrans.

(2) The second stage develops weeks to months later with meningo-encephalitis, cranial nerve and peripheral neuropathies and cardiac problems.

(3) A chronic progressive episodic arthritis. This phase does not seem to occur in the UK.

The treatment is with penicillin or tetracycline.

6. COMMON CAUSES OF RIGHT ILIAC FOSSA PAIN

It is possible to name at least 20 causes of right iliac fossa pain. The list given in this question includes some of the more common ones. In general, like so much of medicine, it is more common to see a common condition presenting atypically than a rare condition presenting typically, e.g. a UTI whilst usually associated with supra-pubic pain may also present with right iliac fossa pain. For a complete list consider the contents of the abdomen anatomically from front to back in the region of the right iliac fossa. Thus: (1) anterior abdominal wall, e.g. rectus sheath haematoma; (2) peritoneal viscera – caecum, small intestine, appendix, right tube and ovary, bladder; (3) retroperitoneal structures – kidney, ureter, iliac artery (leaking aneurysm thereof), iliac vein thrombosis, undescended testis (torsion therof), psoas muscle (abscess).

1. **C – Irritable bowel syndrome**
    The long history and typical symptoms fulfilling the Rome criteria suggest this 'non-diagnosis' which should only be made when an organic cause for the patient's symptoms has been excluded (as in this case). As in this case patients are typically middle-aged females.

2. **E – Non-specific abdominal pain**
    This is the commonest eventual diagnosis in patients presenting with right iliac fossa pain. The description should only be employed for patients in which ALL other relevant causes of pain have been excluded by investigation.

3. **D – Mesenteric adenitis**
    The patient described is typical of this condition in which mesenteric lymph node enlargement causes abdominal pain in response to a systemic, usually viral illness. In this case the patient has a viral upper respiratory tract infection. Evidence of such infections should always be sought, especially in children, to avoid unnecessary appendicectomy.

4. **F – Pelvic inflammatory disease**
    The patient might be assumed to have appendicitis were it not for the symptoms and signs which are typical of PID. The cause is bacterial infection of the tubes/ovaries (salpingo-oophoritis) and is usually contracted primarily from sexual transmission. Organisms include *N. gonorrhoeae* and *C. trachomatis*.

5. **H – Torsion ovarian cyst**
    The history, in particular sudden onset of pain without GI disturbance, suggests this diagnosis which is a common differential in the young female. The diagnosis can usually be confirmed by pelvic ultrasound examination, and commonly requires surgery. A similar presentation is seen with haemorrhage into, and rupture of, an ovarian cyst.

7. THE PAINFUL KNEE

1. B – Chondromalacia patellae
Softening of the articular cartilage of the patella is often associated with anterior knee pain in teenage girls. It is thought to result from mal-tracking of the patella during flexion and extension. On clinical examination, pain can be elicited by the patella femoral crepitation test. Treatment is rest, analgesia and physiotherapy.

2. J – Rheumatoid arthritis
This can occasionally start in the knee as a monoarticular synovitis. With chronicity, the joint may become increasingly deformed. Although deformity can also occur (with chronic pain and swelling) in OA, a valgus deformity is characteristic of rheumatoid whereas a varus deformity is frequently seen with severe OA.

3. D – Meniscal tear
The description given is characteristic of this very common injury. McMurray's test (rotating the knee during various degrees of flexion and extension) aims to catch the torn meniscal fragment between the articular surfaces of the knee and then induce it to snap free with a palpable and audible click. *Whilst you should know the principle of this test, it can be very difficult to convincingly demonstrate in less than very experienced hands. It is also very painful for the patient if positive!*

4. H – Prepatellar bursitis
The occupation gives this away. Commonly called housemaid's knee it is more common now in more contemporary occupations which commonly kneel to work. Treatment is avoidance and bandaging (occasionally aspiration).

5. E – Osgood–Schlatter's disease
This is a traction injury of the tibial apophysis for the patellar ligament. The presentation and findings are characteristic and the radiological findings diagnostic. Treatment is restriction of activity to permit eventual spontaneous recovery.

8. UPPER AIRWAYS OBSTRUCTION

1. **C – Angioneurotic oedema**
    This is a condition of unknown aetiology which most commonly affects young females. Management is by close observation, antihistamines and intravenous steroids/epinephrine nebulisers. Should the condition deteriorate, the patient may require orotracheal intubation. It is distinguished only from anaphylactic shock by the absence of a precipitating allergen (e.g. antibiotics and bee stings).

2. **G – Fracture of the larynx**
    This man has fractured his thyroid cartilage. He is in danger of developing a haematoma of the larynx that could obstruct the airway. Hence he should be admitted to hospital for observation. If the situation deteriorates, tracheostomy may be required as an emergency. A lateral soft tissue view of the neck or tomography of the larynx should be performed and if the cartilages are displaced the larynx should be repaired surgically otherwise scarring can leave lasting damage necessitating a permanent tracheostomy.

3. **N – Thyroid carcinoma**
    This patient has findings consistent with anaplastic carcinoma of the thyroid. Whilst this is one of the less common thyroid malignancies it has a uniformly terrible prognosis because of direct invasion of vital neck structures such as the airway, as in this case. A palliative tracheostomy may relieve symptoms and temporarily prolong life.

4. **A – Acute epiglottitis**
    The rapid onset of the stridor and the high temperature give the clue to the diagnosis. The infecting organism is *Haemophilus influenzae* B, which responds to broad-spectrum antibiotics. If there is any but the mildest degree of stridor, the child must be taken to the operating theatre and anaesthetised on the operating table with a surgeon scrubbed up and the instruments opened so that tracheostomy or cricithyroidotomy can be performed in the event of the anaesthetist being unable to intubate. In this condition the epiglottis is red and swollen and protrudes above the tongue (the rising sun sign). Patients must *never* be examined to see this as to do so may precipitate complete respiratory obstruction. With immunisation, such infections are becoming rarer. The differential diagnosis is acute laryngo-tracheo-bronchitis, and in the third world with an unimmunised population, diphtheria.

5. **J – Inhalation or ingestion of irritants**
    In this case the patient has smoke inhalation with burns to the upper airway. The supraglottic airway is extremely susceptible to obstruction as a result of exposure to heat. When a patient is admitted to hospital after burn injury, the doctor should be alert to the possibility of airway involvement. Clinical indications of inhalation injury include facial burns, singeing of the nasal hairs, carbon deposits in the oropharynx, carbonaceous sputum, hoarseness and a carboxyhaemoglobin level > 10%. The symptom of stridor is an indication for immediate orotracheal intubation. A similar pattern of airway obstruction can be caused by ingestion of corrosives, such as strong acids and alkalis.

9. GYNAECOLOGICAL PROCEDURES

1. **B – Colposcopy**
   A cervical smear result with either moderate or severe dyskaryosis (high-grade smear) is an initial indication for colposcopy. This allows colposcopic assessment of the cervix to see if this agrees with the cytological diagnosis. It is common for punch biopsy to be performed to further gain histological diagnosis (e.g. CIN 1, 2 and 3). It is usually on the basis of histological proof of high-grade CIN or persistent low-grade CIN that LLETZ is performed (though more rarely see and treat LLETZ may be performed).

2. **C – Colposuspension**
   The two commonest causes of stress incontinence are GSI and detrusor overactivity. GSI is diagnosed on UDS when there is demonstrable stress incontinence without aberrant detrusor activity. It must always be performed before any bladder neck surgery. The only procedures that may be helpful from the list are anterior vaginal repair and colposuspension. Anterior vaginal repair only has a small effect on stress incontinence and is mainly used when there are symptoms predominantly of prolapse (cystocele). Therefore when the main complaint is incontinence, colposuspension is still a widely used and highly effective treatment for GSI.

3. **E – Hysteroscopy**
   Abnormal PV bleeding over 40 years of age needs to be investigated as the risks of endometrial pathology (polyp, hyperplasia and carcinoma) increase with age. IMB and PCB can be suggestive of cervical pathology. Their absence and a recent, normal cervical smear and a normal cervix on examination usually rule out the need for colposcopy. Endometrial ablation and hysterectomy may ultimately be required if conservative medical therapy fails but the next logical procedure is diagnostic hysteroscopy (with curettage) to assess the endometrial cavity. Serosal fibroids are not implicated in menorrhagia because they do not affect the size of the cavity unlike submucosal fibroids and are therefore best left alone.

4. **F – Laparoscopy**
   The symptoms and signs are highly suggestive of endometriosis and it is good practice to try empirical treatment in these cases. Up to 80% improve with medical treatment. When there has been no improvement after treatment, either the endometriosis is resistant to medical suppression or the diagnosis is wrong: e.g. PID, adhesions or ovarian pathology. Therefore diagnostic laparoscopy is indicated to assess for pelvic pathology and obtain a diagnosis – it may also be therapeutic, e.g. adhesiolysis performed at the same time. A form of hysterectomy may ultimately be a treatment for endometriosis but this is not indicated at this stage (usually last resort).

5. **A – Anterior vaginal repair**

Prolapse of the pelvis can be divide into anterior compartment prolapse (bladder into vagina – cystocele), middle compartment prolapse (uterus into vagina) and posterior compartment prolapse (bowel or rectum into vagina – entero or rectocele). The appropriate surgery is usually anterior vaginal repair, vaginal hysterectomy or posterior vaginal repair respectively. Mild urinary symptoms are extremely common post-menopause and are often exacerbated by anterior prolapse. The appropriate operation here is an anterior vaginal repair to restore the bladder to its anatomical position. It is often performed with vaginal hysterectomy as multiple compartment defects are common, but in this case there is no clinical evidence of other defects.

10. DISORDERS LEADING TO ABNORMAL COAGULATION

1. **D – Haemophilia A**
    Haemophilia A is an X-linked inherited coagulation disorder with a prevalence of about 1 in 5000 of the male population. Patients with haemophilia A have reduced levels of factor VIII:C in the blood, resulting in abnormal coagulation and excessive bleeding. The extent of the bleeding depends on how severe the reduction in factor VIII:C is, the most severe disease occurring with levels of less than 1% of normal. Factor VIII is involved in the intrinsic coagulation pathway, the integrity of which is tested by measurement of the APTT time. In haemophiliacs, the reduction in factor VIII results in disruption of the intrinsic coagulation pathway and the APTT time is therefore prolonged. The PT ratio, which measures the integrity of the extrinsic pathway, and the bleeding time, which tests the ability of platelets to aggregate and form a platelet plug, are unaffected in haemophilia.

2. **I – Vitamin K deficiency**
    Vitamin K is a fat-soluble vitamin that is essential for the production of clotting factors II, VII, IX and X. Factor VII is involved in the extrinsic pathway, factor IX in the intrinsic pathway and factors II and VII in the final common pathway. Consequently, both the intrinsic and extrinsic pathways are defective in patients with vitamin K deficiency and the PT ratio and APTT time are both prolonged. The bleeding time is not affected as platelet numbers and function are normal. Vitamin K deficiency occurs as a result of inadequate stores, such as in haemorrhagic disease of the newborn, and secondary to fat malabsorption, such as in bile duct obstruction. Oral anticoagulant drugs are vitamin K antagonists.

3. **J – von Willebrand's disease**
    von Willebrand's disease is due to a deficiency or abnormality of von Willebrand factor. This factor plays a role in adhesion of platelets to damaged subendothelium as well as stabilising factor VIII:C in plasma. Consequently, in von Willebrand's disease there is defective platelet function (even though platelet numbers are normal) coupled with rapid destruction of factor VIII:C, leading to factor VIII:C deficiency. The laboratory test profile is therefore similar to that of haemophilia A (namely prolonged APTT time and normal PT ratio), together with evidence of abnormal platelet aggregation, namely prolonged bleeding time. Von Willebrand's disease has been classified into three types with different clinical features and inheritance pattern.

4. **B – Disseminated intravascular coagulation (DIC)**

    In disseminated intravascular coagulation (DIC) there is widespread activation of coagulation by release of procoagulant material and by generalised platelet aggregation or diffuse endothelial damage. This leads to consumption of platelets and coagulation factors and secondary activation of fibrinolysis with production of fibrin degradation products. The clinical consequence of this sequence of events is initial thrombosis followed by widespread bleeding. The bleeding time, PT ratio and APTT time are all prolonged while the levels of clotting factors and the platelet count are reduced. Causes of DIC include septicaemia, haemolytic transfusion reactions, severe trauma, burns, liver disease and obstetric conditions such as placental abruption.

5. **E – Haemophilia B**

    Haemophilia B, also known as Christmas disease, is caused by deficiency in factor IX. The inheritance and clinical features are similar to those of haemophilia A but the incidence is much lower. Not surprisingly, patients with haemophilia B have low levels of factor IX and normal levels of factor VIII:C. In all other aspects, the laboratory test profile of the two diseases is identical.

11. ANATOMY OF THE FEMORAL REGION

1. **C – Femoral nerve**
    The femoral vein lies medial to the artery and these vessels lie within the femoral sheath, formed by the pelvic fascia posteriorly and the transversalis fascia anteriorly, and passing into the thigh deep to the inguinal ligament. The femoral nerve is outside of the sheath.

2. **I – Reflected pectineal part of the inguinal ligament**
    The reflected part of the inguinal ligament passing onto the superior pubic ramus is a medial relationship of the canal, the femoral vein being the lateral relation. The femoral canal lies within the femoral sheath together with the femoral vessels.

3. **G – Pectineal (Cooper's) ligament**
    The ligament passes along the superior pubic ramus. Although of no anatomical note, the pectineal ligament is useful surgically to stitch into in femoral hernia repairs. The anterior relation of the neck is the inguinal ligament.

4. **J – Saphenous opening**
    The femoral canal passes from its neck over the pectineal ligament and pectineus muscle, to the saphenous opening. Femoral hernias emerging at this site are directed proximally over the inguinal ligament, since the superficial fascia is attached to the lower margin of the saphenous opening.

5. **H – Pubic tubercle**
    The pubic tubercle is an important surface marking since it gives attachment to the medial end of the inguinal ligament. The saphenous opening is 1 cm lateral and 3 cm below this point and overlain by the groin crease (exposure of the saphenous opening for venous surgery is in the crease). The superficial inguinal ring is above and medial to the pubic tubercle. This anatomy, although clearly demonstrable in thin people, can be more difficult in the obese, and consequently also the differentiation of femoral and inguinal hernias.

12. MUSCLE ATTACHMENTS OF THE LOWER LIMB

1. **E – Iliopsoas**
   The psoas major arises from the intervertebral discs of the lumbar vertebrae, the adjacent vertebrae and their transverse processes, and fibrous arches crossing over the lumbar vertebral bodies. The iliacus is attached to the upper two-thirds of the iliac fossa and both muscles converge to pass underneath the inguinal ligament and are attached to the lesser trochanter and the adjacent femoral shaft below it.

2. **A, B & J – Adductor longus, Adductor magnus and Vastus lateralis**
   The adductor muscles are attached proximally to inferior pubic ramus, the adductor magnus gaining an additional attachment with the hamstring muscles to the ischial tuberosity. The vastus lateralis arises by an aponeurosis from the lateral side of the greater trochanter and the gluteal tuberosity, as well as the lateral lip of the linea aspera. It joins the rectus femoris, vastus medialis and vastus intermedius to form the quadriceps muscle. These four portions are attached to the upper border and sides of the patella, forming a single musculo-tendinous expansion. From the apex of the patella, a strong tendon descends to attach to the tibial tubercle.

3. **D – Gastrocnemius**
   This is the attachment of the lateral head, the medial head has an equivalent attachment on the corresponding femoral condyle. The muscle is the most superficial in the calf. It descends to join the tendon of the soleus in the mid-calf, forming the tendo calcaneus; this is attached to the middle of the posterior surface of the calcaneus.

4. **F – Peroneus longus**
   The tendon descends behind the lateral malleolus, separated from it by the tendon of peroneus brevis. They cross the lateral surface of the calcaneus separated by the peroneal tubercle. The peroneus longus gains attachment to the sides of the base of the 1st metatarsal and adjacent area on the medial cuneiform bone. The peroneus brevis is attached to the tuberosity on the base of the 5th metatarsal.

5. **I – Tibialis posterior**
   The upper attachment is to the posterior surface of the interosseous membrane and adjoining surfaces of the tibia and fibula. The tendon passes deep to that of the flexor digitorum longus, grooving the back of the medial malleolus before passing under the flexor retinaculum. In the sole, it is attached to the tuberosity of the navicular, and also all other tarsal bones except the talus.

PAPER 8

Paper 8 questions

1. THEME: HYPONATRAEMIA

A   Addison's disease
B   Bendrofluazide
C   Bronchogenic carcinoma
D   Herpes encephalitis
E   Hypothyroidism
F   *Legionella* pneumonia
G   Meningococcal meningitis
H   Paroxetine
I   Pseudohyponatraemia
J   Subarachnoid haemorrhage

The following patients have all presented with hyponatraemia. Please choose the most appropriate cause from the above list. The items may be used once, more than once or not at all.

1. A 31-year-old woman is seen in the medical outpatient department following an admission with severe acute pancreatitis. She is a teetotaller. Examination whilst an inpatient revealed multiple eruptive xanthomata and despite her well-being on discharge her Na^+ is 127 mmol/l.

2. A 26-year-old man is admitted to hospital with a severe headache and photophobia. On examination he is looking unwell, pyrexial (37.4°C) but there are no rashes. A CT head scan is unremarkable other than showing raised intracranial pressure. The diagnosis is confirmed on EEG and polymerase chain reaction of his CSF.

3. A 32-year-old woman is admitted to hospital with confusion and a headache. On examination she is very agitated, GCS of 13/15 but there is no obvious meningism or photophobia. Respiratory examination reveals a mild expiratory wheeze and oxygen saturation of 87% on air. Routine blood tests show FBC: Hb 12.9 g/dl, MCV 87 fl, WCC 7.9 × 10^9/l (relative lymphopenia), Plt 322 × 10^9/l; U&Es: Na^+ 117 mmol/l, K^+ 3.9 mmol/l, urea 3.9 mmol/l, Cr 88 μmol/l.

4. A 71-year-old woman who has previously been treated for polymyalgia rheumatica presents in A&E with low blood pressure, decreased RBG and marked hyponatraemia. Her MSU is positive for nitrites and leukocytes. She improves with intravenous dextrose, cefuroxime, gentamicin and hydrocortisone.

5. An 82-year-old woman with vitiligo is admitted to A&E with confusion having been found on the floor by neighbours. On examination she is described as 'pudgy and overweight', her temperature is 34.3°C and she is bradycardic. Her ECG confirms sinus bradycardia with prominent J waves. Routine blood tests reveal Hb 11.7 g/dl, MCV 103 fl, WCC 13.9 × 10^9/l, Plt 199 × 10^9/l; U&Es: Na$^+$ 125 mmol/l, K$^+$ 3.7 mmol/l, urea 12.9 mmol/l, Cr 133 µmol/l.

2. THEME: SHORTNESS OF BREATH

A   Asbestosis
B   Asthma
C   Atypical pneumonia
D   COPD
E   Fibrosing alveolitis
F   Histiocytosis
G   Pulmonary embolism
H   Sarcoidosis
I   Streptococcal pneumonia
J   Wegener's granulomatosis

The following patients have all presented with shortness of breath. Please choose the most appropriate cause from the above list. The items may be used once, more than once not at all.

1. A 49-year-old woman with known rheumatoid arthritis presents to her GP with a 3-month history of increasing exertional dyspnoea. On examination she has several signs of chronic rheumatoid arthritis and on respiratory examination has fine bibasal inspiratory crepitations.

2. A 61-year-old man who has previously been fit and well is admitted to hospital with a 36-hour history of worsening shortness of breath. On examination he is confused and unwell. Examination of his chest reveals a mild expiratory wheeze but he is unable to co-operate with a peak flow rate. His chest radiograph is relatively unremarkable but his ABGs show marked type I respiratory failure.

3. A 68-year-old man who is still very active and running marathons has noticed increased wheeze and shortness of breath on training runs. On examination he is relatively well but his peak flow rate is only 300 l/min. (predicted 480 l/min). He is given some inhalers and steroids and returns 10 days later. He feels a lot better and peak flow rate = 500 l/min.

4. A 71-year-old woman who was recently diagnosed as having carcinoma of the breast is admitted to hospital with acute onset of shortness of breath. On examination she is tachypnoeic, tachycardic and has oxygen saturation of 86% (on air). Her chest radiograph is unremarkable.

5. A 29-year-old Afro-Caribbean woman is seen by her GP with increasing shortness of breath on exercise. The GP notes a painful lesion over her anterior shin. Chest radiograph reveals bilateral hilar lymphadenopathy and pulmonary infiltrates.

3. THEME: HEPATOMEGALY

A   Alcoholic hepatitis
B   Amyloidosis
C   Autoimmune hepatitis
D   Haemochromatosis
E   HAV infection
F   HBV infection
G   Multiple metastases
H   Polycystic kidney disease
I   Primary biliary cirrhosis
J   Sarcoidosis

The following patients have all presented with hepatomegaly. Please choose the most appropriate cause from the above list. The items may be used once, more than once or not at all.

1. A 29-year-old woman whose grandmother died suddenly of 'stroke' presents in A&E with confusion. On examination she is unwell and hypertensive, with a blood pressure of 210/120 but cardiovascular and respiratory examinations are otherwise unremarkable. Abdominal examination reveals 5 cm hepatomegaly and bilateral ballotable kidneys. Her U&Es: Na$^+$ 129 mmol/l, K$^+$ 6.9 mmol/l, urea 31.2 mmol/l, Cr 729 μmol/l.

2. A 24-year-old man returns from Cambodia with acute jaundice. In the last 2 weeks he is feverish with diarrhoea and vomiting. On examination he is clinically icteric, and has tender 4 cm hepatomegaly below the costal margin. FBC: Hb 13.2 g/dl, MCV 86 fl, WCC 4.1 × 10^9/l (lymphocytes 2.3 × 10^9/l), Plt 349 × 10^9/l; LFTs: TBil 52 μmol/l, AST 397 iu/l, ALT 298 iu/l, Alk phos 296 iu/l, Alb 31 g/l, INR 1.3. Serological tests confirm an RNA virus.

3. A 58-year-old man with known alcohol problems presents to his GP with lethargy and malaise. On examination he looks 'sun-tanned', BM stix reading of 16.4 mol/l, and he has spider naevi, Dupytren's contracture and gynaecomastia. He has 5 cm hepatomegaly below the right costal margin and possible ascites.

4. A 67-year-old man presents to his GP with weight loss and constipation. On examination he is cachectic and abdominal examination reveals 6 cm hepatomegaly and a left upper quadrant mass. An ultrasound scan of the abdomen reveals several hyperechogenic areas in the right lobe of the liver.

5. A 48-year-old woman presents to her GP with a 1-year history of pruritis now associated with increasing jaundice. On examination she is icteric and has 3 cm hepatomegaly. Blood tests reveal anti-smooth muscle antibodies.

4. THEME: PUPILLARY DEFECTS

A Afferent pupillary defect
B Argyll–Robertson pupil
C Cataract
D Fixed, dilated pupil
E Fixed, dilated pupils
F Holmes–Adie pupil
G Horner's syndrome
H Iridectomy
I Opiate narcosis
J Pinpoint pupils

The following patients have all presented with pupillary defects. Please choose the most appropriate cause from the above list. The items may be used once, more than once or not at all.

1. A 79-year-old woman with metastatic carcinoma is brought in by ambulance to A&E with a decreased level of consciousness. She has recently been converted to MST from regular oramorph but her husband has continued to give her the oramorph. She recovers a little with an intravenous dose of naloxone.

2. A 19-year-old student is seen for a routine medical on attending her new medical school. The doctor notices her left pupil is larger than the right and is very slow to react to light. She also finds it difficult to elicit tendon reflexes on the left.

3. A 69-year-old man is admitted to hospital with acute on chronic confusion due to a chest infection. Neurological examination shows an irregular small pupil on the right. A CT head scan shows atrophy but no focal abnormality. A CSF screen for treponemal disease is positive.

4. A 49-year-old man with hypertension and diabetes mellitus presents in A&E with a sudden severe headache associated with 'closure' of his right eye. A subsequent MRI and angiogram shows a ruptured posterior communicating artery aneurysm, which is repaired neurosurgically.

5. A 61-year-old 'heavy smoker' presents to his GP with a 3-month history of weight loss, haemoptysis and a hoarse voice. More recently he has noticed his left eye looks 'closed'.

5. THEME: AUTOANTIBODIES

A   ACh receptor antibody
B   cANCA
C   Endomysial antibody
D   GBM antibody
E   IF antibody
F   JO$_1$ antibody
G   LKM antibody
H   Mitochondrial antibody
I   pANCA
J   SCL-70 antibody

The following patients have all presented with disorders associated with characteristic autoantibodies. Please choose the most appropriate autoantibody from the above list. The items may be used once, more than once, in combination or not at all.

1. A 64-year-old woman with known well-controlled Grave's disease presents to her GP with a three month history of increasing lethargy. On examination she is clinically euthyroid but looks pale. Routine blood tests confirm euthyroid, FBC: Hb 6.1 g/dl, MCV 114 fl, WCC 3.3 × 10^9/l, Plt 104 × 10^9. The blood film shows hypersegmented neutrophils.

2. A 17-year-old woman presents to her GP with a 3-month history of steatorrhoea, weight loss and lethargy. On examination she is thin with a BMI of 17, examination is otherwise unremarkable. Investigations confirm FBC: Hb 8.7 g/dl, MCV 104 fl, WCC 4.9 × 10^{9}l, Plt 293 × 10^{9}l; U&Es/TFTs/LFTs are all normal.

3. A 42-year-old woman presents to her GP with worsening pruritis, malaise and recent onset of jaundice. On examination she is noted to have early Dupytren's contracture, spider naevi and 2–3 cm hepatomegaly. Later investigations confirm a diagnosis of PBC.

4. A 73-year-old man presents to his GP with increasing weakness around the upper and lower limbs. Examination reveals proximal muscle weakness associated with a heliotrope rash. Routine investigations reveal ESR 92 mm/h, CK 21, 000 iu/l and the diagnosis is confirmed on EMG. Chest radiograph reveals a large left apical mass.

5. A 64-year-old man with known carcinoma of the lung presents to his GP with a 3-week history of increasing weakness of his upper and lower limbs and intermittent dysphagia to solids and liquids. On examination there is demonstrated 'fatiguability' but this slowly improves. Diagnosis is confirmed on EMG.

6. THEME: THE ACUTE ABDOMEN

A   Acute (severe) pancreatitis
B   Biliary peritonitis
C   Perforated appendix
D   Perforated caecum
E   Perforated duodenal ulcer
F   Perforated sigmoid disease
G   Perforated small intestine
H   Primary bacterial peritonitis
I   Ruptured abdominal aortic aneurysm
J   Superior mesenteric artery occlusion
K   Urinary peritonitis

The following are descriptions of patients with an acute abdomen. Please select the most appropriate diagnosis from the above list. The items may be used once, more than once or not at all.

1. A 62-year-old man presents with an 8-hour history of increasing upper abdominal pain radiating to the back and associated with nausea and vomiting. On examination he is dehydrated and clinically jaundiced and has widespread tenderness and guarding.

2. A 72-year-old woman with rheumatoid arthritis presents with a rapid onset of severe abdominal pain initially localised to the epigastrium but now present all over the abdomen. There is associated nausea and vomiting and a 4-week preceding history of dyspepsia. On examination she has a rigid abdomen.

3. A 66-year-old woman with a long history of constipation and left iliac fossa pain presents with a 2-day history of increasingly severe left iliac fossa pain associated with nausea and vomiting. On examination there is widespread peritonism, maximal in the left iliac fossa.

4. An 83-year-old woman presents with a 48-hour history of colicky abdominal pain, distension and absolute constipation. She is admitted and has further investigation with a gastrograffin enema. During the night you are called to the ward to find the patient moribund with a rigid abdomen.

5. An 81-year-old man is brought to A&E by ambulance having woken with severe abdominal and back pain associated with collapse. On examination he has a reduced level of consciousness and a distended abdomen. Pulse is 130 bpm, blood pressure = 82/52.

7. THEME: HEMISCROTAL PAIN

A   Acute epididymo-orchitis
B   Haematocele
C   Strangulated inguinoscrotal hernia
D   TB orchitis
E   Testicular seminoma
F   Testicular teratoma
G   Testicular torsion
H   Torsion of an epidymal cyst
I   Torsion of hydatid of Morgagni
J   Varicocele

The following are descriptions of patients with hemiscrotal pain. Please select the most appropriate diagnosis from the above list. The items may be used once, more than once or not at all.

1. A 9-year-old boy presents with sudden onset of severe right scrotal pain and nausea. On examination, the right testis is swollen and lying higher than the left side. Examination reveals the right scrotum to be hot, erythematous and very tender, preventing detailed palpation of the scrotal contents.

2. A 25-year-old man is seen in A&E with a 24-hour history of severe right scrotal pain and swelling. Direct questioning reveals some frequency of micturition and dysuria for several days. On examination he is febrile (38.6°C) and the right hemiscrotum is swollen and tender, the overlying skin being red and hot. Urine dipstix: leucocytes + + +, nitrite +; WCC $14.8 \times 10^9/l$.

3. A 30-year-old man complains of a history of dull left-sided scrotal ache, present for several months. On examination both testes are normal, however the left hemiscrotum appears larger than the right with a soft compressible swelling that feels like a bag of worms, only evident on standing.

4. A 42-year-old man undergoes a routine vasectomy having completed his family. The operation is performed as an inpatient because he has a prosthetic heart valve. The following day you are called to the ward because the patient has woken with left-sided scrotal pain and swelling. On examination the testis is impalpable in an enlarged, tender left hemiscrotum which does not transilluminate.

5. A 33-year-old man presents to his GP with swelling of his left hemiscrotum. He had experienced some dull aching in the scrotum and had been feeling generally unwell for several weeks. The left testis is slightly enlarged and feels hard and irregular in shape. Blood tests show raised βHCG, but normal α fetoprotein (AFP).

8. THEME: SKIN ULCERATION

A   Anthrax
B   Basal cell carcinoma
C   Chancrous ulcer
D   Gummatous ulcer
E   Ischaemic ulcer
F   Marjolin's ulcer
G   Neuropathic ulcer
H   Pyoderma gangrenosum
I   Squamous cell carcinoma
J   Tuberculous ulcer
K   Venous ulcer

The following are descriptions of patients with ulcers. Please select the most appropriate diagnosis from the above list. The items may be used once, more than once or not at all.

1. A 42-year-old man presents 3 weeks after unprotected intercourse with a shallow, indurated, painless, round ulcer on his penis. The ulcer has a raised hyperaemic edge and there is associated shotty inguinal lymphadenopathy.

2. An 80-year-old man presents with a 0.5 cm ovoid ulcer with a central scab and a rolled edge on the inner canthus of the right eye. He thinks that it has been present some years causing only itching and very slight occasional bleeding.

3. A 66-year-old retired Royal Marine with a large scar from a burn sustained in the war in Oman presents with a painless 3 cm area of irregular ulceration within the region of scarring. It is surrounded by a raised edge and has a bloodstained discharge from the base. There is no regional lymphadenopathy.

4. A 58-year-old woman is referred by her GP with an 'extensive' enlarging ulcer above the medial malleolus of the left leg which has now become infected. On examination there is a 12 cm irregular shallow ulcer with a sloping edge and granulation tissue at the base with a seropurulent exudate. There is surrounding erythema, induration and pigmentation.

5. A 42-year-old farmer presents with toxaemia in A&E. A small ulcer with a black base and indurated edge is noticed on his forearm and there is axillary lymphadenopathy. He describes the ulcer starting as a small papule which then broke down to form the ulcer.

9. THEME: EARLY PREGNANCY

A   Anembryonic pregnancy (blighted ovum)
B   Complete miscarriage
C   Ectopic pregnancy
D   Hydatidiform mole (complete)
E   Hydatidiform mole (incomplete)
F   Incomplete miscarriage
G   Inevitable miscarriage
H   Missed (delayed) miscarriage
I   Septic miscarriage
J   Threatened miscarriage

From the above list please choose the item most likely to describe the clinical picture. The items may be used once, more than once, in combination or not at all.

1. A 28-year-old woman, gravida 1, para 0 (G1P0), has 6 weeks' amenorrhoea, moderate PV bleeding and lower abdominal cramps. Pregnancy test-positive. Examination reveals no abdominal or vaginal tenderness and the cervical os is closed. Transvaginal ultrasound scan (TVS) reveals a 20 × 20 mm area in the endometrial cavity suggestive of retained products of conception (RPOC).

2. A 28-year-old woman, gravida 1, para 0 (G1P0), has 6 weeks' amenorrhoea, mild PV bleeding and lower abdominal cramps. Pregnancy test-positive. Examination reveals mild lower abdominal tenderness and also mild tenderness on vaginal examination but the cervical os is closed with no excitation. TVS reveals an empty uterus and free fluid in the rectovaginal pouch. Over the next 48 hours her βHCG levels go from 1200 iu to 1370 iu.

3. A 28-year-old woman, gravida 1, para 0 (G1P0), has 6 weeks' amenorrhoea, moderate PV bleeding and lower abdominal cramps. Pregnancy test-positive. Examination reveals no abdominal or vaginal tenderness and the cervical os is closed. Transvaginal US (TVS) reveals an empty uterus and no free fluid in the rectovaginal pouch. Over the next 10 days her pregnancy test becomes negative.

4. A 28-year-old woman, gravida 1, para 0 (G1P0), has 7 weeks' amenorrhoea, mild PV bleeding and mild lower abdominal cramps. Pregnancy test-positive. Examination reveals no abdominal or vaginal tenderness and the cervical os is closed. TVS reveals an IUP with a measurement (crown–rump length) equivalent to 6 weeks. There is no fetal heart activity. There is no free fluid in the rectovaginal pouch.

5. A 28-year-old woman, gravida 1, para 0 (G1P0), has 7 weeks' amenorrhoea, mild PV bleeding and mild lower abdominal cramps. Pregnancy test-positive. Examination reveals no abdominal or vaginal tenderness but the uterus feels about 12/40 gestation and the cervical os is closed. TVS reveals a large volume of cystic spaces in the endometrial cavity and no fetal pole.

10. THEME: DISEASES OF THE HEART

A   Atrial myxoma
B   Congestive cardiomyopathy
C   Constrictive pericarditis
D   Cor pulmonale
E   Fibrinous pericarditis
F   Hypertrophic cardiomyopathy
G   Infective endocarditis
H   Mitral valve stenosis
I   Myocarditis
J   Ventricular aneurysm

From the above list, please select the disease that each of the following patients is most likely to have. The items may be used once, more than once or not at all.

1. Three days after an anterior myocardial infarct, a 63-year-old man develops a sharp chest pain which is worse on movement and lying down. Auscultation reveals a pericardial rub and his ECG shows 'saddle shaped' ST segment elevation in several leads.

2. A 75-year-old woman with a long history of chronic obstructive airways disease develops pitting oedema of both ankles. On examination she has a palpable liver and moderate ascites. An echocardiogram shows right ventricular hypertrophy.

3. A 19-year-old youth collapses while playing football and cannot be resuscitated. He had no previous history of ischaemic heart disease, hypertension or valve abnormalities. At post mortem the heart weighs 800 g and shows marked left ventricular hypertrophy. The ventricular septum is particularly thick.

4. A 59-year-old man presents with a 1-week history of pyrexia, fatigue, night sweats and muscle pains. Four days before the onset of symptoms he had had a dental extraction and had forgotten to tell the dentist about his past history of rheumatic fever. On examination his temperature is 38.5°C and he has a diastolic murmur. Blood cultures grow *Streptococcus viridans*.

5. A 65-year-old woman suffers a large anteroseptal myocardial infarct. Six months later she presents in acute left ventricular failure, her chest radiograph showing a left ventricular 'bulge'. Echocardiogram shows that the bulge expands during systole.

11. THEME: ANATOMY OF THE INGUINAL REGION

A Conjoint tendon
B Deep inguinal ring
C External oblique muscle
D Inferior epigastric vessels
E Inguinal ligament
F Internal oblique muscle
G Reflected pectineal part of the inguinal ligament
H Superficial inguinal ring
I Transversalis fascia
J Transversus abdominis muscle

For each of the following descriptions, please choose the most appropriate structure from the above list. The items may be used once, more than once or not at all.

1. Inferior relationship of the medial end of the inguinal canal.

2. The structure through which a direct inguinal hernia enters the inguinal canal.

3. The structure through which an indirect inguinal hernia enters the inguinal canal.

4. Superior relationship of the inguinal canal.

5. Medial relation of the neck of an indirect inguinal hernia.

12. THEME: VESSELS OF THE NECK

A   Common carotid artery
B   External jugular vein
C   Facial artery
D   Internal carotid artery
E   Internal jugular vein
F   Maxillary artery
G   Subclavian artery
H   Superficial temporal artery
I   Thoracic duct
J   Vertebral artery

For each of the following descriptions, please choose the most appropriate vessel from the above list. The items may be used once, more than once or not at all.

1. Lies adjacent to the transverse process of the 7th cervical vertebra.   □

2. Is a posterior relation of the opening between the sternal and clavicular heads of sternocleidomastoid muscle.   □

3. Grooves the upper surface of the 1st rib.   □

4. Is crossed from lateral to medial by the hypoglossal nerve.   □

5. Is palpable just above the zygomatic arch.   □

Paper 8 answers

1. HYPONATRAEMIA

1. **I – Pseudohyponatraemia**
   This patient has signs and symptoms consistent with hypertriglyceridaemia as evidenced by the recent pancreatitis and the eruptive xanthomata. Her hyponatraemia is in fact 'pseudohyponatraemia' due to the excess triglycerides.

2. **D – Herpes encephalitis**
   This young man has developed hyponatraemia secondary to raised intracranial pressure and secondary SIADH. All causes of raised intracranial pressure, atypical pneumonias, bronchogenic carcinoma, diffuse pulmonary fibrosis and TB may cause SIADH. The diagnosis is confirmed by paired serum and urinary osmolalities, which show a 'relatively concentrated urine in the presence of dilute serum'. SIADH can only be diagnosed in the presence of normal blood pressure, euvolaemia and euthyroidism.

3. **F – *Legionella* pneumonia**
   This patient has signs and symptoms of an atypical pneumonia, most likely *Legionella pneumophilia*. *Legionella* commonly causes a SIADH with marked hyponatraemia, exacerbating the associated confusion.

4. **A – Addison's disease**
   This patient has been on long-term steroids for polymyalgia rheumatica and this has led to secondary Addison's with hypotension, hypoglycaemia and hyponatraemia. Patients require hydrocortisone replacement, which initially should be given intravenously or intramuscularly.

5. **E – Hypothyroidism**
   This elderly woman has presented with hypothermia, bradycardia, a macrocytic anaemia and hyponatraemia. Her clinical appearance and these results suggest hypothyroidism. The hyponatraemia is thought to be due to a similar mechanism to SIADH although this is still unclear.

2. SHORTNESS OF BREATH

1. E – Fibrosing alveolitis

This woman has developed fibrosing alveolitis secondary to her rheumatoid arthritis. This is a similar picture to idiopathic pulmonary fibrosis (IPF) and may also be associated with finger clubbing. Other respiratory or pulmonary manifestations of rheumatoid disease in the chest include pleuritic chest pain, exudative pleural effusions and intrapulmonary nodules.

2. C – Atypical pneumonia

This man has the signs, symptoms and investigations compatible with an atypical pneumonia. This group of pneumonias are atypical for four reasons; They have ATYPICAL:-

- **Presentation** and symptoms: Multi-system involvement and atypical respiratory findings including shortness of breath, dry cough and wheeze.
- **Signs**: Often respiratory findings are 'unimpressive', the chest is often clear but the patient looks unwell and is very dyspnoeic. The patient may also have multi-system signs, including confusion, drowsiness, jaundice and rashes.
- **Investigations**: The white cell count may be normal but have an abnormal differential. Atypicals can also cause SIADH and hyponatraemia, autoimmune haemolytic anaemia (AIHA), thrombocytopenia and hepatic jaundice. The chest radiograph is often unremarkable but may have diffuse alveolar shadowing resembling pulmonary oedema. The ABGs typically show type I respiratory failure. The atypical organisms are difficult to culture in the laboratory and antibody titres are often necessary. A new urinary *Legionella* antigen test is also being used.
- **Antibiotics**: Atypicals should be treated with high dose erythromycin or clarithromycin, rifampicin or a tetracycline.

3. B – Asthma

This man has probable exercise-induced asthma. He is unlikely to be a smoker (as he is a marathon runner) but others in his household may smoke. He should be advised to use a prophylactic β_2 agonist before exercising but may require regular inhaled steroids if symptoms worsen or persist.

4. G – Pulmonary embolism

This patient has developed a pulmonary embolism on a background of carcinoma of the breast. Malignancy increases the risk of thromboembolic events and any middle-aged to older patient presenting with an unexplained deep vein thrombosis or pulmonary embolism needs investigation, including PSA (male), LFTs and CCa^{2+}, chest radiograph, mammogram (female) and ultrasound of the pelvis and hepatobiliary tree. This patient requires confirmation of the diagnosis by V/Q scan or spiral CT and angiography (CTPA), and long-term treatment with warfarin.

5. **H – Sarcoidosis**

This patient has developed pulmonary sarcoidosis and associated erythema nodosum. The chest radiographic findings are divided into:

Stage	(0)	No changes
	(1)	Bilateral hilar lymphadenopathy (BHL)
	(2)	BHL plus mid-zone changes/infiltrates
	(3)	Diffuse pulmonary infiltrates

All patients require specialist review and some with progressive disease need steroids (with bone-sparing agents) and occasionally immunosuppression.

3. HEPATOMEGALY

1. I – Polycystic kidney disease

This woman has signs of adult polycystic kidney disease leading to renal failure and secondary polycystic enlargement of the liver. Adult polycystic kidney disease can cause cystic changes and enlargement within all of the major intra-abdominal organs including liver, spleen, pancreas and ovaries. Her grand-mother probably died of a ruptured Berry aneurysm causing a fatal subarachnoid haemorrhage.

2. E – HAV infection

This young man has developed an acute hepatitic jaundice secondary to an acute hepatitis A virus (HAV) infection. HAV is a RNA virus and causes an acute jaundice following a 'flu-like illness. This is usually a self-limiting condition. In rarer cases it can cause fulminant liver failure requiring liver transplantation. It is spread by the faecal–oral route and is endemic in areas of poverty and poor water hygiene.

3. D – Haemochromatosis

This man has signs consistent with haemochromatosis as evidenced by his 'suntan' which is due to melanin deposition within the skin, hyperglycaemia secondary to pancreatic infiltration and chronic liver disease as evidenced by the spider naevi, Dupuytren's contracture and gynaecomastia. Haemochromatosis is associated with chronic alcohol excess in 15–20% of cases but alcohol is not suggested as the primary cause. The diagnosis maybe confirmed by a markedly elevated serum ferritin and liver biopsy (if required).

4. G – Multiple metastases

This man has a probable carcinoma of the colon with secondary deposits in the liver. Depending on his general health and wishes he may require surgical, oncological and/or palliative care intervention.

5. J – Primary biliary cirrhosis

This middle-aged woman has developed primary biliary cirrhosis (PBC) which is classically defined by the anti-mitochondrial antibody (AMA) but may also be associated with an anti-smooth muscle antibody (ASmA), more characteristic of autoimmune hepatitis.

4. PUPILLARY DEFECTS

1. J – Pinpoint pupils
This patient is receiving oramorph (morphine elixir) and MST (morphine sulphate tablets) which has led to opiate narcosis. Patient may present with drowsiness, unconsciousness, pinpoint pupils, shallow breathing or even respiratory arrest. With large accidental overdoses the patients may require an intravenous infusion of naloxone or even ventilation until the effects have worn off. Pinpoint pupils and unconsciousness may also be seen in brainstem strokes.

2. F – Holmes–Adie pupil
This patient has a 'Holmes–Adie' pupil. This is a benign, idiopathic disorder in which the pupillary reflexes and ipsilateral tendon reflexes are slow and sluggish. The pupil is mid-dilated and reacts slowly to direct light.

3. B – Argyll–Robertson pupil
This man has an Argyll–Robertson pupil due to neurosyphilis. His CSF confirms treponemal disease and he should receive a course of penicillin. The small, irregular Argyll–Robertson pupil may be uni- or bi- and is now relatively rare. It may also rarely occur in diabetes mellitus.

4. D – Fixed dilated pupil
This patient has developed an acute painful third nerve palsy associated with the rupture of a posterior communicating artery aneurysm. The patient has a ptosis associated with a fixed, dilated pupil which looks 'down and out' due to the unopposed actions of the superior oblique and abductor muscles supplied by the IVth and VIth nerves respectively.

5. G – Horner's syndrome
This patient has developed a left-sided Horner's syndrome associated with a left-sided apical lung cancer. Horner's syndrome is due to an interruption of the sympathetic nerve supply to the pupil anywhere from the hypothalamus, down through the brainstem and cervical cord, as it emerges at T1 and up through the neck, synapsing within the superior cervical ganglion and onto the eye. Horner's syndrome is the association of pupillary constriction (miosis), partial ptosis ± enophthalmos. There may also be unilateral loss of sweating (anhidrosis), which is complete in central nervous causes, partial in precervical ganglionic causes and absent in postcervical ganglionic causes.

5. AUTOANTIBODIES

1. D – IF antibody
This patient has developed a macrocytic anaemia with associated pancytopenia and hypersegmented neutrophils. They all point to a diagnosis of pernicious anaemia where autoantibodies form against (i) intrinsic factor production and release from the gastric parietal cells, (ii) complex formation between the B12 molecule and intrinsic factor, and the complexes subsequent (iii) binding to receptors within the ileum. Pernicious anaemia is commonly associated with other autoimmune diseases including hypothyroidism.

2. C – Endomysial antibody
This young woman has developed coeliac disease, an autoimmune disorder of the upper GI tract. Autoantibodies in this condition include anti-gliadin and anti-reticulin and the more recently discovered anti-endomysial antibody, which is specific for the condition.

3. H – Mitochondrial antibody
This patient has developed primary biliary cirrhosis, an autoimmune condition of the liver primarily seen in middle aged women. There are several autoantibodies associated with the condition but the commonest anti-mitochondrial antibodies (AMA) are found in over 90% of patients. Seven agenic components within the mitrochondria have now been identified as precipitants of the autoimmune reaction. Anti-smooth muscle antibodies (ASmA) are also found in this condition although these are more commonly seen in autoimmune hepatitis.

4. F – JO$_1$ antibody
This man has developed a myositis as evidenced by the limb weakness and associated dramatic elevation of CK. He has a characteristic heliotrope rash around the eyes suggesting a diagnosis of dermatomyositis, which in turn is characterised by the presence of anti-JO$_1$ antibody. In later life dermatomyositis has a significant association with bronchogenic and other cancers.

5. A – ACh receptor antibody
This man has developed Lambert–Eaton syndrome, a myasthenic syndrome, classically associated with small cell carcinoma of the lung. The auto-antibodies in this condition act **pre**-synaptically to block ACh release. In myasthenia gravis the antibodies act **post**-synaptically to block ACh binding, as well as causing down-regulation of the receptors and complement medicated lysis.

6. THE ACUTE ABDOMEN

The term acute abdomen describes a non-traumatic catastrophic event that affects any of the abdominal organs. The characteristic presenting feature is acute severe abdominal pain.

1. **A – Acute pancreatitis**
    This presentation is consistent with several of the diagnoses in the optons list. However, the presence also of jaundice pushes us towards a diagnosis of gall-stone pancreatitis, when in addition to the features of pancreatitis, there may also be features of biliary obstruction caused by a stone impacted at the ampulla of Vater. Treatment in such a case is intensive resuscitation and monitoring as for all cases of pancreatitis and also consideration of an urgent ERCP to remove the stone and thus prevent further disease exacerbation.

2. **E – Perforated duodenal ulcer**
    This is still one of the most common causes of peritonitis despite a huge drop in incidence as a result of the widespread use of H_2 blockers and PPIs. The diagnosis should be suggested in this case by the history of rheumatoid arthritis with the likely use of NSAIDs. Treatment is aggressive resuscitation and then surgery (oversew).

3. **F – Perforated sigmoid disease**
    This is a characteristic presentation of this complication of diverticular disease. The sigmoid colon is by far the most common site hence left iliac fossa pain. Perforation may be small and localised as a paracolic abscess or may lead to purulent or faecal peritonitis. The former may be drained radiologically but peritonitis requires emergency laparotomy and sigmoid colectomy (after appropriate resuscitation).

4. **D – Perforated caecum**
    In this patient, the presentation is with large bowel obstruction. The obstructing lesion is most commonly in the sigmoid or rectum (causes: carcinoma, diverticular disease, volvulus) but the site of maximal dilation is the caecum. When tension in the caecal wall occludes the blood supply, the wall may become gangrenous and eventually perforate leading to faecal peritonitis (and often death). It is for this reason that tenderness in the right iliac fossa in a patient with large bowel obstruction should prompt urgent surgery.

5. **I – Ruptured abdominal aortic aneurysm**
    This diagnosis should be strongly considered in a patient presenting with an acute abdomen and evidence of hypovolaemic shock. An expansile mass may not be palpable after leak or rupture because of haematoma formation.

7. HEMISCROTAL PAIN

1. **G – Testicular torsion**
   This is evidenced by the patient's age, the classic history and examination findings. The commonest age for torsion is 10–15 years (very rarely over 21 years). It is however sometimes difficult to distinguish a torsion from acute epididymo-orchitis in sexually active young males. Whilst the two can usually be clinically separated, surgical exploration is *mandatory* if there is any doubt over the diagnosis to prevent loss of the testis. NB Missed torsion is a recognised source of litigation.

2. **A – Acute epididymo-orchitis**
   Epididymo-orchitis is inflammation usually primarily of the epididymis, most commonly of bacterial aetiology. In younger men, it is usually secondary to sexually transmitted diseases such as *Chlamydia* or gonorrhoea (torsion must be excluded – see above); it also commonly occurs in an older age group when it is secondary to UTI with coliforms.

3. **J – Varicocele**
   This is a bunch of dilated and tortuous veins in the pampiniform plexus (i.e. varicose veins in the spermatic cord). It occurs more commonly on the left and when large causes an aching/dragging sensation in the scrotum.

4. **B – Haematocele**
   This is evidenced by the history of surgery (especially likely with warfarin therapy as would be employed for the prosthetic valve in this case) and examination findings. A haematocele is a collection of blood within the tunica vaginalis. Acute haematocele is a common accompaniment of scrotal trauma (e.g. surgical, football, fighting), however a secondary haematocele can also occur with infection and tumours of the testis. In either case it can be distinguished from hydrocele because it does not transilluminate. If left untreated, the resultant haematoma may form a hard, non-tender mass, which is clinically indistinguishable for a testicular tumour.

5. **E – Testicular seminoma**
   This is evidenced by the age of the patient, history and examination findings, and tumour markers. There are two common primary testicular tumours: teratoma and seminoma. Seminomas most commonly occur in 30–40 year-olds. In contrast, teratoma occurs in a younger age group (20–30 years). Both present as a painless swelling or lump in the testis which is palpable as a hard irregular mass in cases where a secondary hydrocele is absent (see above). AFP is produced by yolk-sac cellular elements and is raised in teratoma but not in seminoma. βHCG is secreted by trophoblastic cells and may be present in either tumour type.

8.   SKIN ULCERATION

Ulcers are correctly described (as in this question) in terms of their location, size, shape, edge, base and discharge; a point that should be remembered by the candidate faced with an ulcer as a short case. The other most favoured examiner's question is probably the definition: 'a discontinuation of an epithelial surface'.

1.   **C – Chancrous ulcer (syphilitic chancre)**
     The classic description, site and short duration after unprotected sex makes this a strong possibility. Classically termed a Hunterian chancre (presumably by first description rather than first-hand experience), this is the pathognomonic lesion of primary syphilis. The other ulcer in syphilis, a gummatous ulcer, occurs as a late manifestation of the infection at a site distant from that of sexual contact and as a result of a granulomatous hypersensitivity reaction.

2.   **B – Basal cell carcinoma**
     The characteristic history/ulcer description and classic site (95% are on the face) suggest this diagnosis. Whilst the lesion grows very slowly, and does not metastasize, if left deep erosion can occur – the so-called rodent ulcer. This is a favourite of pictorial textbooks for its macabre appearance, but is now fortunately quite rare.

3.   **F – Marjolin's ulcer**
     This is an eponym reserved for a squamous cell carcinoma (SCC) which arises in a long-standing area of inflammation or scarring: most commonly in practice a chronic venous ulcer or third-degree burn. Most of the features of an SCC are present although lymphadenopathy is absent since deep scars have no lymphatic drainage.

4.   **K – Venous ulcer**
     This is the commonest site (gaiter area) and typical description of this ulcer which is caused by deep venous insufficiency in the lower limb, usually as a result of previous DVT. In addition to lipodermatosclerosis (described) there may be other features of venous disease (e.g. varicose veins, other healed ulcers, limb swelling). Treatment is with graduated compression bandages/stockings (interestingly, a concept first described by Hippocrates).

5.   **A – Anthrax**
     Caused by the large Gram-positive aerobic spore-forming organism *Bacillus anthracis*, this is the description of cutaneous anthrax (the most common type). The organism is found in cattle and thus those affected are usually dairy or beef farmers, zoo-keepers, cowboys and buffalo hunters (although the latter two are rare in the UK!). Currently uncommon, it is hoped that in the light of terrorist threats this will not become a more topical subject!

9. EARLY PREGNANCY

1. F – Incomplete miscarriage
Moderate to heavy PV bleeding is suggestive of a form of definite miscarriage compared to mild PV bleeding which is more common with threatened miscarriage (PV bleeding before 24/40 with viable IUP) and ectopic pregnancy. Patient reporting of bleeding can however be misleading and is only a guide. No abdominal or vaginal tenderness makes sepsis or ectopic pregnancy less likely. RPOC on TVS tells us this was an intrauterine pregnancy and that, because products were left behind it is an incomplete miscarriage. This gives no indication of the underlying problem with the pregnancy and is purely a description of the stage of the miscarriage at presentation.

2. C – Ectopic pregnancy
All items from the list are possible given the clinical history, but unless it is a very early pregnancy both complete and incomplete miscarriages tend to have more than mild bleeding. The presence of both abdominal and vaginal tenderness makes sepsis or ectopic pregnancy more likely. Empty uteri on TVS with free fluid in the rectovaginal pouch means there may have been haemorrhage due to ectopic pregnancy. Slow rising βHCG is typical with ectopic pregnancy and if an IUP is present it is likely to be visible on TVS with βHCG > 1000 iu.

3. B – Complete miscarriage
Again, moderate to heavy PV bleeding is more suggestive of a form of definite miscarriage (as per Q1) and no abdominal or vaginal tenderness makes sepsis or ectopic pregnancy less likely. The closed cervical os tells us only that any form of miscarriage is not actively occuring at the time of examination. Empty uteri on TVS can be caused by very early IUP (too small), ectopic pregnancy and complete miscarriage. No free fluid in the rectovaginal pouch means there has at least been no haemorrhage due to ectopic pregnancy (less likely). Due to the history and the rapid disappearance of βHCG, a complete miscarriage is the diagnosis as there tends to be either slow fall, stasis or slow rise of βHCG with ectopic pregnancy.

4. H – Missed (delayed) miscarriage
This is by definition not an ectopic pregnancy. This is a non-viable embryo as fetal heart activity should be visible at 6 weeks. This is known as a delayed or missed miscarriage where there has been early embryonic demise. This describes the type of miscarriage rather than its stage of completion. This cannot be a threatened miscarriage (PV bleeding before 24/40 with *viable* IUP).

5. D – Hydatidiform mole (complete)
Large for dates in early pregnancy is usually due to wrong dates, multiple pregnancy and pelvic masses, e.g. fibroids or molar pregnancies. TVS descriptions of complete hydatidiform moles usually have large amounts of cystic spaces (hydropic chorionic villi), 'snowstorm' appearance and no evidence of a fetus. It is therefore most likely to be a complete mole as the TVS images are usually less striking with partial moles and may even show some normal features.

10. DISEASES OF THE HEART

1. **E – Fibrinous pericarditis**

    Fibrinous pericarditis occurs at about the second or third day after a transmural myocardial infarct as an inflammatory response to the necrotic heart muscle. It is usually localised to the area of infarction. Fibrin on the pericardial surfaces manifests clinically as acute onset of pain and fever. The 'rubbing together' of the inflamed visceral and parietal pericardia leads to a pericardial friction rub on auscultation, though this tends to disappear if a pericardial effusion develops. This type of pericarditis usually resolves spontaneously.

2. **D – Cor pulmonale**

    This patient has symptoms and signs of right-sided cardiac failure. Given her history, this is most likely to be due to pulmonary hypertension resulting from long-standing chronic obstructive pulmonary disease (COPD). The resultant right ventricular hypertrophy and/or right ventricular failure are known as cor pulmonale. Acute cor pulmonale is most often caused by pulmonary embolism while chronic cor pulmonale is due to any lung disease that results in pulmonary hypertension. In chronic cor pulmonale the right ventricle develops compensatory hypertrophy and progressively dilates. Ultimately, it is unable to maintain cardiac output at normal levels and when this occurs, symptoms and signs of right-sided congestive cardiac failure, such as dependent oedema, effusions and hepatomegaly, develop.

3. **F – Hypertrophic cardiomyopathy**

    Cardiomyopathy is a general term used to describe heart muscle disease of unknown origin. Hypertrophic cardiomyopathy (HCM), also known as asymmetric septal hypertrophy (ASH), is characterised by myocardial hypertrophy and disorganisation of myocytes on histology. The hypertophy is most pronounced in the left ventricle and interventricular septum, particularly in the area immediately beneath the aortic valve. The normal weight of a heart in an adult male is 300–400 g, so in this patient the weight of the heart is at least twice normal. Because the thick-walled ventricle is abnormally stiff, left ventricular filling (and therefore emptying) is impaired, compounded in about 30% of cases by outflow obstruction, Typical presenting features include chest pain, dyspnoea, syncope, arrhythmias and sudden death.

4. **G – Infective endocarditis**

Infective endocarditis is an infection of either the cardiac valves or the mural surface of the endocardium. It is usually the consequence of two factors: (i) abnormal endocardium, which facilitates bacterial adherence and growth; (ii) the presence of organisms in the bloodstream (bacteraemia). This patient has abnormal endocardium because of chronic rheumatic valvular disease and bacteraemia as a result of dental extraction. Most cases of infective endocarditis are caused by streptococci or staphylococci, though numerous other organisms have been implicated. *Streptococcus viridans* are a group of α-haemolytic streptococci that inhabit the mouth and are often associated with dental disease or procedures. The hallmark of infective endocarditis is the presence of large friable vegetations containing bacteria, fibrin and platelets on the affected cardiac valve. These not only cause destruction of the valve leaflets but can also fragment, resulting in embolic phenomena. Infective endocarditis typically presents, therefore, with features of chronic infection (such as fever and night sweats), valvular damage (such as 'crashing' acute regurgitation or cardiac failure) and emboli (such as stroke and splinter haemorrhages).

5. **J – Ventricular aneurysm**

Ventricular aneurysm is a late complication of transmural myocardial infarction. It results from replacement of the infarcted muscle by a thin layer of collagenous scar tissue that progressively stretches and bulges as the intraventricular pressure rises during systole. Complications of ventricular aneurysms include arrhythmias, left ventricular failure and mural thrombosis with systemic embolisation; rupture of the aneurysm itself is rare.

11. ANATOMY OF THE INGUINAL REGION

1. **G – Reflected pectineal part of the inguinal ligament**
   The inguinal ligament is the lower upturned edge of the external oblique muscle. It is an inferior relationship of the inguinal canal, and in the medial part of the canal the inguinal ligament is reflected backwards onto the superior pubic ramus. This part is also termed the lacunar ligament.

2. **I – Transversalis fascia**
   A direct inguinal hernia protrudes through a weakness in the posterior wall of the canal, beneath the conjoint tendon, and protrudes through the superficial inguinal ring alongside the spermatic cord.

3. **B – Deep inguinal ring**
   Indirect inguinal hernias pass within the spermatic cord through the deep ring, the canal and the superficial inguinal ring, and may follow the cord into the scrotum, whereas direct inguinal hernias passing through the superficial inguinal ring do not have a natural pathway to descend into the scrotum.

4. **F – Internal oblique muscle**
   The internal oblique muscle arises from the lateral two-thirds of the inguinal ligament lying initially anterior to the deep inguinal ring. It then arches over the inguinal canal and is joined by the aponeurotic fibres of the transversus abdominis muscle to form the conjoint tendon; this passes behind the medial end of the inguinal canal to the superior pubic ramus.

5. **D – Inferior epigastric vessels**
   A direct inguinal hernia emerges medial to the vessels through Hesselbach's triangle, the other two sides being the lateral border of the rectus abdominis muscle and, below, the inguinal ligament. Pressure over the deep inguinal ring (just above the midpoint of the inguinal ligament) controls a reduced indirect inguinal hernia but on coughing the direct inguinal hernia still bulges into the canal and out through the superficial inguinal ring.

12. VESSELS OF THE NECK

1. **J – Vertebral artery**
    The artery arises from the first part of the subclavian artery and passes adjacent to the 7th vertebra on its way to the vertebral arterial canal of the 6th and upper cervical transverse processes.

2. **E – Internal jugular vein**
    This is a valuable landmark for closed or open insertion of a central venous line.

3. **G – Subclavian artery**
    At this point the attachment of the scalenus anterior muscle separates it from the subclavian vein. The latter lies behind the clavicle and can be approached from above or below the bone for the insertion of venous access lines. The T1 nerve root lies posterior to the artery.

4. **D – Internal carotid artery**
    The hypoglossal nerve descends between the internal jugular vein and the internal carotid artery, before passing forwards over the internal and external carotid arteries and hyoglossus to innervate the tongue.

5. **H – Superficial temporal artery**
    The artery is palpable over the squamous temporal bone and is a useful and accessible monitor of the pulse in anaesthetised patients. It is also subject to temporal arteritis, an important diagnosis to make and to initiate treatment before the onset of visual complications.

PAPER 9

Paper 9 questions

1. THEME: LESIONS SEEN ON OPHTHALMOSCOPY

A A-V nipping
B Blot haemorrhage
C Dot haemorrhage
D Hard exudates
E Maculopathy
F Optic atrophy
G Papilloedema
H Retinitis
I Silver wiring
J Soft exudates

The following patients have all presented with lesions seen on ophthalmoscopy. Please match with the most appropriate findings from the above list. The items may be used once, more than once, in combination or not at all.

1. A 29-year-old man with poorly controlled type 1 diabetes mellitus is seen in diabetes outpatient clinic for his 6-monthly review. His latest HbA1c is 9.7%. His visual acuity is reduced two lines since his last visit and ophthalmoscopy shows severe pre-proliferative retinopathy with lesions particularly seen around the centre of the retina, temporal to the disc. He is referred urgently to the ophthalmologist.

2. A 64-year-old type 2 diabetes mellitus man is seen in the diabetic outpatient clinic for his annual review. His visual acuity is 6/12, which is the same as for the last 2 years but ophthalmology shows signs of background retinopathy.

3. A 49-year-old woman is seen in medical outpatient department with resistant high blood pressure. She is on lisinopril, nifedipine and atenolol but despite these medications her BP = 200/90, lying and standing. Ophthalmoscopy shows grade II hypertensive retinopathy.

4. A 47-year-old woman is admitted to A&E with a tonic–clonic seizure. On examination she has left-sided weakness grade 4/5 and equivocal plantar responses. A contrast-enhanced CT head scan shows a large right-sided space-occupying lesion with a mass effect to the left and associated oedema.

5. A 24-year-old homosexual man presents with severe diarrhoea which is later confirmed as cryptosporidiosis. He is also noted to have several violaceous lesions on his palate and chest. Three weeks later he is admitted with severe visual blurring and is seen to have 'cottage cheese and tomato ketchup' lesion of the left retina.

2. THEME: CHEST RADIOGRAPH FINDINGS

A   Bilateral hilar lymphadenopathy
B   Cardiomegaly
C   'Double' left heart border
D   Depression of the horizontal fissure
E   Elevation of the horizontal fissure
F   Loss of the hemidiaphragm
G   Obscuration of the right heart border
H   Pleural effusion
I   Tracheal deviation to the left
J   Tracheal deviation to the right

For each of the disorders below please list the possible radiological abnormalities from the above list. You may use the options once, more than once, in combination or not at all.

1. Chronic heart failure.

2. Left lower lobe collapse.

3. Right apical mass.

4. Right middle lobe pneumonia.

5. Right lower lobe collapse.

6. Sarcoidosis – stage 1.

7. Right-sided tension pneumothorax.

3. THEME: SPLENOMEGALY

A   Acute myeloid leukaemia
B   Chronic granulocytic leukaemia
C   Cytomegalovirus
D   Gaucher's disease
E   Hodgkin's lymphoma
F   Infective endocarditis
G   Malaria
H   Myelofibrosis
I   Thalassaemia
J   Visceral leishmaniasis

The following patients have all presented with splenomegaly. Please choose the most appropriate cause from the above list. The items may be used once, more than once, or not at all.

1. A 33-year-old woman is admitted to hospital with lethargy and a low grade pyrexia 6 weeks after having her wisdom teeth removed. On examination she is anaemic and has a temperature of 37.4°C. Cardiovascular examination reveals a pansystolic murmur heard primarily at the apex. She is also noted to have a 'tippable' spleen. Urinanalysis is positive for blood.

2. A 29-year-old diabetic woman with a recent renal transplant is admitted to hospital with a pyrexial illness, lethargy and respiratory distress. On examination she is unwell with a temperature 38°C and ophthalmoscopy reveals microvascular retinopathy with a 'cottage cheese and tomato ketchup' appearance in the the left retina. She is also noted to have 3 cm hepatomegaly and 2 cm splenomegaly below the costal margins.

3. A 51-year-old man is admitted to hospital with increasing lethargy and shortness of breath. On examination he is clinically anaemic, has a purpuric rash over his lower limbs and has 6–8 cm splenomegaly below the left costal margin. Blood tests reveal FBC: Hb 6.1 g/dl, MCV 82 fl, WCC 20.2 × 10^9/l (70% blasts), Plt 17 × 10^9/l.

4. A 23-year-old student presents to her GP with night sweats and non-tender lymphadenopathy. Of note she had a severe Epstein–Barr virus infection aged 14 years old. On examination she has generalized lymphadenopathy with associated 6cm splenomegaly. Routine investigations reveal FBC: Hb 8.7 g/dl, MCV 87 fl, WCC 22.9 × 10^9/l (marked eosinophilia), Plt 299 × 10^9/l; ESR 89 mm/h. A lymph node biopsy confirms the presence of Reed–Sternberg cells.

5. A 49-year-old woman is admitted from the medical outpatient department with weight loss, increasing shortness of breath on exercise and spontaneous epistaxis. On examination she is clinically anaemic and is heavily bruised with 10 cm splenomegaly. Her FBC reveals Hb 5.2 g/dl, MCV 81 fl, WCC 250 × 10⁹/l, Plt 79 × 10⁹/l.

4. THEME: SEIZURES

A   Astrocytoma
B   Cerebral abscess
C   Cerebral infarct
D   Cerebral metastases
E   Herpes encephalitis
F   Hypocalcaemia
G   Hyponatraemia
H   Subarachnoid haemorrhage
I   Sturge–Weber syndrome
J   Tuberose sclerosis

The following patients have all presented with seizures. Please choose the most appropriate cause from the above list. The items may be used once, more than once or not at all.

1. A 19-year-old female with a deeply pigmented 'birth mark' on the left side of her face presents in A&E with several tonic–clonic seizures during the past 4–5 hours.

2. A 31-year-old HIV-positive man presents in A&E with a 2-day history of worsening headaches, fever, vomiting and weakness of the left upper limb. Whilst being examined by the medical SHO he has a tonic–clonic seizure. A contrast-enhanced CT scan of the head confirms a large 'ring-enhancing' lesion in the right frontoparietal region with associated mass effect and oedema.

3. A 71-year-old woman is placed on paroxetine for depression. Of note she is already on bendrofluazide for hypertension. Six weeks later she is brought to A&E by ambulance having had several seizures. Her husband says she has been increasingly confused for several days but has otherwise been well.

4. A 52-year-old smoker with long-standing hypertension presents in A&E with acute onset of a severe generalised headache and a reduced level of consciousness. Whilst in the department he has a 'violent' prolonged tonic–clonic seizure. He is paralysed and ventilated, and a CT head scan shows hyperdense areas within the ventricles and around the brainstem.

5. A 42-year-old devout Moslem woman is brought to A&E with a collapse. On examination she is very pale and noted to have a positive Chvostek's and Trousseau's sign. Examination is otherwise unremarkable. Her son tells the doctor that she has had three or four 'funny turns' during the last 24 hours.

5. THEME: ACUTE RENAL FAILURE

A   Anti-GBM disease
B   Benzylpenicillin
C   *E. coli* O157
D   Gentamicin
E   IgA nephropathy
F   *Legionella* pneumonia
G   Multiple myeloma
H   Ramipril
I   Streptococcal pneumonia
J   Wegener's granulomatosis

The following patients have all presented with acute renal failure. Please choose the most appropriate cause from the above list. The items may be used once, more than once or not at all.

1. A 29-year-old man presents acutely unwell in A&E. He has a decreased level of consciousness, confusion and diarrhoea. Investigation revealed FBC: Hb 11.9 g/dl, MCV 91 fl, WCC 13.6 × 10⁹/l, Plt 24.9 × 10⁹/l; U&Es: Na⁺ 124 mmol/l, K⁺ 3.9 mmol/l, urea 11.1 mmol/l, Cr 207 μmol/l. The diagnosis is confirmed by urinary antigen titres.

2. A 78-year-old woman is admitted with a severe cellulitis of her left anterior shin. She is started on appropriate intravenous treatment but 5 days later investigations show U&Es: Na⁺ 131 mmol/l, K⁺ 6.4 mmol/l, urea 19.3 mmol/l, Cr 516 μmol/l. She also has marked proteinuria and peripheral oedema.

3. A 19-year-old man presents to his GP 10 days after developing a sore throat with increasing ankle oedema and lethargy. He has marked proteinuria on his dipstix, and U&Es: Na⁺ 130 mmol/l, K⁺ 6.6 mmol/l, urea 14.9 mmol/l, Cr 488 μmol/l.

4. A 38-year-old woman is admitted to hospital with a 10-day history of 'flu-like' illness, shortness of breath with marked haemoptysis and ankle oedema. Her chest radiograph reveals 'patchy shadowing in both lung fields, consistent with pulmonary haemorrhage'. Urinalysis: protein +++; U&Es: Na⁺ 128 mmol/l, K⁺ 6.9 mmol/l, urea 22.3 mmol/l, Cr 516 μmol/l.

5. A 31-year-old man presents to his GP with 'nasal congestion', episodes of frank haemoptysis and a 1-week history of increasing shortness of breath and peripheral oedema. U&Es: Na⁺ 128 mmol/l, K⁺ 7.2 mmol/l, urea 21 mmol/l, Cr 736 μmol/l; ESR 129 mm/h; CCa²⁺ 2.34 mmol/l; plasma electrophoresis – increased β2 globulin.

6. THEME: DYSPHAGIA

A Achalasia
B Bulbar palsy
C Chagas' disease
D CREST syndrome
E Gastro-oesophageal reflux disease
F Myasthenia gravis
G Oesophageal candidiasis
H Oesophageal carcinoma
I Paraoesophageal hernia
J Pharyngeal pouch
K Pharyngeal web
L Pseudobulbar palsy

*The following patients have all presented with difficulty swallowing (dysphagia).
Please select the most appropriate diagnosis from the above list. The items may be
used once, more than once or not at all.*

1. A 42-year-old man presents with a long history of epigastric burning pain
    which is worse at night. He also suffers from severe burning pain in the
    chest when drinking hot liquids. Recently he has noted some difficulty
    swallowing solids. Endoscopy reveals confluent circumferential erosions
    and stricturing in the lower oesophagus. Twenty-four hour ambulatory
    oesophageal pH measurement demonstrates a pH of less than 4 for 10%
    of the recording.

2. A 69-year-old man presents with a 3-month history of difficulty
    swallowing. He initially felt solids sticking at chest level but now has
    difficulty drinking. He has lost 8 kg in weight. Examination is
    unremarkable apart from his gaunt appearance.

3. A 50-year-old man from Brazil is an inpatient on the cardiology ward with
    heart failure. You are asked to give an opinion regarding his additional
    symptoms of dysphagia. He has regurgitation of solids and liquids equally,
    both occurring shortly after swallowing and has hypoalbuminaemia
    leading to a worsening of his peripheral oedema.

4. An 80-year-old woman presents to the ENT clinic with a history of
    progressive dysphagia. She notes that initially food stuck at the back of her
    throat causing her discomfort which was relieved on regurgitation. The
    latter was assisted by pressing on her neck.

5. A 59-year-old patient is admitted to hospital from A&E with severe upper abdominal and chest pain associated with vomiting. On questioning he admits to having had several less severe previous episodes and some dysphagia. An erect chest radiograph is performed to look for free gas under the diaphragm with a working diagnosis of perforated duodenal ulcer. The radiograph however demonstrates a large bubble of gas lying in the chest behind the heart.

7. THEME: GENETIC RISK FACTORS FOR COLORECTAL CANCER

A   Acromegaly
B   *APC* gene
C   Familial adenomatous polyposis
D   Hereditary non-polyposis colorectal cancer (HNPCC)
E   K-RAS gene
F   Microsatellite instability
G   Mismatch repair genes
H   Peutz–Jeghers syndrome
I   P53 gene
J   Ulcerative/Crohn's colitis

The following are descriptions of patients with an increased risk of colorectal cancer. Please select the most appropriate diagnosis from the above list. The items may be used once, more than once or not at all.

1.   A hereditary autosomal dominant condition caused by germline mutations in the *APC* gene.

2.   A condition in which the 40–80% of cases are caused by germline mutations in mismatch repair genes leading to DNA microsatellite instability.

3.   An autosomal dominant condition characterised by perioral pigmentations and upper and lower gastrointestinal hamartomatous lesions, and small bowel, pancreatic and colorectal cancer.

4.   When it affects the colon throughout its length, this condition is associated with a 1% risk of colorectal cancer after 10 years of active disease and a further 1% per year approximate increase in risk thereafter.

5.   A condition defined by clinical and pedigree criteria called the Amsterdam criteria.

8. THEME: NECK LUMPS

A   Branchial cyst
B   Carotid body tumour
C   Cervical lymphadenopathy
D   Cervical rib
E   Cystic hygroma
F   Pharyngeal pouch
G   Sternomastoid tumour
H   Supraclavicular lymphadenopathy
I   Thyroglossal cyst
J   Thyroid disease

The following patients have all presented with a palpable lump in the neck. Please select the most appropriate diagnosis from the above list. The items may be used once, more than once or not at all.

1. A 22-year-old man presents with an asymptomatic slowly growing painless lump in the posterior triangle of the neck above the clavicle. Direct questioning reveals a 3-month history of malaise, weight loss, pruritis and episodic night sweats. The lump is 3 cm in diameter, firm and non-tender.

2. A 68-year-old man presents with an asymptomatic slowly growing painless lump in the neck. On examination he has a hard 2 cm mass lying laterally in the anterior triangle of the neck, deep to the middle third of the right sternomastoid muscle. You notice that the patient has dysphonia.

3. An infant attends with his mother who is concerned because he has a right torticollis. On examination there is a swelling in the middle third of the sternomastoid muscle.

4. A 12-year-old girl presents with a history of recurrent sore throats. On examination she has a firm 2 cm mass lying laterally in the anterior triangle of the neck, deep to the upper third of the left sternomastoid muscle just below the angle of the mandible. Oropharyngeal examination reveals enlarged tonsils.

5. A 26-year-old woman presents with a slow-growing smooth painless lump in the anterior triangle of the neck. The mass is just to the left of the midline and overlying the laryngeal cartilage and moves on swallowing.

9. THEME: INFECTIONS IN PREGNANCY

A   Cytomegalovirus
B   Group B β haemolytic streptococcus
C   Hepatitis B
D   HIV
E   Parvovirus B19
F   Rubella
G   Syphilis
H   *Toxoplasma gondii*
I   Urinary tract infection
J   Varicella zoster virus

From the above list please choose the infection or infectious agent most likely to cause the clinical picture described. The items may be used once, more than once or not at all.

1. Often asymptomatic, easy to treat but if left untreated is associated with maternal sepsis, hyperemesis gravidarum and premature labour.

2. If found to be positive for this infection, it is an indication for antenatal therapy, delivery by Caesarean section, neonatal therapy and refraining from breastfeeding.

3. If found to be positive for this rare infection, it can cause teratogenesis in the fetus and long-term neurological sequelae for the mother. It is very easy to treat once identified.

4. If acquired in the first 20 weeks of pregnancy it may cause mental retardation, congenital deafness and heart defects.

5. Present in 15–20% of the pregnant population and asymptomatic. 1 per 1000 neonates will suffer life-threatening sepsis as a result of this.

10. THEME: AUTOIMMUNE DISEASES

A   Addison's disease
B   Graves' disease
C   Hashimoto's thyroiditis
D   Pernicious anaemia
E   Polymyositis
F   Primary hypoparathyroidism
G   Scleroderma
H   Sjögren's syndrome
I   Systemic lupus erythematosus
J   Type 1 diabetes mellitus

From the above list, please select the disease that each of the following patients is most likely to have. The items may be used once, more than once or not at all.

1. A 66-year-old woman presents with increasing tiredness, dyspnoea on exercise and swollen ankles. On examination she has pallor of the mucous membranes and pitting oedema of both ankles. Investigations show Hb 4.0 g/dl, MCV 121. Serum levels of folate are normal but vitamin B12 is grossly reduced.

2. A 38-year-old woman presents with a 2-month history of symmetrical joint pains in the hands and feet. More recently she had developed a rash over both cheeks and the bridge of her nose. On examination she is hypertensive. Investigations show a high ESR, reduced levels of complement and a high titre of antinuclear antibodies in the serum. Dipstick of the urine shows the presence of protein.

3. A 45-year-old woman presents with a 3-month history of tiredness, weight gain, constipation and amenorrhoea. On examination she has dry skin, bradycardia and a mild proximal myopathy. Investigations show Hb 8.6 g/dl with a normal MCV, a low serum T4, a high serum TSH and raised serum creatine kinase.

4. A 38-year-old woman presents with a 4-month history of recurrent conjunctivitis, dry mouth, mouth ulcers and swelling in the neck. On examination, she has bilateral parotid enlargement. A Schirmer tear test shows reduced tear production. Laboratory investigations show moderately raised antinuclear antibodies, positive rheumatoid factor and anti-Ro antibodies.

5. A 52-year-old woman presents with a 3-month history of progressive difficulty in getting up from a chair, walking up stairs and combing her hair. On examination, she has severe proximal weakness of the arms and legs. Investigations show a raised serum creatine kinase, positive rheumatoid factor and antibodies to tRNA synthetase (Jo-1). Muscle biopsy shows a lymphocytic infiltrate between the muscle fibres associated with fibre necrosis and regeneration.

11. THEME: UROGENITAL ANATOMY

A   Left kidney
B   Left suprarenal gland
C   Left ureter
D   Membranous urethra
E   Ovary
F   Pelvis of the right kidney
G   Prostate
H   Right suprarenal gland
I   Right ureter
J   Trigone of the bladder

For each of the following descriptions, please choose the most appropriate structure from the above list. The items may be used once, more than once or not at all.

1. A posterior relation of the left colic artery.

2. A posterior relation of the second part of the duodenum.

3. An anterior relation of the right common iliac artery.

4. A superior relation of the deep perineal pouch.

5. A posterior relation of the obliterated umbilical ligament.

12. THEME: SURFACE MARKINGS OF THE HEART

A   Left costoxiphoid angle
B   Left 5th intercostal space in the anterior axillary line
C   Left 5th intercostal space in the midclavicular line
D   Left 3rd costosternal junction
E   Medial end of the 2nd right intercostal space
F   Medial end of the 6th left intercostal space
G   Medial to the 4th costosternal junction
H   Medial to the 3rd left intercostal space
I   Midsternal at the level of the 4th intercostal space
J   Right sternal border

For each of the following descriptions, please choose the most appropriate markings from the above list. The items may be used once, more than once or not at all.

1. Surface marking of the tricuspid valve. ☐

2. Optimal site for auscultation of the mitral valve. ☐

3. Surface marking of the right border of the heart. ☐

4. Optimal site for auscultation of the aortic valve. ☐

5. Access site for intracardiac injection. ☐

Paper 9 answers

1. LESIONS SEEN ON OPHTHALMOSCOPY

1. **B, C, D, E & J – Blot haemorrhage, dot haemorrhage, hard exudates, maculopathy and soft exudates**
   This patient has pre-proliferative diabetic retinopathy, which is characterised by background changes (dot and blot haemorrhages and hard exudates) and cotton wool spots (areas of retinal oedema). This patient has also developed maculopathy which is characterised by hard exudates at its periphery, known as a 'macular star'. Maculopathy is a reason for urgent ophthalmology referral as it needs rapid treatment. Failure to identify this problem can lead to rapid deterioration of the patient's acuity and blindness.

2. **B, C & D – Blot haemorrhage, dot haemorrhage and hard exudates**
   This patient has developed background diabetic retinopathy characterised by dot haemorhages (capillary microaneurysms), blot haemorrhages (leakage of blood into the retina) and hard exudates (lipid and protein deposits which have a yellowish/white colour and well defined edge). Background disease heralds the onset of microvascular disease and is associated with early nephropathy. Patients should be placed on an ACE inhibitor and their glycaemic and BP control maximised.

3. **A & I – A-V nipping and silver wiring**
   Hypertensive retinopathy is divided into four grades:
   Grade I   The vessels show increased tortuosity and there is 'silver wiring' which is a result of increased reflectivity of the vessels.
   Grade II   Includes Grade I changes but is characterised by arteriovenous (A-V) nipping at points of crossing of the vessels.
   Grade III   This heralds the onset of retinal ischaemia and is characterised by cotton wool spots and 'flame' shaped haemorrhage.
   Grade IV   This stage includes changes of Grades I–III together with papilloedema.
   Grades III and IV are associated with 'malignant' or accelerated hypertension and require urgent medical treatment. The **BP** needs titrating down **SLOWLY**. Rapid reduction with antihypertensives may lead to acute cerebral infarction.

4. **G – Papilloedema**
   This patient has a large space occupying lesion with associated oedema and mass effect leading to raised intracranial pressure. This has caused papilloedema which is seen as loss of the borders of the optic disc, which in turn becomes engorged with dilatation of the surrounding vessels and small haemorrhages.

5.   H – Retinitis

This HIV positive man has features of AIDS, as defined by the cryptosporidiosis, Kaposi's sarcoma and the CMV retinitis. The retinitis has a characteristic appearance which has various descriptions including cottage cheese and raspberry jam, scrambled eggs and tomato ketchup or even cottage cheese and ketchup.

2. CHEST RADIOGRAPH FINDINGS

1. **B & H – Cardiomegaly and pleural effusion**
   The signs of chronic heart failure are associated with the enlarged heart (cardiomegaly) and fluid within the spaces of the pleural cavity, i.e. pleural effusions, interlobar (fluid in the fissure), interlobular (fluid between the lobules – Kerley B lines), alveolar (causing the 'hazy' alveolar shadowing, classically in the batwing pattern) and as a result, upper lobe diversion of the blood vessels.

2. **C & F – 'Double' left heart border and loss of the hemidiaphragm**
   Left lower lobe collapse classically produces a 'double left heart border' as the collapsed lobe 'falls' behind the heart. It may also cause obscuration of the left hemidiaphragm. Causes of lobar collapse include proximal obstruction due to infection, plugging of major bronchi, aspiration of foreign bodies and most commonly proximal obstructing tumours.

3. **E, H & I – Elevation of the horizontal fissure, pleural effusion and tracheal deviation towards the left**
   A right apical mass may cause tracheal deviation to the left due to the trachea being 'pushed away', however if it causes right upper lobe collapse this will lead to tracheal deviation towards the lesion as it 'pulls' the trachea across. Lobar collapse will also lead to elevation of the horizontal fissure, and may be associated with hilar lymphadenopathy and possibly a pleural effusion.

4. **G & H – Loss of the right heart border and pleural effusion**
   A right middle lobe pneumonia causes loss of the right heart border and may be associated with a pleural effusion.

5. **D & F – Depression of the horizontal fissure and loss of the hemidiaphragm**
   Right lower lobe collapse will cause obscuration of the right hemidiaphragm and 'depression' of the horizontal fissure. Causes of lobar collapse are similar to those in question 2.

6. **A – Bilateral hilar lymphadenopathy**
   Sarcoidosis classically causes bilateral hilar lymphadenopathy, which in turn may be associated with midzone or more diffuse interstitial shadowing and eventually 'honeycombing'.

7. **I – Tracheal deviation to the left**
   Tension pneumothoraces produce mediastinal shift and tracheal deviation away from the side of the pneumothorax.

3. SPLENOMEGALY

1. **F – Infective endocarditis**
   This patient has developed several stigmata of infective endocarditis as evidenced by the mitral regurgitant murmur, low grade fever, anaemia, dipstix positive haematuria and a 'tippable' spleen. For the spleen to be palpable it must be at least two to three times its normal size.

2. **C – Cytomegalovirus**
   This patient with a recent renal transplant has developed systemic CMV infection. She has the typical features of CMV retinitis and has palpable hepatosplenomegaly and evidence of pneumonitis. This diagnosis is confirmed by antibody titres with an acute IgM response or by tissue biopsies which show the pathognomonic intranuclear 'owls' eyes' inclusions. In the immunocompromised patient an antiviral such as ganciclovir should be used.

3. **A – Acute myeloid leukaemia**
   This man has a normocytic anaemia, thrombocytopenia but a leukocytosis with predominant blast cells. The diagnosis may be confirmed on bone marrow examination which characteristically shows hypercellularity and blast cells. Depending on the patient's general health and wishes he should be offered chemotherapy with expert haematological and oncological follow up.

4. **E – Hodgkin's lymphoma**
   This young woman has developed Hodgkin's lymphoma which is strongly associated with previous EBV infection. She has the characteristic 'Reed–Sternberg' cells in her lymph node biopsy, which represent abnormal lymphocytes. The disorder is classified by the affected lymphoid tissue involved above and below the diaphragm and the presence or absence of systemic symptoms such as night sweats, weight loss, malaise and lethargy, the so called 'B-symptoms'. Diagnosis is usually confirmed on the peripheral blood film and lymph node biopsy.

5. **B – Chronic granulocytic leukaemia**
   This woman has a diffusely enlarged spleen associated with a normocytic anaemia, thrombocytopenia and a 'massive' leukocytosis. This picture is in keeping with CGL which is one of the five worldwide causes of a 'giant spleen'. The other four are chronic malaria, visceral leishmaniasis (Kala-Azar), myelofibrosis and Gaucher's disease.

4. SEIZURES

1. **I – Sturge–Weber syndrome**
   This young woman has Sturge–Weber syndrome, the association of a diffuse facial port-wine stain or naevus in a division of the trigeminal nerve and intracranial angiomata. Patients may present at any age with seizures.

2. **B – Cerebral abscess**
   This HIV patient has developed an intracerebral abscess which may be caused by tuberculosis, toxoplasmosis, streptococcal or staphylococcal infection. Ring-enhancing lesions may also represent a primary or secondary malignant tumour as well as lymphomatous deposits.

3. **G – Hyponatraemia**
   This woman has developed severe hyponatraemia due to the combination of paroxetine and bendrofluazide. Both of these tablets are relatively common causes of hyponatraemia.

4. **H – Subarachnoid haemorrhage**
   This man has had a large subarachnoid haemorrhage leading to fresh blood (which appears white in an unenhanced scan) within the ventricles. He requires nimodipine to stop secondary bleeds through vasospasm, correction of any clotting abnormalities and urgent neurosurgical opinion. If the GCS is 7/15 or below he should also be electively paralysed and ventilated.

5. **F – Hypocalcaemia**
   Devout Moslem women who cover up with traditional robes have little or no sun exposure. If they do not have adequate calcium and vitamin D intake through other sources they run the risk of osteomalacia and hypocalcaemia which rarely may be severe enough to cause seizures.

5. ACUTE RENAL FAILURE

1. **F – *Legionella* pneumonia**
   This patient has developed an atypical pneumonia secondary to *Legionella pneumophila*. As with many atypicals there may be few respiratory signs or symptoms, and the patient may principally present with signs and symptoms of a multi-system involvement. The renal impairment is caused by the effects of overwhelming sepsis and resulting multi-organ failure.

2. **B – Benzylpenicillin**
   This patient has developed acute renal impairment and a possible nephrotic syndrome due to the intravenous penicillin she has been placed on for her cellulitis. Drugs such as penicillin can cause acute tubulointerstitial nephritis or an immune-mediated glomerulonephritis.

3. **E – IgA nephropathy**
   This young man has developed acute renal failure 10 days after a sore throat. IgA nephropathy classically occurs 7–10 days after an acute infection, whereas post-streptococcal glomerulonephritis occurs a little later at 14 days.

4. **A – Anti-GBM disease**
   This woman has developed anti-GBM disease, previously called Goodpasture's syndrome. The common basement membrane antigen is found in the kidney and lung and leads to an acute glomerulonephritis and pulmonary haemorrhage with subsequent nephrotic syndrome and respiratory failure.

5. **J – Wegener's granulomatosis**
   This man has both upper and lower respiratory tract symptoms associated with acute renal failure. This combination is classical of Wegener's granulomatosis, which causes a glomerulonephritis and acute renal failure. The diagnosis may be confirmed by the presence of cANCA and typical biopsy findings.

6. DYSPHAGIA

1. E – Gastro-oesophageal reflux disease
This patient has gastro-oesophageal reflux disease (GORD) as evidenced by the long history of 'classic' symptoms. The diagnosis is confirmed by endoscopy in which he has grade III disease, i.e. circumferential disease leading to a stricture. The pH study confirms an increased lower oesophageal acid exposure (pH < 4 for > 4% of the time).

2. H –Oesophageal carcinoma
The history of rapidly progressive dysphagia in a man of this age should prompt this diagnosis. The weight loss is also strongly suggestive. A histological diagnosis would be confirmed at endoscopy, and the size of the lesion by barium swallow which usually has the typical irregular shouldered 'apple core' appearance.

3. C – Chagas' disease
This disorder is caused by the parasite *Trypanosoma cruzi* and is endemic in large parts of rural South America making it one of the commonest diseases in the world. Infection follows a bite of a rather unpleasant nocturnal insect (Reduviid bug) that lives particularly in the roofs of adobe dwellings. There is a long incubation period followed by manifestations of the disorder, which are largely immune-mediated, and include cardiomyopathy and megaoesophagus/megacolon. The oesophageal manifestations are similar to achalasia clinically and pathologically (destruction of the myenteric plexus) and occur in 25% of cases.

4. J – Pharyngeal pouch (AKA Zenker's diverticulum)
This disorder first described by Ludlow in 1767 is a pulsion diverticulum of the lateral pharynx at a point of congenital weakness between the crico- and thyropharyngeal portions of the inferior constrictors called Killian's dehiscence. Food sticks in the diverticulum and causes dysphagia by compressing the upper oesophagus. Treatment is largely surgical. The condition is important to remember for the unwary endoscopist who can easily perforate the diverticulum on intubation of the patient.

5. I – Paraoesophageal hernia
Unlike the very common sliding hernia (hiatus hernia) which may be a cause of reflux disease/dyspepsia, the rolling type although much less common is a serious condition that requires surgical intervention. A variable portion of the stomach 'rolls' through a defect in the diaphram to one side of the oesophagus where it may become strangulated leading to the acute presentation presented. Barium swallow aids diagnosis. Treatment is by gastropexy with or without an anti-reflux procedure.

7. GENETIC RISK FACTORS FOR COLORECTAL CANCER

A variety of hereditary conditions are linked with the development of colorectal cancer (CRC), and the genes responsible for tumour development continue to be elucidated. Whilst such conditions are rare compared with sporadic tumours, representing only 5–10% of all such cancers, they are important not just for the families that have them (especially for screening and surveillance implications), but also as an example of the increasing role of genomics and genetics in medicine and surgery.

1. **C – Familial adenomatous polyposis**
   This condition represents < 1% of all patients with CRC. The patient develops hundreds of adenomas, principally in the distal colon and rectum from the age of approximately 10 years old. Untreated, 100% of those affected will progress with time to development of CRC. Treatment is proctocolectomy. Relatives should undergo genetic testing and close endoscopic surveillance. Depending on the exact allelic site of sequence alteration in the *APC* gene, the patient may have other abnormalities such as desmoid tumours, carcinoma of the ampulla of Vater and osteomata of the mandible.

2. **D – Hereditary non-polyposis colorectal cancer (HNPCC)**
   These are the genetic defects classically associated with this condition in which affected individuals have a much greater than average chance of developing CRC. It represents approximately 3% of all cases of CRC. Compared with sporadic carcinomas, carcinomas develop at a younger age (typically in the 30–50 year age group), are often multiple (synchronous lesions), and are more commonly right-sided. The two commonest mutations are of the mismatch repair genes *MLH1* and *MSH2*. Mutations lead to conformation abnormalities and disordered function of the mismatch repair enzymes that the genes encode with subsequent acquisition of other DNA sequence aberrations of CRC oncogenes such as *APC*, *K-RAS* and *P53*.

3. **H – Peutz–Jeghers syndrome**
   The classic findings of this rare hereditary disorder are described. It is one of three clinically similar hamartomatous polyposis syndromes associated with CRC, the others being even rarer (Cowden's disease and familial juvenile polyposis). The mutant genes responsible have been elucidated for most cases.

4. **J – Ulcerative/Crohn's colitis**
   These are the classically cited risks for patients with ongoing active pancolitis (the risks are similar for both disorders). Lifetime risk is 17 × that of an average risk population (NB the risk of developing CRC in an average risk population is 1/18). Patients require regular colonoscopic surveillance after 8 years of disease and subsequent proctocolectomy if areas of dysplasia are found on biopsies. Patients with left-sided colitis have a lower risk and should be screened after 15 years of disease.

5. **D – HNPCC**

   This condition described in (2) is currently defined within families affected by CRC on the basis of the Amsterdam criteria (I and II). The former more stringent, Amsterdam I criteria require at least three relatives with histologically verified CRC. One must be a first degree relative of the other two, at least two successive generations must be affected and at least one relative must have received the diagnosis before the age of 50 years. Amsterdam II criteria are similar but allow for relatives with other cancers associated with HNPCC (endometrial, stomach, ovary, upper urinary tract and small bowel.

8. NECK LUMPS

1. **H – Supraclavicular lymphadenopathy**
   This patient has supraclavicular lymphadenopathy as evidenced by the anatomical position given. The diagnosis in a male of this age with the constitutive symptoms given is most likely to be lymphoma. The student should remember that this is also a site for metastatic carcinoma from bronchogenic, breast and some gastrointestinal malignancies, e.g. colorectal, stomach (Virchow's node, Troisier's sign).

2. **C – Cervical lymphadenopathy**
   This is evidenced by the anatomical position given. In this case the cause of the lymphadenopathy is metastatic carcinoma from a laryngeal primary. This is one of the commonest causes of swelling of the deep cervical nodes, which lie behind the sternomastoid muscles. Primary lesions may occur in the skin of the head and neck, the lips, tongue and buccal cavity, and the larynx.

3. **G – Sternomastoid tumour**
   This condition of infancy may represent an organising haematoma, or an area of fibrosis secondary to ischaemia. It is either caused by birth trauma or some other late intrauterine event. The condition may present with a lump or torticollis.

4. **C – Cervical lymphadenopathy**
   This is evidenced by the anatomical position given. In this case the cause of the lymphadenopathy is acute inflammation, probably tonsillitis. Other acute inflammatory causes of cervical lymphadenopathy are pharyngitis/laryngitis and EBV. Chronic inflammatory causes include TB and sarcoid. NB: you have now had all four main causes of cervical lymphadenopathy: acute inflammation, chronic inflammation, lymphoma and metastatic carcinoma.

5. **J – Thyroid disease**
   This patient has a solitary thyroid nodule and requires investigation to exclude a papillary carcinoma (differential includes dominant nodule within a multi-nodular goitre, simple cyst and thyroid adenoma).

9. INFECTIONS IN PREGNANCY

1. I – Urinary tract infection

Many of the listed infections are asymptomatic and can cause maternal sepsis. Urinary tract infection (UTI) in pregnancy is commonly asymptomatic and picked up on routine antenatal urine testing rather than symptoms. Due to the relative immunosuppression of pregnancy once it becomes systemic it can quickly lead to sepsis if not treated. The high pyrexia and systemic prostaglandin release may cause premature labour and it is the only infection in the list that is actively associated with hyperemesis gravidarum.

2. D – HIV

HIV infection has a perinatal transmission rate of about 15% which can be reduced to approximately 1% after antenatal maternal anti-retroviral treatment (AZT), elective Caesarean section, neonatal anti-retroviral treatment (AZT) and not breastfeeding. Hepatitis B needs none of these as it is easily prevented by neonatal vaccination and HB Ig. None of the other infections require refraining from breastfeeding.

3. G – Syphilis

Syphilis, rubella, CMV, *Toxoplasma* and VZV (very rarely) can all cause teratogenesis. Parvo B19 causes hydrops fetalis due to fetal anaemia. Syphilis (tertiary) is the only one likely to cause maternal long-term neurological sequelae in an immunocompetent host and it is the only one easily treated (with high dose penicillin). *Toxoplasma* treatment is more complex and as all the others are viral they are also difficult to treat.

4. F – Rubella

Mental retardation, congenital deafness and heart defects are the classic triad of congenital rubella if contracted during the first 20 weeks of pregnancy. CMV and toxoplasmosis can cause microcephaly, hydrocephalus and mental retardation but not usually heart defects or specific deafness.

5. B – Group B β haemolytic streptococcus (GBS)

Group B streptococcus (GBS) is a commensal organism in the vagina in up to 15–20% of the population and by definition is therefore asymptomatic. Parvo B19, CMV, rubella and VZV are much more commonly found to be seropositive (60%, 70%, 97% and 97% respectively). *Toxoplasma* seropositivity is only found in around 10% in the UK. HIV and hepatitis B are much rarer than this. 1 per 1000 neonates become infected during labour and delivery and can suffer a life threatening sepsis. Therefore if a woman is found to be positive for GBS she is treated with penicillin during labour to prevent transmission to the fetus.

10. AUTOIMMUNE DISEASES

1. **D – Pernicious anaemia**

   This patient has symptoms and signs suggestive of cardiac failure due to anaemia. Investigations confirm a severe macrocytic anaemia due to vitamin B12 deficiency. Pernicious anaemia is an autoimmune disease of the stomach in which there is chronic inflammation and atrophy of the gastric mucosa leading to destruction of parietal cells, failure of intrinsic factor production and consequent malabsorption of vitamin B12. The disease is most prevalent in elderly women and is associated with other organ-specific autoimmune diseases such as thyroid disease, Addison's disease and vitiligo. Antiparietal cell antibodies are found in 90% of patients with pernicious anaemia, but can also be found in other conditions. Anti-intrinsic factor antibodies are more specific but are found in only 50% of cases.

2. **I – Systemic lupus erythematosus**

   Systemic lupus erythematosus (SLE) is a multisystem disease that has a variable clinical presentation and behaviour. Arthralgia and skin rashes are the most common features, but involvement of the kidneys, lungs, heart, CNS and eyes are also frequent. This patient exhibits the classical 'butterfly' rash on the cheeks, but other cutaneous manifestations include vasculitic lesions and purpura. Renal involvement is indicated by hypertension and proteinuria. The fundemental defect in SLE is thought to be a failure to maintain self-tolerance. Consequently, a large number of autoantibodies are produced that can damage tissue either directly or in the form of immune complex deposits. Anti-nuclear antibodies are present in 90% of patients with SLE, but other antibodies such as rheumatoid factor and antiphospholipid antibodies are also detected. Low serum complement levels, a high ESR, and leukopenia or thrombocytopenia are also commonly present.

3. **C – Hashimoto's thyroiditis**

   This patient shows the typical symptoms, signs and thyroid function test profile of hypothyroidism. Hashimoto's thyroiditis is the commonest cause of hypothyroidism in the UK. As with other autoimmune diseases it is much more common in women than men (in a ratio of about 9:1) and is associated with other organ-specific autoimmune diseases. Several autoantibodies are detected in the serum, most commonly anti-thyroid peroxidase and anti-thryoglobulin. These lead to atrophy of the thyroid parenchyma and intense lymphoid infiltration of the gland. The anaemia seen in Hashimoto's thyroiditis is usually of normochromic normocytic type but may be megaloblastic if there is associated pernicious anaemia. In this patient, the raised serum creatine kinase is due to the myopathy.

4. **H – Sjögren's syndrome**

Sjögren's syndrome is a disorder characterised by dry eyes and dry mouth resulting from immune-mediated destruction of the lacrimal and salivary glands. It can occur as an isolated disorder (primary form) or in association with other autoimmune diseases (secondary form). 90% of cases occur in middle-aged women. Salivary gland enlargement is common and is due to lymphocytic infiltration. A number of autoantibodies is found in the serum including antinuclear antibodies, rheumatoid factor and autoantibodies to the ribonucleoprotein antigens SS-A (Ro).

5. **E – Polymyositis**

Polymyositis is one of the inflammatory myopathies, a heterogeneous group of uncommon disorders characterised by immune-mediated muscle injury and inflammation. The main clinical feature is symmetrical muscle weakness initially affecting large muscles of the trunk, neck and limbs. Thus, tasks such as getting up from a chair and climbing stairs become increasingly difficult. Muscle biopsy demonstrates chronic inflammation and myopathic features. Several autoantibodies are found in the serum including antinuclear antibodies and rheumatoid factor. Jo-1 antibodies (to tRNA synthetase) are specific for this disorder and their presence is predictive of pulmonary involvement.

11. UROGENITAL ANATOMY

1.   C – Left ureter
The ureter descends on the psoas muscle and common iliac vessels, over the sacroiliac joint, and on reaching the ischial spine it passes forwards to the bladder. It is crossed by the root of the sigmoid mesentery and in males by the vas deferens. In females it is crossed by the broad ligament and uterine artery and has a close relationship with the neck of the cervix.

2.   I – Right ureter
The right kidney is capped by the suprarenal gland, the hilum being covered by the descending part of the duodenum, and the lower pole by the right colic flexure laterally and the duodenum medially. The remainder of the surface is related to the visceral surface of the liver.

3.   H – Right ureter
The right ureter descends on the psoas muscle and crosses the genitofemoral nerve. Anteriorly it is crossed by the descending part of the duodenum, the right colic, iliocolic and gonadal vessels, and the root of the small gut mesentery. Elsewhere, it is covered by adherent peritoneum. Its pelvic relations in males and females are as described in the answer to question 1 above.

4.   G – Prostate
The prostate lies under the bladder surrounding the prostatic urethra; it sits on the perineum. The prostatic urethra becomes the membranous urethra, passing through the deep perineal pouch to pierce the perineal membrane and become the bulbous urethra. The prostate is divided into a median lobe that lies posteriorly between the urethra and the ejaculatory ducts, and lateral lobes that are below and lateral. They are continuous anteriorly but separated posteriorly by a midline sulcus that is palpable on rectal examination.

5.   E – Ovary
The posterior relations of the ovary are the internal iliac vessels and the ureter. Superiorly, the external iliac vessel completes the triangle of the ovarian fossa on the lateral wall of the pelvis. The ovary, however, is clasped by the infundibulum and lies on the posterior aspect of the broad ligament; the lateral relationship described varies with changes in uterine size and position.

12. SURFACE MARKINGS OF THE HEART

1. **I – Midsternal at the level of 4th intercostal space**
    The optimal site for auscultation of the tricuspid valve is at the right sternal border in line with the 4th intercostal space.

2. **C – Left 5th intercostal space in the midclavicular line**
    This is also the marking for the apex of the heart and where the cardiac impulse can be seen and palpated. Murmurs from the mitral valve may radiate to the axilla and are accentuated by lying on the left side; the opening snap of mitral stenosis is heard more prominently over the 4th left costal cartilage when leaning forward.

3. **J – Right sternal border**
    The maximum convexity of this line is opposite the 4th intercostal space, bulging beyond the sternal border and in line with the superior vena cava above and the inferior vena cava below.

4. **E – Medial end of the 2nd right intercostal space**
    Aortic murmurs may radiate into the right side of the neck and occasionally across towards the apex.

5. **F – Medial end of the 6th left intercostal space**
    At this site, and also at the medial end of the left 5th intercostal space, the pleura is reflected away from the midline in the cardiac notch. Substances, eg adrenaline after cardiac arrest, can be delivered directly into the ventricles at this site.

PAPER 10

Paper 10 questions

1. THEME: THYROID FUNCTION TEST RESULTS

	TSH (mU/l)	fT$_4$ (pmol/l)	fT$_3$ (nmol/l)
A	48.9	3.2	0.4
B	< 0.01	64.8	7.3
C	< 0.01	15.9	8.8
D	7.3	14.3	1.8
E	3.2	18.7	2.4
F	0.71	7.0	1.2
G	18.9	14.3	2.8

The following patients have all been shown to have abnormal thyroid function tests. Please match their presentations to the thyroid function tests in the above table. The items may be used once, more than once or not at all.

1. An 81-year-old woman on thyroxine for long-standing primary hypothyroidism is seen in medical outpatient department for her 6-monthly check up. She is clinically well and euthyroid but her AMTS is 6/10. Routine investigations show her to be poorly compliant with her thyroid medication.

2. A 19-year-old woman presents to her GP with palpitations and sweats. On examination she appears to be agitated, tremulous and is tachycardic at 130 bpm in atrial fibrillation. She is admitted to hospital and improves with β blockers and carbimazole.

3. A 69-year-old woman is admitted to A&E with fast atrial fibrillation and pulmonary oedema. On examination she is thin, sweaty and has marked palmar erythema. Her initial investigations reveal normal cardiac enzymes and echocardiogram but her TFTs confirm T$_3$ thyrotoxicosis.

4. A 34-year-old woman presents to her GP with a 3-month history of worsening lethargy, malaise and amenorrhoea. Examination reveals her to have a pale complexion, postural hypotension and a BM is 3.1 mmol/l. Examination is otherwise unremarkable.

5. A 78-year-old woman presents in A&E with pneumonia and fast atrial fibrillation. Investigations reveal sick euthyroid syndrome.

2. THEME: PLEURAL EFFUSION

A   Alcoholic cirrhosis
B   Amyloidosis
C   Bronchogenic carcinoma
D   Chronic HBV
E   Constrictive pericarditis
F   Diabetic nephropathy
G   Ischaemic cardiomyopathy
H   Pulmonary emboli
I   Renal cell carcinoma
J   Tuberculous pericarditis

The following patients have all presented with a pleural effusion. Please choose the most appropriate cause from the above list. The items may be used once, more than once or not at all.

1.   A 38-year-old man presents to his GP with increasing exertional dyspnoea and abdominal swelling. On examination he has ascites, bilateral pleural effusions and is noted to have several spider naevi. An abdominal ultrasound scan shows a 'hypoechogenic mass in the liver ?hepatoma'.

2.   A 49-year-old smoker presents to his GP with increasing shortness of breath and peripheral oedema. On examination he has *no* clubbing or palpable lymphadenopathy but has a large right pleural effusion. An ECG shows sinus tachycardia, left axis deviation and poor anterior R wave progression.

3.   A 51-year-old smoker presents to his GP with increasing abdominal swelling and shortness of breath. On examination he has tar staining of the fingers and is clinically anaemic. His chest radiograph confirms a left pleural effusion with three large lesions spread through the two lung fields.

4.   A 62-year-old female is admitted to hospital with a 2-month history of insidious worsening of shortness of breath which has acutely worsened in the last 10 days. On examination she is tachycardic, tachypnoeic and unwell. She has signs consistent with a large right and smaller left pleural effusion, a raised JVP and a third heart sound. Her ECG shows large dominant R waves in V_1 and V_2 with associated T wave inversion, right axis deviation and sinus tachycardia.

5.   A 32-year-old man presents in A&E with weight loss, haemoptysis and exertional dyspnoea. Examination reveals a low volume pulse, pulsus paradoxus and positive Kussmaul's sign. The heart sounds are poorly heard. His ECG shows low voltage complexes but is otherwise unremarkable. The diagnosis is confirmed by pericardiocentesis which drains 50 ml of blood stained fluid.

3. THEME: NEUROLOGICAL DEFICIT/DISABILITY

A   Agraphia
B   Aphasia (global)
C   Astereognosis
D   Ataxia
E   Dysarthria
F   Dysdiadochokinesia
G   Dyspraxic gait
H   Expresssive dysphasia
I   Nystagmus
J   Resting tremor

The following patients have all presented with neurological disability. Please choose the most appropriate cause from the above list. You may use the items once, in combination, more than once or not at all.

1. A 31-year-old man with known epilepsy is placed on erythromycin for a chest infection. Ten days later he presents in A&E with phenytoin toxicity.

2. A 63-year-old man visits his GP complaining of falls. On examination he is bradykinetic with 'mask' like facies and he improves with L-dopa therapy.

3. A right-handed 71-year-old woman presents in A&E with symptoms suggestive of a dominant hemisphere stroke. She is able to follow three-stage commands but is unable to produce any coherent words. Sensory examination is normal but she cannot recognise objects placed in her right hand when her eyes are closed.

4. A 61-year-old man with known type 2 diabetes mellitus attends his GP with worsening burning pains and numbness in his feet associated with falls. On examination his gait is abnormal and he has a glove and stocking distribution of peripheral sensory neuropathy.

5. A 74-year-old man is admitted to hospital with worsening mobility, confusion and urinary incontinence. Routine investigations including FBC, U&Es, RBG, LFTs, TFTs and calcium are normal, his CXR is unremarkable as is his MSU. A CT head scan shows marked ventricular dilatation and he improves with ventriculoperitoneal shunt.

4. THEME: COLLAPSE

A Aortic stenosis
B Complete heart block
C Neurocardiogenic syncope
D Postural hypotension
E Sick sinus syndrome
F Tachy–brady syndrome
G Tonic–clonic seizure
H Transient ischaemic attack
I Ventricular tachycardia
J Vertebrobasilar insufficiency

The following patients have all presented with an episode of collapse. Please choose the most appropriate cause from the above list. The items may be used once, more than once or not at all.

1. A 76-year-old man with a known history of ischaemic heart disease presents in A&E with an episode of collapse preceded by 'a feeling of light-headedness'. On examination he is pale but is otherwise haemodynamically stable. The medical SHO in A&E thinks he can see cannon waves in the JVP. His ECG shows atrioventricular dissociation with a narrow complex escape rhythm at a rate of 48 bpm.

2. An 83-year-old woman is sent for a tilt table test after an episode of collapse in the street. Her routine blood tests, CXR and ECG were within normal limits as was her 24-hour tape. She becomes extremely hypotensive and bradycardic associated with presyncope, sweating and clamminess within 2 min of carotid sinus massage and tilting to 70°.

3. A 74-year-old widow is seen in medical outpatients with three episodes of collapse in the past 4 months related to washing the top shelves of her kitchen cabinets and more recently whilst looking up watching an air display at her local airport.

4. An 81-year-old woman presents in the medicine for the elderly outpatient clinic with two episodes of collapse associated with dizziness whilst out playing golf. On examination her blood pressure = 110/100 and has an 'abnormal feel' to her carotid pulse. The ECG shows voltage criteria of left ventricular hypertrophy.

5. An 87-year-old man with known IHD, cardiac failure and hypertension is admitted to hospital with an episode of collapse leading to a fractured left neck of femur. On examination he is well but in obvious distress with a shortened, externally rotated left leg. His pulse is 60 bpm and regular and BP = 100/70. The SHO notes he is on bendrofluazide, atenolol, isosorbide mononitrate and ramipril. His ECG shows sinus rhythm, left axis deviation and an old anterior MI but no acute changes. The subsequent 24-hour tape is normal sinus rhythm throughout.

5. THEME: HAEMATOLOGICAL MALIGNANCIES

A Acute lymphoblastic leukaemia (ALL)
B Acute myelogenous leukaemia (AML)
C Chronic lymphatic leukaemia (CLL)
D Chronic myeloid leukaemia (CML)
E Hairy cell leukaemia
F Hodgkin's lymphoma
G Multiple myeloma
H Myelofibrosis
I Non-Hodgkin's lymphoma
J Waldenstöm's macroglobulinaemia

The following patients have all presented with a haematological malignancy. Please choose the most appropriate disorder from the above list.

1. A 46-year-old man presents to his GP with a 2-month history of increasing lethargy, vague abdominal pains and recurrent chest infections. On examination he is clinically anaemic and has multiple areas of bruising over his limbs and torso. He has a massively enlarged spleen extending down into the right iliac fossa. His blood film shows 'pancytopenia with atypical B-cell lymphocytes with spiky projections'.

2. An 81-year-old man presents in haematology outpatients with a vague, non-specific systemic upset and an ESR of 129. On examination he is clinically anaemic but has no lymphadenopathy or organomegaly. Routine investigations reveal FBC: Hb 7.8 g/dl, MCV 89 fl, WCC 3.6 × 10⁹/l, Plt 17 × 10⁹/l; U&Es: Na⁺ 137 mmol/l, K⁺ 4.7 mmol/l, urea 4.7 mmol/l, Cr 86 μmol/l, CCa²⁺ 2.45 mmol/l. The plasma electrophoresis shows 'an IgM monoclonal band with associated immunoparesis'.

3. A 38-year-old woman presents in A&E with a 1-month history of painful enlargement of her cervical and axillary lymph nodes, lethargy and severe oral ulceration. On examination she has gross cervical, axillary and inguinal lymphadenopathy associated with splenomegaly. Her blood film shows 'occasional blast cells'. The diagnosis is subsequently proven on lymph node biopsy.

4. An 87-year-old man presents in A&E with a chest infection and malaise. Routine investigation reveal FBC: Hb 11.3 g/dl, MCV 80 fl, WCC 126 × 10⁹/l, Plt 347 × 10⁹/l; blood film shows 'predominantly lymphocytes with no blast cells seen'. He is seen by the haematologist and started on chlorambucil.

5. A 41-year-old woman is seen by her GP with increasing neck swelling associated with night sweats and weight loss. Routine investigations reveal FBC: Hb 8.5 g/dl, MCV 84 fl, WCC 7.6 × 10⁹/l, Plt 216 × 10⁹/l; U&Es Na$^+$ 135 mmol/l, K$^+$ 4.9 mmol/l, urea 5.7 mmol/l, Cr 91 μmol/l; ESR 109 mm/h. A subsequent lymph node biopsy confirms the presence of Reed–Sternberg cells.

6. THEME: DIARRHOEA

A   Amoebic dysentery
B   Autonomic neuropathy
C   Bacterial enteritis
D   Colorectal carcinoma
E   Crohn's disease
F   Diverticulitis
G   Irritable bowel syndrome
H   Overflow diarrhoea
I   Pseudomembranous colitis
J   Thyrotoxicosis
K   Ulcerative colitis
L   Viral enteritis

The following patients have all presented with diarrhoea as a predominant symptom. Please select the most appropriate diagnosis from the above list. The items may be used once, more than once or not at all.

1. A 67-year-old man presents with a history of several months' diarrhoea (loose stool, three times per day) and has now noticed rectal bleeding and passage of mucus. He previously opened his bowels once every 2 days with formed stool. He has lost approximately 1 stone in weight. He is afebrile, pulse 78 bpm. Hb 9.1 g/dl.

2. A 1-year-old child is brought to A&E by his parents with diarrhoea, vomiting and fever. His siblings and several children at the creche have had the same problem recently and one required admission for correction of dehydration. On examination, the child is listless, dehydrated and febrile, 39.5°C, pulse 120 bpm. Hb 13.4 g/dl, WCC 6.2 × 10⁹/l.

3. A 72-year-old lady develops acute cholecystitis and is treated with intravenous cefuroxime. She is due to go home but then develops lower abdominal pain associated with severe diarrhoea (10–15 times per day). She is febrile, 39.5°C, pulse 100 bpm. Hb 10.2 g/dl, WCC 21.4 × 10⁹/l.

4. A 35-year-old patient with severe cerebral palsy has long-standing constipation for which he has a routine prescription of laxatives in his nursing home. He has been having increasing abdominal pain and the nurses say that the abdomen has become distended and that he has copious diarrhoea. He is afebrile, pulse 90 bpm. Hb 14.2 g/dl; WCC 8.7 × 10⁹/l.

5. A 66-year-old woman presents in A&E with a 3-day history of increasing lower abdominal pain associated with diarrhoea. On examination temperature is 37.7°C with tenderness and guarding in the left iliac fossa. Hb 12.4 g/dl, WCC 15.6 × 10⁹/l.

7. THEME: EVIDENCE-BASED MEDICINE

A   Case–control series
B   Case series
C   Cohort study
D   Controlled clinical trial
E   Cross-sectional survey
F   Experimental research paper
G   Guidelines
H   Meta-analysis
I   Non-systematic review
J   Randomised controlled trial
K   Systematic review

The following are descriptions of types of publication. Please select the most appropriate descriptive term from the above list. The items may be used once, more than once or not at all.

1. The gold standard in medical research. Usually designed to prospectively assess the effects of an intervention.

2. An overview of primary studies that contains a statement of objectives, materials and methods and has been conducted according to explicit and reproducible methodology.

3. A statistical synthesis of the numerical results of several trials which all addressed the same question.

4. A study in which two or more groups of people are selected on the basis of differences in exposure to a particular agent and followed up to observe differences in outcome between the groups.

5. A study in which medical histories of more than one patient with a particular condition are described to illustrate one interesting aspect of the condition or treatment.

8. THEME: MELANOTIC SKIN LESIONS

A   Acral melanoma
B   Amelanotic melanoma
C   Blue naevus
D   Café au lait patch
E   Compound naevus
F   Hutchinson's lentigo
G   Intradermal naevus
H   Junctional naevus
I   Nodular melanoma
J   Superficial spreading melanoma

The following are descriptions of pigmented lesions of the skin. Please select the most appropriate descriptive term from the above list. The items may be used once, more than once or not at all.

1. A 50-year-old Afro-Caribbean man presents with a 2 cm irregular pigmented lesion on the palm of the hand.

2. A 75-year-old gentleman presents with a slowly growing irregular area of brown/dark brown pigmentation on the face. He consults a dermatologist who informs him that whilst the lesion is potentially malignant, it should be completely cured by local excision.

3. A pathology report describes a benign pigmented lesion in which melanocyte proliferation is observed within the basal epithelial layer.

4. A 60-year-old patient presents with anal pain and bleeding. On examination there is a tumour at the anal verge which is suspected to be an anal carcinoma. Biopsies under anaesthesia are reported as showing undifferentiated anaplastic cells of unknown origin. Subsequent immunostaining is positive for S100.

5. A large (3 × 4 cm) irregular melanotic lesion with varying degrees of pigmentation is widely excised from the leg of a 25-year-old woman who has been resident in Australia for the last 2 years. The pathologist reports that the thickness of the lesion is 1 mm and that the lesion is confined to the epidermis.

9. THEME: PERINATAL AND NEONATAL MORTALITY

A Birth asphyxia
B Congenital abnormality
C Early pregnancy complications, e.g. ectopic pregnancy
D Hypertensive disorders
E Maternal genital tract sepsis
F Maternal medical conditions
G Maternal obstetric haemorrhage
H Neonatal sepsis
I Prematurity
J Thromboembolic disease

From the above list please choose the item most likely to describe the following statements. The items may be used once, more than once, in combination or not at all.

1. This condition is the biggest contributor to perinatal mortality. ☐

2. This is the single biggest cause of indirect maternal mortality. ☐

3. This condition is the single biggest contributor to direct maternal mortality. ☐

4. This condition is a cause of direct maternal death usually due to pulmonary oedema associated with inappropriate fluid balance management. ☐

5. This condition is only a small contributor to perinatal mortality but is the commonest cause of complaint in cases that reach litigation. ☐

10. THEME: DISEASES OF THE UPPER GASTROINTESTINAL TRACT

A   Acute erosive gastritis
B   Adenocarcinoma
C   Adenoma
D   Barrett's oesophagus
E   Chronic peptic ulcer
F   Coeliac disease
G   Crohn's disease
H   Giardiasis
I   Lymphoma of mucosa associated lymphoid tissue (MALT)
J   Squamous cell carcinoma

From the above list, please select the disease that each of the following patients is most likely to have. The items may be used once or not at all.

1. A 63-year-old man presents with a three month history of 'acid heartburn'. Endoscopy shows red velvety patches in the lower oesophagus, extending 5 cm above the oesophagogastric junction. Biopsies of the red patches show gastric-type glandular epithelium with foci of intestinal metaplasia.

2. A 27-year-old woman presents with a 9-month history of weight loss, abdominal pain and diarrhoea. Barium follow-through reveals a stricture and mucosal cobblestoning in the mid-ileum. Endoscopy reveals several small ulcers in the stomach and duodenum. Gastric and duodenal biopsies show non-necrotising granulomas.

3. A 51-year-old man presents with a 3-month history of burning epigastric pain relieved by antacids and food. He had recently had two episodes of vomiting coffee grounds. Endoscopy reveals a 3 cm antral ulcer with 'punched-out' edges. Biopsies of the ulcer reveal inflammatory debris and granulation tissue only. Biopsies of the gastric mucosa adjacent to the ulcer show an infiltrate of lymphocytes, plasma cells and neutrophils. None of the lymphocytes are atypical and there is no evidence of epithelial malignancy.

4. A 25-year-old man presents with a six month history of abdominal discomfort and more recently steatorrhoea. He had also felt tired in the past few weeks and had been taking iron supplements. Blood tests show a megaloblastic anaemia. Vitamin B12 levels are normal but serum and red cell folate concentrations are low. Anti-endomysial antibodies are present in the serum. A duodenal biopsy shows subtotal villous atrophy with an increased number of intra-epithelial lymphocytes.

5. A 75-year-old man presents with a two month history of anorexia, weight loss and epigastric pain. Blood tests done by his GP reveal an iron deficiency anaemia. Endoscopy shows a polypoid mass in the gastric antrum. Biopsies show sheets of atypical glands infiltrating into the submucosa with clusters of signet-ring cells.

11. THEME: ANATOMY OF THE LIVER

A Bare area of the liver
B Caudate lobe
C Caudate process
D Coronary ligament
E Falciform ligament
F Gall bladder
G Left lobe
H Left triangular ligament
I Porta hepatis
J Right lobe

For each of the following descriptions, please choose the most appropriate structure from the above list. The items may be used once, more than once or not at all.

1. Lies on the lateral side of the quadrate lobe.

2. Is the superior relationship of the aditus of the lesser sac.

3. Site of the entry of the hepatic artery into the liver.

4. Anterior relationship of the upper pole of the right kidney.

5. Forms the upper limit of the lesser sac.

12. THEME: BLOOD SUPPLY OF THE HEART

A   Anterior interventricular artery
B   Circumflex artery
C   Coronary sinus
D   Diagonal artery
E   Great cardiac vein
F   Left coronary artery
G   Left marginal artery
H   Posterior interventricular artery
I   Right coronary artery
J   Right marginal artery

For each of the following descriptions, please choose the most appropriate vessel from the above list. The items may be used once, more than once or not at all.

1.   Opening in the anterior aortic sinus.

2.   Gives rise to the diagonal artery.

3.   Supplies the apex of the heart.

4.   Supplies the sinoatrial (SA) node.

5.   Lies between the left auricular appendage and the pulmonary trunk.

Paper 10 answers

1. THYROID RESULTS

1. G

Patients with cognitive impairment often take their medication intermittently Thus, their TSH is raised but their fT¾ are within normal limits. This is because they have often taken several thyroxine tablets over the preceding week prior to their TFTs being checked. A dosset box may improve things but failing this a carer or district nurse should be instructed to help the patient take their medications regularly.

2. B

This young woman has developed signs and symptoms consistent with primary thyrotoxicosis, the most likely cause of which is autoimmune thyroid disease. She may be treated with carbimazole or propylthiouracil to block her thyroid hormone production, and β blockers for the systemic symptoms.

3. C

This woman has signs and symptoms of thyrotoxicosis but her T_4 is normal. She has therefore developed the less common T_3 thyrotoxicosis which may present with similar signs and symptoms.

4. F

This woman has developed secondary hypothyroidism due to pituitary failure. She has signs consistent with Addison's (low blood pressure and low BM) as well as amenorrhoea. Causes include postpartum infarction (Sheehan's syndrome), stroke and infiltration, e.g. sarcoid, amyloid or haemochromatosis.

5. D

Patients who are acutely unwell with severe systemic illness often have abnormal thyroid function tests which do not fit into any 'obvious' pattern. This is because the thyroid stops hormone synthesis, more T_3 is converted peripherally to rT_3 than T_4, and less T_3 and T_4 are bound to albumin.

2. PLEURAL EFFUSION

1. D – Chronic HBV

The three major metabolic 'failures' – hepatic, cardiac and renal – all lead to fluid overload, peripheral oedema, ascites and transudative pleural effusions. This patient has signs of chronic liver disease and a possible hepatoma. (This picture is primarily associated with chronic viral hepatitis but can also occur with any condition leading to cirrhosis.)

2. G – Ischaemic cardiomyopathy

This man has signs of old ischaemic heart disease on his ECG including left axis deviation and poor anterior R wave progression. Common causes of cardiomyopathy include ischaemic heart disease, hypertension, alcohol, post-viral and idiopathic.

3. I – Renal cell carcinoma

Although this man initially presents with the signs and symptoms of bronchogenic carcinoma the radiographic findings are more in keeping with 'cannon ball' metastases of renal cell carcinoma. Primary and secondary carcinoma may produce an exudative effusion.

4. H – Pulmonary emboli

This woman has a history suggestive of multiple pulmonary emboli leading to right heart strain and cardiac failure. Her ECG confirms signs of right ventricular strain (dominant R waves with T wave inversion in leads V_1 and V_2 and right axis deviation). The diagnosis should be confirmed (after initiating anticoagulation with LMW heparin) by V/Q scan or spiral CT scan of the chest with angiography. PEs classically produce an exudative effusion.

5. J – Tuberculous pericarditis

This patient has signs consistent with a significant pericardial effusion/tamponade. The most likely cause is a tuberculous infection, others include ischaemic heart disease, malignant infiltration, pericarditis, rheumatic fever and uraemia.

3. NEUROLOGICAL DEFICIT/DISABILITY

1. **D, E, F and I – Ataxia, dysarthria, dysdiadochokinesia and nystagmus**
   This man has been placed on erythromycin which is a liver enzyme inhibitor. This will reduce the metabolism of phenytoin and lead to toxicity. Phenytoin toxicity is manifest as cerebellar syndrome and paradoxically causes seizures. The phenytoin should be stopped until the levels are back in the therapeutic range and the patient should be told about future antibiotic and other medications which may affect his phenytoin therapy.

2. **J – resting tremor**
   This man has Parkinsonism as evidenced by his bradykinesia 'frozen' facial expression and falls. This is classically associated with a resting tremor, rigidity, (hypertonia) leading to 'cogwheeling' of the upper limbs.

3. **C & H – Astereognosis and expressive dysphasia**
   This patient has had a left cerebral hemisphere stroke leading to expresssive dysphasia and astereognosis. Other features of a middle cerebral artery stroke include visuospatial problems and motor/sensor deficit of the contralateral limbs.

4. **D – Ataxia**
   This patient has a peripheral sensory neuropathy, which may lead to a sensory ataxia which is characterised by a high-stepping, foot slapping, gait.

5. **G – Dyspraxic gait**
   This man has signs and symptoms suggestive of normal pressure hydrocephalus. The classical triad of this condition is cognitive impairment, gait dyspraxia and urinary incontinence. Patients with a good history of the triad and CT head scan findings in keeping with the disorder should benefit from the insertion of a ventricular peritoneal shunt.

4. COLLAPSE

1. **B – Complete heart block**
   This patient has developed symptomatic complete heart block. He has characteristic cannon waves in his JVP due to the associated atrioventricular dissociation which means his right atrium contracts against a closed tricuspid valve. He needs the insertion of a permanent pacemaker.

2. **C – Neurocardiogenic syncope**
   This patient has developed symptomatic bradycardia and hypotension two minutes after tilting her to 70° and carotid sinus massage. This is known as neurocardiogenic syncope and is thought to be a result of an abnormal response to venous pooling in the legs. The pooling leads to a reduced cardiac filling pressure which in turn leads to an increased 'vigorous' ventricular contraction. This response stimulates mechanoreceptors, which send afferent messages to medullary centres which in turn send out efferent messages leading to increased vagal-mediated hypotension and bradycardia. This is known as the Bezold–Jarisch reflex. It is unclear how to treat this syndrome successfully and several therapeutic interventions may be required. Paradoxically, β blockers are used which block the afferent part of the pathway and lead to an improved vasomotor response. Permanent pacemakers may also have a role.

3. **J – Vertebrobasilar insufficiency**
   This patient has symptoms suggestive of vertebrobasilar insufficiency. This is caused by compression of the vertebrobasilar arteries by bone (cervical spondylosis) or through atherosclerosis. Unlike similar disease in the carotid arteries, operative intervention carries excessive risks and supportive therapy is the only treatment at present. The appropriate management of co-existent severe carotid artery disease may improve her symptoms.

4. **A – Aortic stenosis**
   This patient has significant aortic stenosis as evidenced by her narrow pulse pressure, slow rising pulse and the voltage criteria of LVH on her ECG. She needs an echocardiogram to estimate the degree of stenosis, pressure gradient across the valve and her left ventricular function. Subsequent management including cardiac catheterisation and possible valve replacement depends on the patient's wishes, her comorbidity and the left ventricular function.

5. **D – Postural hypotension**
   Patients presenting with a fractured neck of femur should have the reason for their fall investigated. Common causes include mechanical falls due to poorly fitting footwear, loose fitting fixtures in the home and accidental falls which may happen to anyone. However pathological falls due principally to cardiovascular and neurological conditions must be excluded by history and investigation, particularly in the presence of loss of consciousness or amnesia with regard to the fall. Postural hypotension may occur as a result of degenerate autonomic responses but is principally iatrogenic induced by antihypertensive agents, as in this case. The patient should have all possible hypotensive agents stopped and his anti-anginal therapy reconsidered.

5. HAEMATOLOGICAL MALIGNANCIES

1. **E – Hairy cell leukaemia**
    This man has developed hairy cell leukaemia, so called because of the appearance of the abnormal B-cells. It is a disease of middle age and is more common in men than women, usually presenting with clinical features of pancytopenia and splenomegaly.

2. **J – Waldenstöm's macroglobulinaemia**
    This man has a pancytopenia, ESR > 100 mm/h and has evidence of a monoclonal gammopathy with associated immunoparesis. However, he has a normal serum calcium, no evidence of renal impairment and no symptoms suggestive of bony lesions. These features differentiate the patient with Waldenstöm's macroglobulinaemia from multiple myeloma. Waldenstöm's is generally a more benign condition but requires similar supportive treatment with blood transfusions and rapid treatment of sepsis.

3. **B – Acute myelogenous leukaemia**
    Acute myelogenous leukaemia (AML) is the principal leukaemia of adults. It presents in middle to late middle age with symptoms of pancytopenia (anaemia, recurrent infection and spontaneous bruising and bleeding), lymphadenopathy and splenomegaly. AML is differentiated by the predominant cell morphology of the abnormal leukaemic blast cells and these dictate the various treatment options which include chemotherapy, bone marrow transplantation and supportive treatment with blood transfusion, blood products and rapid treatment of sepsis.

4. **C – Chronic lymphatic leukaemia**
    Chronic lymphatic leukaemia (CLL) is the predominant leukaemia of older people. It is often discovered as an incidental finding when the patient has a routine full blood count or may present insidiously with non-specific symptoms such as malaise, weight loss and fever. The peripheral blood film shows anaemia, a leukocytosis with a lymphocytosis of abnormal B-cells. Most patients only require observation and regular blood transfusion but the more symptomatic and those with higher white cell counts are placed on hydroxyurea. Patients are very susceptible to severe sepsis as the abnormal B-cells cause an immunoparesis and thus patients can not mount an effective immune response.

5. **F – Hodgkin's lymphoma**

This middle-aged woman has developed painless lymphadenopathy, night sweats and weight loss. Her lymph node biopsy confirms the presence of Reed–Sternberg cells which are pathognomonic of Hodgkin's lymphoma. These are malignant giant cells which are characterised by their binuclear, bilobed appearance or multilobed, polypoid mononucleus containing inclusion like 'owl eyes' nucleoli surrounded by a clear halo. Hodgkin's lymphoma has a bimodal distribution of incidence, the first peak in young adults and the second in middle age. Patients present with gross lymphadenopathy, particularly of the cervical region, and systemic features, known as B-symptoms, including weight loss, fever and night sweats. Patients may also complain of pain in the enlarged lymph nodes on drinking alcohol and tobacco intolerance. Treatment depends on patient's wishes, staging, site and bulk of the disease, and includes chemotherapy, radiotherapy and supportive haematological treatments.

6. DIARRHOEA

1. **D – Colorectal carcinoma**
    This gentleman has the commonest clinical presentation of colorectal carcinoma with a change in bowel habit (usually to diarrhoea), rectal bleeding and weight loss. This particular case is typical of a rectal or left-sided colonic cancer. Caecal carcinomas more often present with diarrhoea anaemia, but no evident bleeding.

2. **L – Viral gastroenteritis**
    This is a very common condition in infants and children and typically occurs in outbreaks as described. Common enteroviruses are RNA viruses such as rotavirus and Norwalk virus. Treatment is supportive.

3. **I – Pseudomembranous colitis**
    This is caused by overgrowth of the bacteria *Clostridium difficile* following treatment with oral or intravenous broad-spectrum antibiotics. Diagnosis is confirmed by stool culture. Treatment involves stopping the causative agents and starting metronidazole or vancomycin. The disorder takes its name from the pseudomembrane observed if the colonic mucosa is examined endoscopically. In an 80-year-old inpatient, overflow diarrhoea and incontinence caused by faecal impaction should be excluded by rectal examination as in this case.

4. **H – Overflow diarrhoea**
    Overflow occurs as a consequence of faecal impaction which prevents the normal anorectal mechanisms of defaecation and continence from functioning. Whilst severe impaction can be manifest as large bowel obstruction, liquid faeces and air more commonly circumnavigate the impacted bolus periodically presenting as diarrhoea. In this case the cause of constipation is neurogenic, and this is a serious management problem in many degenerative central neurological disorders and spinal cord injuries.

5. **F – Diverticulitis**
    Diverticular disease of the colon can manifest itself in many ways: constipation, diarrhoea, bleeding, obstruction and perforation. When a diverticulum becomes inflamed the condition is described as diverticulitis, some of the findings of which are described in this case. With increasing severity there may be localised perforation and abscess formation or free perforation with purulent or even faecal peritonitis. Treatment of diverticulitis is principally intravenous antibiotics and bowel rest.

7. Evidence-based medicine

1. **J – Randomised control trial (RCT)**
   Such trials, which are by necessity prospective, evaluate by randomisation the effect of a single variable in a precisely defined patient group. They potentially eradicate bias and should use hypotheticodeductive reasoning (aim to falsify not confirm a specific hypothesis).

2. **K – Systematic review**
   Overview-type studies include systematic reviews, meta-analyses and non-systematic reviews. The former two types of overview have a much higher relative weighting in the traditional hierarchy of evidence when making decisions about clinical interventions. The Cochrane database is a database of systematic reviews and meta-analyses.

3. **H – Meta-analysis**
   When reviewing the impact of new therapies, evidence can come from several studies of modest size and with slightly differing conclusions. One solution might be to carry out a definitive RCT but might require considerable time, effort and expense. An alternative is to combine data from several modest studies into a meta-analysis. By combining studies in a coherent (statistically-robust) way, conclusions can thus be reached based on a larger pool of subjects.

4. **C – Cohort study**
   This differs slightly from an RCT in that it generally takes two or more large cohorts of subjects (rather than a specific sample size of patients) and follows them up long term for the effects of a certain agent, e.g. environmental factor on the basis of which they are selected. An example is that of Sir Richard Doll's work associating lung cancer with smoking by observing a cohort of 40,000 doctors in 4 cohorts according to number of cigarettes smoked over 10 years.

5. **B – Case series**
   This is really synonymous with a series of case reports illustrating together an interesting aspect of condition or treatment. Although they are not randomised and rarely prospective, and represent a low relative weight in the traditional hierarchy of evidence, they are easy for the less scientifically minded to digest and can still convey very important information rapidly before a definitive trial can be performed; eg McBride's 1961 *Case series of two infants with limb absence born to mothers taking Thalidomide* first alerted the world to this terrible drug complication.

8. MELANOTIC SKIN LESIONS

1. **A – Acral melanoma**
   This is one of the five classically described clinicopathological types of malignant melanoma which are: Hutchinson's lentigo, acral lentiginous, mucosal, superficial spreading and nodular. The diagnosis is suggested by the race of the patient and site of the lesion (the latter giving its name). It is the only type to affect black people and occurs on the palms or soles or under the nail bed. It is the rarest form in white people (0.5–1%). The two commonest types are superficial spreading (65%) and nodular melanoma (25%).

2. **F – Hutchinson's lentigo (AKA malignant lentigo, lentigo maligna)**
   The diagnosis is given by the clinical description and the prognosis given to the patient. This is considered as a type of *in situ* malignant melanoma by some pathologists and a premaligant lesion by others. Regardless, pathologically the tumour is confined to the epidermis. Slowly growing, it carries an excellent prognosis after local excision. Left it can progress to the more aggressive invasive form, that of superficial spreading melanoma.

3. **H – Junctional naevus**
   Proliferating benign melanocytic lesions are pathologically classified into intradermal (proliferation deep to the basal layer of the epidermis, i.e. confined within the dermis), junctional (as described) and compound (both junctional and intradermal elements). The importance lies in the increased risk of malignant change in lesions with junctional proliferation. A specific variant which is the exception to this rule is the juvenile naevus (pre-puberty).

4. **B – Amelanotic melanoma**
   This is a variant usually of nodular melanoma, in which the cell of origin is the melanocyte but melanin production is not evident (had this been the case, the diagnosis of mucosal melanoma would have been obvious). The diagnosis is finally made by staining for the neural marker S100 which stains melanocytes because they share a common tissue of origin embryologically with some neural tissues (the neural crest). Mucosal melanoma carries the worst prognosis of all melanomas because of late presentation and early lymphatic spread (other melanoma sites, i.e. excluding skin include ocular and subungual).

5. **J – Superficial spreading melanoma**
   The clinical and pathological descriptions fit with this diagnosis which has the best prognosis of melanoma variants because of the late vertical invasion (compared with nodular) and therefore decreased risk of tumour spread. There are two local microstaging systems for melanoma which are complementary reliable indicators of prognosis and are described in the vignette. Breslow's system measures the depth of invasion in mm (subdivided into 4) whereas Clark's defines the depth of invasion by histological level: epidermis (I) through to subcutaneous fat (V).

9. PERINATAL AND NEONATAL MORTALITY

1. **I – Prematurity**
    Complications of prematurity (RDS, intraventricular haemorrhage, sepsis, necrotising enterocolitis) are by far the largest cause of perinatal mortality (death after 24/40 gestation and up to 28 days post delivery) reported by the Confidential Enquiry into Stillbirths and Deaths in Infancy (CESDI). Not surprisingly the mortality rate decreases with increasing gestation.

2. **F – Maternal medical conditions**
    Indirect maternal deaths are defined as deaths due to previously existing conditions that may have been exacerbated by the physiological effects of pregnancy but not directly due to obstetric causes. The only cause of indirect maternal death in the list is maternal medical conditions. Important examples are maternal congenital cardiac disease resulting in high output heart failure due to the increased cardiac output (40%) and epilepsy leading to status epilepticus due to the altered handling of anti-epileptic medication in pregnancy.

3. **J – Thromboembolic disease (TED)**
    Direct maternal deaths are defined as deaths during pregnancy and up to 42 days after delivery due to causes directly related to pregnancy or its management including omissions and incorrect management. Thromboembolic disease (TED), particularly pulmonary embolism, has repeatedly been by far the leading cause of direct maternal death in the triennial Confidential Enquiries into Maternal Death (CEMD). There are often multiple risk factors for TED and guidelines for the use of thrombo-prophylaxis in pregnancy and the puerperium to reduce the occurrence of TED and thus maternal mortality are used nationally.

4. **D – Hypertensive disorders**
    Hypertensive disorders of pregnancy (pre-eclampsia, PET) cause a number of maternal deaths each year. Unfortunately the commonest mode of death is iatrogenic failure to manage fluid balance appropriately resulting in fluid overload and pulmonary oedema. PET (particularly severe cases) causes a small vessel angiopathy resulting in a tendency for fluid to shift to the extravascular space with renal dysfunction, leading to an inability to excrete excess fluid. Due to this pathophysiology a relatively small amount of fluid overload can cause overwhelming pulmonary oedema. Pulmonary oedema can also occur in obstetric haemorrhage and maternal sepsis but the mode of death is usually hypovolaemia and multi-organ failure respectively.

5. **A – Birth asphyxia**
    Deaths due to birth asphyxia are actually rare and therefore only a small contributor to perinatal mortality. Recent Australian epidemiological studies have shown that the majority of deaths in which birth asphyxia may be implicated are in fact probably due to pre-existing intrinsic fetal problems. However the public perception is that it is much more common and as such is the commonest complaint in obstetric litigation in relation to perinatal death.

10. DISEASES OF THE UPPER GASTROINTESTINAL TRACT

1. **D – Barrett's oesophagus**
    The most common cause of 'acid heartburn' is gastro-oesophageal reflux, during which gastric acid refluxes from the stomach into the lower oesophagus. The oesophagus is normally lined by stratified squamous epithelium. This type of epithelium cannot easily withstand the damage caused by gastric acid so meta-plasia occurs to gastric-type glandular epithelium, which is better able to bear the damage. Endoscopically the metaplastic mucosa has a red, velvety appearance in contrast to the smooth white appearance of normal oesophageal epithelium. This condition is known as Barrett's oesophagus. Like many other metaplastic conditions, Barrett's oesophagus is associated with an increased risk of malignancy, particularly when there is associated intestinal metaplasia.

2. **G – Crohn's disease**
    The only granulomatous disease on this list is Crohn's disease. This can affect any part of the alimentary tract from mouth to anus, and there is often micro-scopic involvement of the stomach and duodenum, even in the absence of referable symptoms or macroscopic disease. In this patient, the barium meal findings of cobblestoning and stricture formation are typical of Crohn's disease.

3. **E – Chronic peptic ulcer**
    The main differential diagnosis of a gastric ulcer lies between a chronic peptic ulcer and an ulcerating malignant tumour. Chronic peptic ulcers have sharply defined punched-out borders in contrast to ulcerating malignancies which tend to have raised, rolled, everted edges. The floor of a peptic ulcer is composed of fibrous scar tissue overlaid by granulation tissue, inflammatory exudate and necrotic slough. The endoscopic and histological findings in this patient therefore support a diagnosis of chronic peptic ulcer. The mucosa adjacent to a chronic peptic ulcer often shows chronic gastritis, particularly when *Helicobacter pylori* infection is the underlying cause.

4. **F – Coeliac disease**
    This patient has symptoms and signs of fat malabsorption, suggestive of small intestinal disease. The fact that the duodenal biopsy shows subtotal villous atrophy confirms an enteropathy, so the differential diagnosis lies between coeliac disease and Crohn's disease. The presence of anti-endomysial antibodies in the serum and the intra-epithelial lymphocytosis are diagnostic of coeliac disease. This is an immune-mediated disorder in which there is sensitivity to the α-gliadin component of gluten. Anaemia is common in coeliac disease due to malabsorption of iron and/or folic acid. The dietary iron supplements have probably prevented significant iron deficiency and the most likely cause of this patient's anaemia is therefore folate deficiency. Treatment of coeliac disease with a gluten-free diet usually causes a rapid clinical and histological response.

5. **B – Adenocarcinoma**

   Epigastric pain is a non-specific symptom of upper gastrointestinal pathology, but the weight loss and anorexia are more sinister, and the anaemia implies chronic GI bleeding. The endoscopic appearance of a polypoid mass is suspicious of malignancy and the differential diagnosis lies between an adenocarcinoma and a lymphoma. The finding on biopsy of atypical glands that infiltrate the submucosa, together with signet ring cells, confirms an adenocarcinoma.

11. ANATOMY OF THE LIVER

1. **F – Gall bladder**
   The gall bladder descends along the lateral border of the quadrate lobe. The falciform ligament with the ligamentum teres in its lower border lies on the medial side.

2. **C – Caudate process**
   The opening of the lesser sac from the peritoneal cavity passes anterior to the inferior vena cava and behind the free margin of the lesser omentum, above the first part of the duodenum.

3. **I – Porta hepatis**
   The hepatic artery lies medial to the common bile duct, both lying in front of the portal vein within the free margin of the lesser omentum. The three structures enter the porta hepatis and divide into right and left branches, which then ramify within the right and left lobes of the liver.

4. **A – Bare area of the liver**
   The upper pole of the right kidney and adjacent suprarenal gland and a part of the inferior vena cava are surrounded by the coronary ligament within the bare area on the posterior aspect of the liver.

5. **B – Caudate lobe**
   The lesser omentum extends upwards into the liver and surrounds the caudate lobe, the reflections from the posterior abdominal wall peritoneum completing the surround. The sac extends downwards behind the stomach within the greater omentum and across to the left into the hilum of the spleen, behind the stomach.

12. BLOOD SUPPLY OF THE HEART

1. I – Right coronary artery
From its origin in the anterior aortic sinus, the artery lies between the right auricular appendage and the pulmonary trunk, before descending in the anterior atrioventricular groove. It passes around the inferior margin of the heart, giving off the right marginal, and becomes the posterior interventricular artery.

2. A – Anterior interventricular artery
The diagonal artery is a prominent branch of the anterior interventricular artery.

3. A – Anterior interventricular artery
The artery has two to nine branches that supply the anterior surface of the left ventricle as it passes to the apex of the heart. It often passes onto the posterior surface as well as supplying the left ventricle through its prominent diagonal branch.

4. B – Circumflex artery
The SA node is usually supplied by a branch of the circumflex artery. The atrioventricular (AV) node in 80–90% of individuals is supplied by the 1st septal branch of the posterior interventricular artery.

5. F – Left coronary artery
The left coronary artery lies between the left auricular appendage and the pulmonary trunk, and gives off the anterior interventricular artery to become the circumflex artery. This passes around the upper border of the heart to lie in the posterior atrioventricular groove.

Index

Numbers refer to papers, and questions within each paper